# CUSTOMER-CENTERED REENGINEERING

## Remapping for Total Customer Value

# CUSTOMER-CENTERED REENGINEERING

## Remapping for Total Customer Value

*Edwin T. Crego, Jr.*

*Peter D. Schiffrin*

*Foreword*
*Karl Albrecht*

**IRWIN**
*Professional Publishing*
Burr Ridge, Illinois
New York, New York

Senior sponsoring editor: Cynthia A. Zigmund
Project editor: Paula M. Buschman
Production manager: Ann Cassady
Designer: Heidi J. Baughman
Art coordinator: Heather Burbridge
Compositor: TCSystems, Inc.
Typeface: 10.5/12 Palatino
Printer: Quebecor Printing Book Press, Inc

**Library of Congress Cataloging-in-Publication Data**

Crego, Edwin T.
  Customer-centered reengineering : remapping for total customer value / Edwin T. Crego, Peter D. Schiffrin; foreword, Karl Albrecht.
    p.    cm.
  Includes index.
  ISBN 0-7863-0298-4
  1. Organizational change. 2. Corporate reorganization.
3. Consumer satisfaction. I. Schiffrin, Peter D. II. Title.
HD58.8.C74  1995
658.4'063—dc20                        94-10544

*Printed in the United States of America*

1 2 3 4 5 6 7 8 9 0  BP  1 0 9 8 7 6 5 4

# Foreword

In many ways, this book is a plan for escape—escape from flatland, that mythical and metaphorical land of perception in which people are constrained by their experience to see in only two dimensions. This book shows you how to escape to a higher level of perception and consciousness regarding the effectiveness of organizations.

My colleagues and longtime personal friends Ed Crego and Peter Schiffrin offer you the benefit of over 40 years of collective experience in observing and dealing with organizational craziness of almost all kinds. They understand the need to revise and revolutionize the perspectives of leadership in today's organizations. They know that, in many ways, "you can't get there from here." You have to rise above the planar concepts of traditional structural thinking in business and get to the why that lies behind the how. This is the real promise of the concept of reengineering.

We all know that buzzwords and buzzideas come and go. Management fads, fancies, and fallacies are coming and going these days faster than ever before. The fad cycle from birth to gospel to grave is becoming shorter and shorter. Yet, for all of our healthy skepticism, we know at some level of thinking that we've got to find better ways to run businesses. It's no longer just a matter of doing things better, but of doing better things.

Strange and amazing things happening in today's business environment, not only locally and nationally but globally, are forcing business leaders to rethink, reinvent, and reengineer their enterprises. Many of these changes, and the adaptations to them, are painful, but in the long run most will be healthy. We're witnessing an unprecedented rearrangement of the elements of business, under the driving influence of various economic, technological, and social shock waves. The order of the day is deconstruction and reconstruction. Downsizing, delayering, outsourcing, partnering, alliances, and leverage are the new constructs for deploying resources in the post-capitalist era.

The greatest single asset of this book, I believe, is the focus of its treatment. In sound-bite language, "It's the customer, stupid." Ed Crego and Peter Schiffrin have taken the lead in reengineering the concept of reengineering toward a focus on customer value. They understand that much of what passes for reengineering these days is merely rearranging the deck chairs on a sinking ship. What is needed is a fundamental commitment to aligning the strategy, people, and systems of the organization around the core premise of customer value. It's no longer good enough to expound about being customer focused. We've got to build the driving concept of customer value into the very psyche of the organization and reflect it faithfully in every dimension of the infrastructure.

I believe their message is the right one for our times. Please read it carefully and thoughtfully. You're in good hands.

**Karl Albrecht**

# Preface

We believe that the United States of America is a nation at risk—not because of crime, or drugs, or threats to the environment, but because of what is going on in our organizations. For more than a decade, organizations have been making radical cuts to their staffing complement.

They know that they have cut into flesh and bone. However, they are unaware that unwittingly, at the same time, they have also cut into the heart and the soul. And organizations without hearts or souls cannot long survive.

Within the past few years a new management tool, *business process reengineering*, has been introduced that offers great promise and a possible alternative to the slash and thrash techniques that have created these "amputated" organizations. There are several different definitions for and approaches taken to reengineering. However, in general, it is a methodology for rethinking and redesigning the organization's core processes from ground zero to make them significantly more effective and efficient. Some reengineering delivers on that promise. However, there is evidence to suggest that the majority—up to 70 percent—doesn't.

Why? We believe that it's because much of what passes for reengineering is simply downsizing or cost cutting in disguise or information system consulting "gussied up" in new clothes. Consequently, at best, what it can deliver is incremental improvement or change rather than the *breakthroughs* that are desired.

The second primary deficiency is the focus of reengineering itself. Most reengineering addresses business processes. Processes are just part of what comprise an organization. An organization is a complex organic system defined by its *strategy, structure, subsystems (processes), and people.* Therefore, process redesign only deals with the tip of the organizational iceberg.

The third major deficiency of most reengineering is an internal fixation. It concentrates on the company and what it does rather than on *the customer* and what he or she expects or experiences. As a result, the changes that are made may benefit a firm in the short term but do nothing over time to enhance customer satisfaction or to build continuing loyalty.

We need an approach that overcomes these deficiencies and addresses the 21st century business imperative, which we believe will be to ensure *Total Customer Value*—a state in which the *quality* of a total experience, as perceived by the customer, exceeds its *cost*. To create this level of value, an organization must be willing and able to *remap* everything about the way that it is organized, operated, and does business. It must be willing to reinvent itself from the outside in, based on an understanding that the world is not flat and the customer should be at the center of the organization's universe.

*Customer-Centered Reengineering* provides an approach that an organization can employ to satisfy these conditions.

The TQS Group has evolved this comprehensive and tested methodology based on a decade of consulting with and studying the best practices of those organizations in the United States and worldwide that have successfully reengineered themselves around their customers in order to create a sustainable competitive advantage.

Through our research and experience, we have identified three critical success factors for major organizational change efforts such as reengineering:

- Transformational leadership.
- Strategic remapping.
- Transition management.

We have brought these factors together to construct what we call the Customer-Centered Reengineering Superhighway. An organization that wants to maximize the potential success for a reengineering intervention needs to build all three lanes of this superhighway.

As the superhighway implies, the reengineering journey is not just a mechanical one. In fact, at its very core, it is and must be a human one. America's space program provides us with an important lesson in this regard.

In his book, *The Right Stuff,* Tom Wolfe tells an interesting story. It seems that when the NASA scientists and engineers were preparing for the first "manned" space launch they did not intend to put any windows into the astronaut's capsule. They hadn't put in any for the monkeys that were put into space and they didn't see why it needed to be any different for the humans, America's finest pilots. After all, everything would be scientifically programmed and controlled perfectly from the ground.

When the astronauts heard this, they were outraged. They went on strike and refused to go into space until they at least got a window to look out of. They also wanted more control over the capsule while in flight. There was an enormous fight between the engineers and the pilots (astronauts). Eventually, the astronauts got a small window but little else for the initial launch into space.

In the intervening years, NASA came to a remarkable conclusion. Everything can't be engineered or controlled from the ground. For a variety of reasons, astronauts are best qualified to maneuver a spaceship during flight and landing. Programmed systems, technical procedures, and robots couldn't fix the Hubble telescope; people could. Wonder of wonders. Man (person) beats machine.

What does this tell us about reengineering? First, you need a window to the real world—customer insights. Second, not everything can be controlled from the ground—by the reengineers. Third, to make reengineering work, you need to turn it over to the pilots—the employees who create value for the customer.

Along with this there is another learning. Organizations are not machines. They were never engineered in the first place. They are complex, dynamic, and living organisms with dominant values, attitudes, habits, attributes, and behaviors that exist in environments that are changing at warp speed.

Because of this, the reengineering journey must entail much more than making radical changes to business processes. It demands creating an entirely new organization—not a virtual organization, but a veritable one. A *veritable organization* is one that speaks the truth, demonstrates consistency in word and action, and makes a lifetime commitment to each of its key constituencies—customers, employees, shareholders, and community.

The remainder of this book is dedicated to those organizations and executives who have the courage to consider such a total transformation and undertake the journey. It is a journey not only of the head, but also of the heart and soul. For some organizations, it will be a journey to restore the heart and soul. We hope that this book will serve as a compass and resource for those who are willing to set sail and chart a course into unknown territory. We believe that the journey will be worth it.

Edwin T. Crego, Jr.
Peter D. Schiffrin

# Acknowledgments

This book was easy to produce because it is basically a story written about and by our heroes and friends.

The heroes are the employees, managers, and executives in organizations that we have consulted with and studied who are developing new rules for the game and reengineering the way that business is done—both in terms of how the organization relates to the customer and how the individuals in the organization relate to each other. They have given us the evidence to build and support our theories and contributed significantly to our learning and knowledge creation process.

Our friends include many talented individuals with whom we have collaborated in our client work—too many to name here without devoting a full chapter to the task. Most importantly, they include our colleagues and associates at The TQS Group: Karl Albrecht, chairman of the Group, who encourages us all to innovate continuously and to stretch the outer edge of the envelope on behalf of the customer; Jim Dauner and Becky Glime—fellow toilers in the customer value vineyard; Ron Gunn and Ed Wilt—whose contribution of radical rhetoric and pragmatic prose helped to shape parts of these chapters; and Veronica Vasquez, our secretary, who ensured that this manuscript was produced in a high-quality manner within nearly impossible timelines.

Finally, we want to thank our families, Beverly Ginsburg and David Schiffrin, Sheila Smith and Lisa Crego, respectively, for being our partners in the process of lifelong learning and continuous improvement and for giving us constructive and caring feedback that we can use to *reengineer* ourselves.

# Contents

*Chapter One*

# There's Something Happening Here . . .

*"You cannot step twice into the same river, for fresh waters are ever flowing in upon you."*

Heraclitus

Streator, Illinois, is a city of 14,800 located in north central Illinois.

## THE GLASS CONTAINER CAPITAL OF THE WORLD

As you drive into Streator from the north on Route 23, you see a brown and blue sign with a globe of the world on it that reads, *"Welcome to Streator. Glass Container Capital of the World."* The sign conjures up images of a thriving local economy, a vibrant industry, and international competitive superiority.

There's something seriously wrong with this picture, however. Streator's unemployment rate is among the highest in the state of Illinois. They don't make many glass containers in the city anymore. Most significantly, projections are that the glass industry, as we know it, will continue its decline to the point of virtual demise in the first part of the 21st century.

It wasn't always this way. Just 30 years ago, glass dominated and Streator ruled. In 1964, Owens-Illinois Glass and Thatcher Glass, the two glass manufacturers in Streator, employed close to 5,000 employees. They contributed significant amounts to the local tax base, school system, and charities. They created hundreds of jobs for college students during the summer months. Whenever there was a community event, such as a high school reunion or a senior class night, you could rest assured that the momento given out would be a glass container of some type made especially for the occasion.

In recognition of these contributions, Streator's city council passed an ordinance that prohibited selling certain products such as milk, soda pop, and beer in other than glass bottles within the city limits. They approved closing the street that ran in front of the Owens-Illinois plant so that the company could build an addition. Streator was a company town and what was good for the company was good for the city.

Then, in the late 70s and early 80s, things began to change. The glass container industry matured. Plastics, aluminum cans, cardboard containers, and other more advanced forms of packaging became acceptable and lower-cost substitutes for glass bottles. Streator's glass manufacturers suffered.

They responded by trying to cut costs and improve productivity. They laid off. They downsized. They attempted to restructure. Then, the seemingly inevitable happened. Thatcher Glass closed its doors for good in the mid 1980s and Owens-Illinois shrank. Today, the company employs a skeleton staff whose primary function is to keep the furnaces going and to melt down scrap and recycled glass. Yet, the sign still reads, *"Welcome to Streator. Glass Container Capital of the World."*

## FOR WHOM THE BELL TOLLS

Streator's story is symbolic. Over the past decade, it has been repeated in various iterations in countless cities and companies across the United States and around the world.

To illustrate, consider the well-documented closings of the textile mills in Fall River, Massachusetts; the myriad manufacturing companies in Trenton, New Jersey; the automotive plants in Flint, Michigan; the steel mills in Gary, Indiana; and the meat packing facilities in Waterloo, Iowa. More recently, look at Sears' elimination of its entire catalog operation, Woolworth's shuttering of 970 stores throughout North America, and Kmart's selling all of its discount warehouse stores to Wal-Mart.

One might argue that this shakeout is natural—part of the evolutionary cycle of business. Main Street is changing and the dinosaur industries—steel, glass, meat packing, and so on—are consolidating, purifying, or disappearing. This may be partially true. But these changes are not just going on in the older and more established industries or businesses. They are affecting everyone.

Witness the conflagration in the airline industry. Carriers as diverse as Pan-Am, Eastern, Braniff, and Peoples Express are grounded permanently. TWA and Continental just recently emerged from Chapter 11 bankruptcy. And the two domestic titans, United Airlines and American Airlines, are struggling for their very existence and considering breaking apart into regional carriers to achieve economies and selling off units such as their food service operations to raise revenue.

The message is clear. In the United States, there were nearly 900,000 bankruptcy cases filed in both 1991 and 1992.[1] The bell can and will toll for anyone.

## REMAPPING ERRORS

What happened to these businesses? Didn't their owners or executives see the handwriting on the wall? Weren't they smart enough? Tough enough? Quick enough? Hadn't they read *In Search of Excellence?* Didn't they try to make changes? What prevented them from turning things around?

As students of and consultants to businesses, these questions have perplexed and bothered us and caused us to search for answers for some time. Obviously, there is no single or simple answer to any of them because, although the statistics and stories may be similar, each business's situation is unique. So, we can't detail the specific reasons for the collapse of any one business or why megacorporations like Sears, General Motors, and IBM and thousands of other less well-known organizations have had such extreme difficulties in *teaching the elephant to dance.*

We are certain, though, that none of these organizations sat idly by watching their fortunes whither away or go down the tubes. They have all attempted some form of radical organizational surgery or "remapping."

Remapping, as we define it, is any *major* change to the nature of the business. Remapping occurs in four stages:

1. **Reading the current map.** Assessing the present state of the business in terms of the company's organization and operations, and its customers, competition, and industrial and environmental context.

2. **Developing a new map.** Defining a new desired state that will improve organizational health and performance.

3. **Mapping out a new course.** Selecting a methodology and strategy to take the business from its current troubled state to the desired "success" state.

4. **Following the map.** Implementing the action plan intended to improve the organization's performance.

After more than two decades of research and working with hundreds of organizations, we have discovered that an organization can make errors in any or all of the stages. We have classified these remapping errors into four major problem types.

*Remapping error types*

**Type I: Diagnosis error.** Incorrectly assessing the root cause of the company's problem.

**Type II: Anticipation error.** Developing time-based or short-term solutions that underestimate the rate of change being faced and do not address the future needs of the market or the customer.

**Type III: Selection error.** Choosing the wrong problem-solving strategy or methodology.

**Type IV: Application error.** Making a mistake in implementing the selected strategy or methodology.

## LIFE CYCLES, SHOCK WAVES, AND BREAKPOINTS

The Type I diagnosis and Type II anticipation errors are the most fatal. The reason for this is apparent. There has been more change in most industries over the past decade than in all other years combined. In fact, in many of the more technologically competitive industries, such as telecommunications, consumer electronics, and computers, the half-life of differentiating new product or service concepts is probably no more than six months.

As many unsuccessful organizations are learning in the *Nanosecond Nineties*, as Tom Peters labels them, it is just not enough anymore to practice continuous improvement or to make incremental adjustments. Success on a going forward basis demands radical or breakthrough change. Consequently, the old tools and methods for planning and responding to industry and business trends, such as life cycle analysis, are becoming increasingly irrelevant or immaterial. Let's examine why.

Traditional business life cycle theory hypothesizes that all businesses move through three major stages: early, middle, and late. In the *early* stage, the product or service is new, relatively unique, or both. Competition is limited. Demand outstrips supply and the price is high. In the *middle* stage, markets may still be growing, but competition increases, prices stabilize, and the customer's sophistication increases. In the *late* or mature stage, market growth declines, prices drop, customers are more and more demanding, the marginal and least well-managed businesses fail, and growth flattens. For those remaining firms, new products or services are created and a new but related business life cycle begins.

Movement through these stages is a function of many forces, including the product life cycle; the industry life cycle; market growth and size; the nature of the competitive arena; barriers to entry to the industry; the influence of suppliers; and the desires, sophistication, and purchasing behavior of customers.

Larry Grenier, a Harvard professor, was one of the first academicians to write about this life cycle phenomenon. According to Grenier, growing companies pass through a series of developmental stages involving both *evolution*, prolonged periods of growth where no major upheaval occurs in organizational practices, and *revolution*, periods of substantial turmoil and change in organizational practices.[2]

We would argue that, as we move into the turbulent and potentially traumatic 21st century, the length of these evolutionary and revolutionary periods will be almost exactly reversed. The revolutionary or choppy wave periods will be extremely long and the evolutionary periods of relatively calm waters or rolling waves will be short or nonexistent. As a result, to succeed in the future, organizations are going to have to become shock-wave riders and masters of continuous and discontinuous change.

These shock waves will be created not only by what is going on in the industry and business itself, but in the society surrounding it. As examples, consider the far-reaching implications of the following international events: the signing of the NAFTA treaty; the collapse of Communism; and the peace accord being negotiated between the Palestinians and Israel.

There was a time when external events such as these used to unfold more slowly, and much more predictably, than they do today. Anticipation of the future and its effects on one's business was, in those simpler times, more often a matter for casual speculation than it was a matter of survival. This is no longer the case. Knowledgeable planning and continuous innovation are now essential for ongoing business success.

The rate of change continues to accelerate and the sheer magnitude of change increases constantly. Magnitude of change refers both to the degree of the adjustment and to the number of people affected by or adopting some innovation, whether that innovation is a new technological adaptation or an altered set of social attitudes. The speed and magnitude of our change has been heightened by a society in which commerce is increasingly not merely based upon the exchange of information, but is the exchange of that information itself using a multiplicity of media.

The "information highway" is upon us. The future is here now. Consequently, those businesses that want to succeed into the 21st century must not only be capable of being shock-wave riders, but also be able to anticipate, exploit, and create *breakpoints*—to cause shock waves within their own industry.

As defined by Paul Strebel in his excellent new book with the same title, breakpoints are "sudden or radical shifts in the rules of the business game." These shifts can be caused by events peculiar to the industry or business itself or within the broader societal context.[3] As we will discuss later in Chapter Three, creating strategic breakpoints is at the very heart of reengineering in a way that creates a sustainable competitive advantage for an organization.

## FROM MEGATRENDS TO MICROFOCUS

These breakpoints will vary dramatically from industry to industry and business to business. However, as we scrutinize today's business landscape and project ourselves forward into the 21st century, we see one general overriding shift that we expect to impact the way business is done across the board. This is the shift from megatrends to microfocus.

We see evidence of this shift all around us. There are microbreweries, microtoys, microcomputers, micromakeup kits, and microchips. Perhaps the best example of this shift to the "small is beautiful" perspective is provided by Cray Research.

Cray Research basically invented the super computer industry. Super computers process amazing amounts of information at blinding speed. Cray developed the original vector technology for its supercomputers by building very large, very expensive, custom-designed processors to serve as the supercomputer's brain. These processors solve problems sequentially.

In contrast, Cray's competitors, companies like Intel, Thinking Machines, and MPP, developed their supercomputers using a "massively parallel" processing technology by linking together thousands of inexpensive, commodity-like microprocessors to serve as the brains of their machines. These microprocessors break problems apart and into smaller pieces and then solve them simultaneously.

For years, Cray's executives said these strung-together smaller machines would never rival the capacities and capabilities of their big megamachines. However, on September 27, 1993, Cray's chairman and research chief, John Carlson, announced the introduction of the company's first "massively parallel" machine, the Cray 3TD supercomputer, with the pronouncement, "We can for the first time anticipate overcoming some of the barriers to the grand challenges."[4]

Cray had decided that it would rather switch than fight. And the switch was from mega to micro.

What are the other microfoci? We're not futurists, so we may not be fully qualified to comment. Or, maybe, that makes us qualified.

In any case, here, in no particular or priority order, are a "baker's dozen" of the most important microfoci that we see underway today with the potential for transforming the way business is done tomorrow.

**Microfocus No. 1: From big business to small business.** Not only will small business growth and job creation continue to outstrip that of big business, even big businesses will break themselves into smaller, more entrepreneurial units in order to be more competitive, flexible, and responsive to customer needs. Best example—the "Baby Bells" and AT&T. Others—Aetna Insurance, Prudential Insurance, and Arthur Andersen.

**Microfocus No. 2: From global to local.** As trade barriers come down, more and more firms will expand and do business in the international marketplace. However, they'll do it not as mega-monoliths—a lesson that Federal Express learned as it tried to expand its express service into other countries—but by adjusting to local customs and standards. In addition, those franchise type businesses doing business within a country—fast-food restaurants, food stores, and so on—will give local managers more autonomy and authority to customize their operations and marketing to the needs and desires of the local neighborhoods and customers.

**Microfocus No. 3: From organizational pyramid to networks.** Middle management levels and jobs will continue to disappear. Self-directed work teams will become more prevalent. Most importantly, information technology will be used to link organizational units together in new and creative ways and to minimize organizational structure and redundancy.

**Microfocus No. 4: From vertical/horizontal integration to constellations.** Strategic alliances, joint ventures, and virtual organization type arrangements will become even more prevalent and popular.

**Microfocus No. 5: From bureaucracy to adhocracy.** Organizational policies and procedures will continue to be streamlined. Rule books will be tossed out in order to make it easier for the customer to do business and for the organization to respond to the customer's needs in a timely and effective manner.

**Microfocus No. 6: From corporate mentality to collective intelligence.** It will no longer be assumed that Big Brother knows it all. People will be seen as the organization's primary resources. The wealth of the organization will not be its land or capital but the knowledge created by these employees. The learning organization will become a basic paradigm for business success.

**Microfocus No. 7: From company men to free agents.** As companies continue to downsize, the concepts of corporate loyalty, the "man in the gray flannel suit," and "bleeding IBM blue" will become vestiges of the past. They will be replaced with a free agency-type arrangement in which employees and employers enter contracts for specified periods of time that are renegotiated based upon performance.

**Microfocus No. 8: From high risers to homesteaders.** Many big office buildings will stand empty. More and more work will be done by individuals out of the home. Flexible work schedules and piecework arrangements will become a much preferred mode of doing business.

**Microfocus No. 9: From main street to minimalls.** This trend has been upon us for almost three decades now. It will continue until every possible site that can be used for a minimall is occupied and the main streets of America are grown over with weeds.

**Microfocus No. 10: From expressways to information highways.** With the mergers of telephone and cable companies, the integrated media era of shopping, entertainment, and every other activity imaginable at home will develop at an accelerated pace. And, eventually, the minimalls may suffer main street's demise.

**Microfocus No. 11: From mass marketing to one-to-one marketing.** Using scanner technology and increasingly sophisticated computerized organizational databases on their customers' behavior, businesses will target and tailor their messages directly to each individual customer.

**Microfocus No. 12: From mass production to customization.** Just as one-to-one marketing will become an emergent mode for reaching the customer, producing unit lots of one will become the emergent focus for bundling services and products into a package to meet the needs of the customer.

**Microfocus No. 13: From company-centered to customer-centered change.** More and more organizations will discover the folly of implementing downsizing, quality improvement, reengineering, and other performance improvement "fads" that do not take the needs of their key customers into account. Realizing that the only thing that counts in the long term are changes that matter to the customer, they will finally make the customer connection correctly.

## FAD-BASED FAILURE CYCLE

Many organizations commit the Type III selection error—choosing the wrong problem-solving methods or strategy. They rush to judgment and are prone to the "cart before the horse" syndrome. They arrive at the answer (methodology or strategy selection) before they have adequately analyzed the situation (problem diagnosis).

This normally happens in the following manner. A senior executive in Company A reads or hears about the latest, breakthrough management technique—benchmarking, employee empowerment, self-directed work teams, skill-based pay—and the wondrous results that it has achieved for Company B.

He or she wants the same results for company A and gets it to take the "miracle cure." They try it. It doesn't work immediately or as desired. They stop taking the prescription. They're off in search of the next wonder drug or diet fad. They repeat the same process, again. The fad-based failure cycle continues.

Downsizing and total quality management were the most popular management or performance improvement techniques of the 80s. It appears that business process reengineering will become the methodology of choice for the 90s. To gauge the extent to which fad-based failures occur, it is instructive to note the results that have been achieved to date using these three methods.

### Downsizing

A recent study of 1,000 companies that had downsized revealed the following:

- Only 19 percent of the companies reported an increase in competitive advantage because of their downsizing.
- Almost 90 percent hoped to reduce expenses; less than 50 percent did.
- Three-quarters hoped for productivity improvements; only 22 percent achieved them.

- More than 50 percent expected to reduce bureaucracy and speed decisions; only 15 percent did.[5]

## Total Quality Management

Over the past two years, there have been several studies of the results achieved through "total quality" initiatives. The most significant was released in 1992 by the American Quality Foundation. That international study, which was based on a survey of 584 companies in the health care, automotive, computer, and banking industries in the United States, Canada, Germany, and Japan, disclosed major failings in quality improvement activities around the world, with American companies seriously lagging behind foreign competitors in their quality improvement efforts.[6]

Other research findings related to the state of quality improvement efforts in the United States include the following:

- Only 36 percent of 500 executives at major US companies believed that their quality process had improved their competitiveness, as found in an Arthur D. Little survey.
- 38 percent of the senior managers from 95 US corporations gave their quality programs failing grades in response to a poll conducted by Rath & Strong, a Boston-headquartered consulting firm.[7]
- A mere 10 percent of 450 respondents had a logistics process in place to support customer satisfaction, as reported in a 1991 survey by A. T. Kearney, a Chicago-based management consulting firm.[8]

## Reengineering

Because of its more recent emergence as a preferred methodology, there is very little systematic data available on the results accomplished under the reengineering mantle. However, Michael Hammer and James Champy, authors of *Reengineering the Corporation* and the foremost proponents of this *new* improvement technology, estimate that "50 to 70 percent of organizations that undertake reengineering efforts do not achieve the dramatic results they intended."[9] Combine this estimate with reports in the popular press regarding problems associated with reengineering in companies such as American Express's International Division[10] and it seems reasonable to assume that the success rate of traditional reengineering approaches will approximate and be no better than that achieved through downsizing, total quality management, and the other popular management improvement methodologies of the 80s and early 90s.

## CRITICAL SUCCESS FACTORS FOR ORGANIZATIONAL CHANGE

These statistics are dismal and discouraging, most especially so for those organizations that have spent millions of dollars in search of solutions. Why aren't the results any better?

As we noted earlier, it may be because an organization is doing the *wrong thing right*—applying a methodology that is inappropriate given its particular problem and circumstances. Or it can be that it is *doing the right thing wrong*, and that the root cause of failure is not in what was done but in how it was done.

We in The TQS Group found evidence of this Type IV application error through a survey that we conducted in 1991 on the implementation processes and methods used and results achieved through quality improvement initiatives in Fortune 500 companies. Senior quality executives from 78 organizations responded to the survey.

Only one-third of those executives reported that their programs had had a substantial positive impact on organizational performance in terms of revenues, market share, or profit margin. Two-thirds reported that their programs had had no marked impact on organizational performance.[11]

As we analyzed these responses, we uncovered the source of this failure. As displayed in Figure 1–1, slightly more than half (51 percent) of all the survey respondents indicated that they had active executive involvement in their change efforts. A much smaller percent reported that they used customer research (40 percent) to form their quality programs or had developed a comprehensive program strategy (34 percent) for guiding their change efforts.

As we analyzed these data further, we found that, of those firms that reported substantial performance improvement from the quality program, 85 percent said that they had all three of these factors present. In stark contrast, of those companies that indicated little or no performance improvement, only 10 percent stated that they had all three of these factors present. This finding has caused us to identify these elements as the central success factors for quality improvement. Based on our experience and a review of the literature on downsizing and reengineering, we found that these factors are also central to achieving positive results through these major organizational performance improvement methodologies. As a result, we

**FIGURE 1–1**
*Quality Program Success Factors*

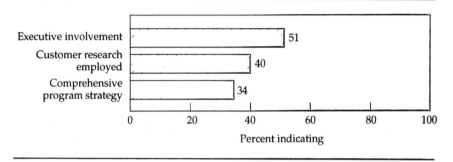

have labeled them as the critical success factors for organizational change initiatives (see Table 1–1).

## THE REINVENTION IMPERATIVE

There is something happening here . . . As we review the success and failure factors in trying to remap the organization to improve its performance, the message in the bottle becomes clear: **Master change. Reinvent yourself.**

The old adage goes: *Manage change or it will manage you.* As this chapter illustrates, managing change will not be enough in the future. Those organizations that want to succeed in the 21st century will have to lead change and reinvent their businesses from the outside in. They must become masters of the art of *creative destruction and self-renewal.*

Joseph Schumpeter, the economist, coined the term *creative destruction* to describe the process whereby those hidebound companies that can't keep up in the marketplace fail and go out of business and their places are taken by more innovative and progressive organizations. High-performing organizations of the future will do their own pruning and self-destructing. They will continuously reinvent themselves and their industries. Their credo will be: *Do it to ourselves, before others do it unto us.*

To excel, these organizations will:

- **Read the tea leaves.** Stay externally focused and maintain a constant and vigilant eye on the market and the customer rather than obsess over organizational policies and internal politics.
- **Avoid emus.** Not too long ago, we heard a story about a fellow who had ridden his motorcycle around the world. He had

**TABLE 1–1**
*Organizational Change Critical Success Factors*

---

- **Executive involvement and leadership**—throughout the entire improvement effort.
- **Strategic customer-centered connection**—through original customer research and ongoing customer satisfaction measurement.
- **Comprehensive change program strategy**—with clearly articulated strategic goals and a well-defined framework for improvement integrated and linked to the business's purpose and processes.

---

traveled successfully through every variety of traffic and terrain because he was always alert. Then, as he was driving through the Australian outback where the road is flat for hundreds of miles and there is virtually no population, his attention wandered for just a moment. He ran into an emu, a large flightless Australian bird related to the ostrich, and was killed. The 21st century changemasters will not suffer the fate of that motorcyclist. No matter how well they are doing, they will expect and be prepared for the unexpected.

- **Become protean.** Structure themselves along the lines of an "office building without walls" so that they can reframe and reform readily and easily in response to customer and marketplace needs. They will be organized and operated to maximize flexibility, agility, and adaptiveness.

- **Create breakpoints.** Lead, not lag the market. They will innovate constantly and take the necessary but calculated risks required to cause industry and organizational realignment. They will create shock waves that others must ride.

- **Think small.** Ensure an appropriateness of size for the organization and focus on *the* customer in order to win big.

- **Follow the North Star.** Recognize that there should not be "1,000 points of light" or competing priorities and that the customer's expectations and experience should be the single guiding light for all of the changes that are to be made throughout the organization.

Most important, these organizations will draw upon all of these skills in order to *reengineer around the customer.* They will bring the power of the customer into their center and use it to change everything about the way that they do business.

This will entail much more than just making radical changes to business processes. It will involve transforming the entire organization including its strategy, systems, structure, and people practices. It will require a journey not only of the head but also of the heart and soul.

The remainder of this book is dedicated to those organizations and executives who have the courage to consider such a total transformation. We hope that it will serve as a compass for those who are willing to set sail and chart a course into unknown seas. We believe that the journey will be worth it.

## Chapter Two

# It's the Customer, Stupid!

*"I am sick and tired of visiting plants to hear nothing but great things about quality and cycle time . . . and then to visit customers who tell me of problems."*

John Akers
*Ex-CEO, IBM*

John Akers used to be the CEO of IBM.

## MIRROR, MIRROR ON THE WALL

During Mr. Akers's tenure, IBM's fortunes plummeted. Earnings fell. Market share and stock price declined. And IBM's average annual revenue growth ran significantly behind that of the computer industry as a whole.[1]

Many factors contributed to IBM's decline. Books have been and will be written providing detailed facts, opinions, and insights into the IBM case. However, it is widely acknowledged that one of the central reasons for IBM's precipitous fall was that the company lost focus of its customers.

Carol Loomis highlighted this failure in a *Fortune* article by writing:

> Those companies [IBM, Sears, and General Motors] did not fix their gaze on the customer. Rather, they looked inward and backward, remembering how it used to be and somehow expecting those glories to reappear. As a result, they were always behind the curve.[2]

As the opening quote to this chapter shows, Mr. Akers recognized IBM's lack of customer focus. He held a mirror up to the organization, but no one on the inside wanted to look. Or, if they did, they couldn't see what he saw. In the end, he paid the ultimate organizational price—his job—for not being able to convince others that his view of the world was correct and theirs was flawed.

Was John Akers's assessment correct? Only time will tell. It is ironic to note, however, that his successor at IBM, CEO Lou Gerstner, just 30 days after replacing Mr. Akers, disclosed that his number two priority for the company was to spend a lot more time with customers. As he put it, "We're also going to start talking to our customers about what we think we can do to define for them the computing model of the nineties . . . IBM used to be the company that did that. IBM could be the company to do it again."[3] Only time will tell whether Mr. Gerstner will be better at getting the IBMers to look into the mirror than his predecessor was.

## P. T. BARNUM WAS WRONG

IBM isn't the only organization having a tough time achieving a strong customer focus. Over the past few years, we have spoken to scores of groups and thousands of people about the critical business importance of making the organization customer-centered. Wherever we speak, the idea resonates with almost everyone in the audience and there appears to be almost a religious fervor to making the customer commitment. Nevertheless, when we ask for questions, inevitably the first one that we get goes something like this:

> How do we get our top executives to buy into this concept? Or, if they do start to buy in, how do we get them to understand and make a *total* commitment to it in terms of really changing the way that the business is organized and managed to become customer-centered?

It appears that, in spite of all the rhetoric to the contrary in annual reports and public pronouncements, a lot of companies are still being operated according to the old P. T. Barnum philosophy that the market is a monolith, customers are fungible, and there's one born every minute. This type of thinking leads to cases like:

• Sears automotive centers implementing an "incentive" compensation system that rewarded mechanics and managers for the size of the repair bill. As might be expected, this system led to substantial fraud including doing repair work that was not necessary and charging customers for work that wasn't even done.

• JC Penney's advertising gold chains for sale at prices deeply discounted from the original retail price. The problem was that these chains had never been sold at anywhere near the retail price quoted in the ad.

• Hoover launching a marketing campaign in Scotland to attract new customers for their vacuum cleaners by promising that any customer who bought a vacuum cleaner would get one free round-trip ticket from Edinburgh Airport in Scotland to Miami or New York City. The Scots, who are noted for knowing a good deal when they see one, bought up every vacuum cleaner in sight. As a result,

Hoover reneged on its promise to give a free ticket to everyone. As might be imagined, this led to a spate of lawsuits, counter claims, and an ongoing public relations nightmare for Hoover.

The true tragedy of these cases is that these three organizations were American stalwarts who built their original reputations around concern for and devotion to their customers. Somehow, somewhere, something went wrong. What was it?

We believe that a large part of the answer is attributable to the "conquest sale" mindset. This mindset has predominated for years in industries as diverse as automotive, insurance, and the airlines. It operates something like this:

- There is a virtually endless market for our product or service.
- It is more important to get new customers than to do a good job of serving our existing customers.
- We should devote our primary marketing energy and resources to bringing "new business" through the door.
- We should structure our compensation system to give greater rewards for getting new business rather than repeat business.
- Our competition operates with the same mindset and in the same manner that we do. As a result, the worst thing that will happen to us by following this course is that we'll end up trading off customers.
- There isn't room for any new competitors in our industry.

This mindset may have been appropriate at some point in time. However, this dinosaur logic doesn't apply anymore. Increased competition, most notoriously from Japan, but also domestically, and an increasingly sophisticated and demanding marketplace have spelled the end of the replaceable customer. The truth is that even if you're running P. T. Barnum's circuses and sideshows nowadays, you won't find any suckers being mass produced out there anymore.

## LEARNING THE 3 R's

So, it's time to adopt a new mindset. Unfortunately, that's easier said than done. Old habits are hard to kick—especially when they're thinking habits. There are still a lot of corporate executives who operate with an "I'm from Missouri" attitude regarding the need for becoming more customer-centered. We've also learned this from our speaking engagements. Next to how to get the CEO to buy into customer focus, the other question that we are asked most frequently is:

Is there any evidence that I can give my boss that a superior level of quality or customer satisfaction translates into increased profits or improved business performance?

The answer is yes!! Study after study has revealed that satisfying the customer and delivering a higher relative level of quality than the competition pays huge dividends in terms of the 3 R's—*repeat, referral, and renewal*. The Profit Impact of Marketing Strategy (PIMS) and the Technical Assistance Research Programs (TARP) Institute produced the two most well-known studies documenting the positive returns from being customer-centered.

The PIMS research was conducted to determine how key dimensions of strategy affect profitability and growth in business. The study involved 450 corporations for periods ranging from 2 to 10 years. In exploring the relationship between quality and profitability, the PIMS researchers examined two different kinds of quality: conformance quality and perceived quality. *Conformance quality* is achieving zero defects as measured against prescribed product specifications. *Perceived quality* refers to quality as defined by the customer.

The PIMS researchers did not find any positive relation between conformance quality and profitability. However, they discovered a strong correlation between perceived quality and organizational performance.

The PIMS research disclosed that businesses that offer a product or service with superior quality as perceived by customers clearly outperform those with inferior quality, whether the performance measure is return on sales or return on investment. It also disclosed that those "superior quality" businesses enjoy

- Stronger customer loyalty.
- More repeat purchases.
- Less vulnerability to price wars.
- The ability to command higher relative price without affecting market share.
- Lower marketing costs.
- Significant improvements in market share.[4]

The TARP research was conducted to assess the effectiveness of various practices of American companies in handling consumer complaints. Noteworthy findings from this study include the following:

- Dissatisfied customers tell 11 people of their problems. Satisfied customers tell four people of their good experiences.
- Nearly 70 percent of customers who experience a problem with products or services do not complain.
- Merely getting the customer to complain about a problem, even if nothing is done about the complaint, will increase the chances by about 10 percent that the consumer will purchase again from that organization.

- Resolving a customer's problem satisfactorily significantly increases the chance that the consumer will repurchase: 70 percent of consumers with minor complaints will repurchase and 54 percent of consumers with major complaints will repurchase.
- Resolving the customer's problems quickly has an even more beneficial effect. For those consumers whose problems are resolved in a short period of time, 95 percent with minor complaints will repurchase and 82 percent with major complaints will repurchase.[5]

Linda Lash, Director of Customer Satisfaction for Avis Europe, Ltd., provided a specific example of the strong positive relationship between improved customer satisfaction and improved business performance at a Conference Board conference on Profiting from Total Quality. She reported that by using customer survey data, Avis had developed a customer income balance sheet to track the cost of lost customers and a "customer care" income statement to track complaint resolution and results. These tools allowed Avis to pinpoint critical problem areas and to develop strategies for correcting them immediately and positively. By using these tools over the period from 1989 to 1992, Avis made a 22 percent improvement in lost rentals and posted a 37 percent increase in its return on investment from handling complaints.[6]

## RECOGNIZING THE NEED FOR CUSTOMER DELIGHT AND LOYALTY

Customer satisfaction makes dollars and sense. However, in the 21st century merely satisfying the customer is not going to be good enough. This is true because a *satisfied* customer is a *vulnerable* customer. This is illustrated in the simple customer decision-making and behavior model presented in Figure 2–1.

As the model shows, the customer comes to an encounter with existing attitudes or expectations. He or she has a contact with the organization in a *moment of truth* or a series of moments. If that contact occurs as expected—that is, it's nothing special—the customer is satisfied. And guess what? He or she is vulnerable and may or may not return.

Why? Because today's customer has an almost endless variety of options from which to choose. There are automobile dealerships, fast-food restaurants, computer stores, and hotels on every corner. If the customer has no compelling reason to choose one over another because of a prior positive experience, the customer will continue to experiment or just rotate purchases among several providers.

**FIGURE 2–1**
*Customer Satisfaction Performance-Attitude-Behavior Model*

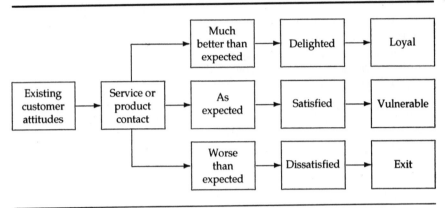

Source: Services Marketing Council, *Customer Satisfaction Measurement, Analysis and Use* (Chicago: American Marketing Association, 1993).

Recent research has shown that depending on what industry you are looking at, anywhere between 65 percent to 85 percent of customers who switch from one product or service to another state that they were satisfied with the product or service from which they switched.[7] On the other hand, very satisfied or "delighted" customers become loyal customers. They would rather stay than switch. By staying, they generate significant additional revenues and profits for the company to which they are loyal. For example, a loyal customer generates an average of

- $100,000 in revenue for an automobile firm over a lifetime.
- $500 in profit for a bank on a checking account.
- Four or five new customers for a business.

Loyal customers affect the expense side of the ledger too. On average, it costs $1 to get more business from an existing customer compared to $5 to get business from new customers. In the insurance industry, a 5 percent increase in customer retention translates into an 18 percent reduction in operating costs.

To sum it up, customer loyalty pays off in big ways. Those organizations that recognize this will reengineer themselves *first* to bring the customer in and *then* to drive costs out, rather than vice-versa. They will organize and manage themselves to promote customer delight and loyalty. As a result, they will be perfectly positioned to respond to the needs and demands of the 21st century customer.

# THE 21st CENTURY IMPERATIVE: TOTAL CUSTOMER VALUE

Unfortunately for businesses, there will be no single 21st century customer. Indeed, in the 21st century with the shift to a *micro focus*, there will be no such thing as *the customer*. Rather, there will only be *this customer*—an individual who makes buying decisions based on expectations for and experiences with any given organization.

There will be one single issue, however, that unites this individual customer with other customers. That is *customer value*. As Peter Drucker noted more than 20 years ago, "What is value to the customer may be the most important question for a business and the one that is asked least often."[8]

The reason for this is simple. Until recently, businesses were able to dictate what constituted value. Traditionally, value has been defined from the organization's perspective as the quality "built into" a product or service related to its price. Quality was achieved by conforming or complying to a set of standards in the production of goods or service.

This is an antiquated and irrelevant definition. It no longer matters what the company thinks value is. The only thing that matters is what the customer thinks it is.

Today's customers are far shrewder, tougher, and more demanding than yesterday's. They take their *entire experience* with an organization's product or service into account in evaluating quality. They judge the whole bundle. They are not just interested in base price. They also consider those *hidden* costs such as the personal waiting time invested to get a product delivered or fixed correctly as part of their construct for judging the worth of a product or service.

The customer value equation is changing and will continue to change. In the 1980s value was quality as defined by the company, at almost any price. In the 1990s, value has become quality, as defined by the customer, at the right cost. To be successful, organizations must be able to solve this new equation correctly and respond to the emerging expectations and evolving demands of their customers.

Yankelovich Clancy Shulman released a study in 1992 of customers' changing needs and attitudes related to the automotive industry. Although the study was done for the automotive industry, we believe that it has implications for companies in many other fields. Here are some of its key findings:

- **Customers no longer buy to impress others.** The emphasis is on owning products that are personally satisfying.
- **People feel less need to consume.** The 80s era of hyperconsumption is over.

- **Buying the "best" is no longer so important.** Instead, value is sought at every price level—even in luxury items.

- **Customers are sophisticated marketplace strategists.** They wait for the deals and specials to buy. They are prepared to negotiate almost anything.

- **Products must be able to deliver on the basics.** Performance, reliability, and ease of maintenance count.

- **Customers are not interested in technology per se.** They want to know that the technology can make the product better and their lives easier.

- **Service is critically important to any product.**[9]

Customer characteristics and conditions such as these caused the American Marketing Association to label the 90s as the *Value Decade* and Jack Welch, chairman of General Electric, to pronounce, "The value decade is on us. If you can't sell a top quality product at the world's lowest price, you're going to be out of the game."

More and more businesses have begun to acknowledge and accept the fact that they're playing in the value decade. This ranges from McDonald's saying on their placemats that, "At McDonald's today, value means a lot more than just low price. It means fast, courteous service. Clean restrooms, and a smile with your change. It's what you deserve" to Neiman Marcus informing us that value is "the very finest quality for the money."

Everybody's getting into the value game. The only problem is that few companies realize that we're still playing in the preliminaries and that we haven't gotten to the main event yet. As the saying goes, "We ain't seen nothing yet." If the 90s are the value decade, the strategic business imperative for the 21st century will be to ensure total customer value, which we define as follows:

---

*Total Customer Value*

A state in which the *quality* of a total experience, as perceived by the customer, exceeds its cost.

---

Every organization that wants to be successful in the 21st century is going to have to reengineer itself to satisfy this imperative. This is true even if a business excels at delivering customer value today. As we noted earlier, the customer value equation will continue to change.

> **Joint Value Creation**
>
> A *virtual partnership* between company and customer, that is designed to yield the maximum benefits for each party.

The customer will become even more sophisticated. Expectations will escalate. Requirements for satisfying experiences will become tougher. Demands for cost reduction will increase.

The 21st century will be a *brave, new world*. It will belong to the customers and those few businesses that are flexible, quick, and courageous enough to reengineer themselves around the customer.

## JOINT VALUE CREATION: THE FUTURE ADVANTAGE

Some organizations have already begun to respond to this imperative by radically restructuring their relationships with their customers and/or suppliers. They are establishing a new way of doing business that we call joint value creation.

Companies that are using the joint value creation approach to achieve a future advantage for themselves include IKEA, Federal Express, General Electric, Motorola, and ValueLink, a division of Baxter HealthCare.

IKEA, the Swedish furniture retailer, has established a partnership with the customer that is based on a deal: We'll give you good, affordable merchandise, which we market in a pleasant and helpful environment; you provide the delivery service and whatever assembly is required for the furnishings you buy. IKEA is not just trying to make it easier for the customer. On the contrary, they are pushing them to do more, to do things they have not been accustomed to doing. According to one explanation, "IKEA wants its customers to understand that their role is not to *consume* value but to *create* it."[10] The customers think this is an excellent partnership, apparently, and IKEA flourishes.

Federal Express has been in partnership with its customers from the outset. They provide us with packaging materials—and user-friendly, good quality stuff it is—and labels; we do our own packaging and labeling, helping to make it possible for speedy delivery at a cost we can afford. Now they have carried the partnership even further, with their tracking software. Before, we could call Fed Ex's 800 number to get a near-real-time report on where a package is, who received it, at what time, and so on. By providing customers with their new tracking software, Fed Ex has transferred some of the job to the customers. Result: you don't have to call Fed Ex to get the information, and Fed Ex doesn't have to pay as many people to answer your phone calls.

Computer technology, combined with leaps in telecommunications, has made customers partners in other ways, too. General Electric's retailers (customers) now rely on GE's "virtual inventory," a computer-based system that puts them on-line with GE, so that they can check inventory and availability, and promise next-day delivery to *their* customers.[11] The customer is GE's partner, examining inventory, ordering, and scheduling delivery: tasks GE previously undertook. And the retailer doesn't have to carry the costs of hundreds of appliances in inventory in order to satisfy his own customers' needs.

One of the most astonishing examples of how customers can participate in telling business how to operate through technology is found in Motorola's Bravo pager factory. The variables in the design of a paper run to some 29 million possible combinations. But a customer can describe the qualities he wants to a Motorola salesperson, and together they can design the customer's pager, on a laptop computer, which forwards the specifications to the factory by modem. In a matter of hours, the factory can produce the customer-designed pager in lots as small as one![12]

ValueLink is a program set up by Baxter HealthCare Corporation to help hospitals reduce the large amounts of money that they spend on storing and distributing supplies within the hospital. The program is based on the core concepts of the "stockless environment" and "just-in-time" delivery. It works like this.

ValueLink takes over the inventory management from a hospital. It houses the required inventory in a distribution center. The hospital requests its supplies electronically. Baxter fills these orders within 24 hours. The net result of this partnership—major hospitals save as much as $1 to $2 million in operating expenses and Baxter earns a service fee and frequently becomes the hospital's sole supplier of medical items. Joint value creation par excellence.

## REENGINEERING THE ORGANIZATION'S MENTAL MAP

Most organizations today are not positioned to deliver total customer value or to engage in joint value creation. They are still operating with company-centered maps. They are victims of their own past success. They have a hard time understanding that what got them here will not get them there, and that in the future, good enough will not be good enough.

The executives in these company-centered organizations devote most, if not their exclusive, attention to and talk about those reports, measures, and indicators that relate to the company's performance, productivity, and profits. They are internally focused and think from the inside out. Consequently, if they undertake a reengineering initiative, their primary focus is to improve organizational efficiency or effectiveness.

Given this situation, the first step that these organizations must take in order to satisfy the 21st century imperative of reengineering for total customer value is to reconstruct their mental maps or, to use the current jargon term, to make a *paradigm shift* from company-centered thinking to customer-centered thinking.

Organizations with customer-centered mental maps stand in bold relief to company-centered organizations. They are externally focused upon the customer. They think from the outside in rather than from the inside out. Their executives are most concerned with customer contact measures. They believe that increased customer satisfaction and loyalty translate into enhanced organizational performance. Consequently, if they undertake a reengineering initiative, the primary focus is to address customer expectations and experience.

Customer-centered organizations have several key defining characteristics. They

- **Practice TLC.** That's not "tender loving care." It's thinking like a customer. These organizations think customer not company; problem not product; satisfaction not service.

- **See the customer as their primary asset.** They recognize that their real assets are not the balance they have in the bank, their rolling stock, or their inventory, but their customer base. They realize that if the company loses its customers, all of their other assets can disappear very quickly. Consequently, they do lifetime value calculations for their key customers and do everything they can to capture that full value.

- **Define their business purpose as customer satisfaction.** They concentrate not on what they do but on managing the customer's expectations and experience to promote satisfaction.

- **Operate with a marriage mindset.** They establish long-term relationships and create incentives to promote loyalty and allegiance from both customers and employees.

Customer-centered organizations also emphasize a different vocabulary. The key words in their language and the core concepts for customer centering are presented in Figure 2–2. We have defined

**FIGURE 2–2**
*Key Customer Centering Concepts*

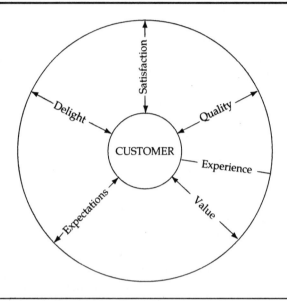

Source: Services Marketing Council, *Customer Satisfaction Measurement, Analysis and Use*
(Chicago: American Marketing Association, 1993).

some of the terms earlier. However, it is worthwhile to review them
here:

- **Expectations**—the attributes or attitudes that a customer has that
  form the framework for judging performance.
- **Experience**—an interaction of the customer with any aspect of the
  organization in a "moment of truth."
- **Satisfaction**—the measure of the extent to which a customer's
  experience matches expectations.
- **Quality**—what the customer says it is. The whole bundle of
  tangibles and intangibles that a customer takes into account when
  evaluating an experience.
- **Value**—the quality of an experience as perceived by the customer,
  related to its cost.
- **Delight**—a condition in which experience exceeds expectations.

Finally, the customer-centered organization operates with an entirely different perspective than does the company-centered organization in terms of the importance of organizational priorities as reflected in the chart that follows.

## Organizational Priorities

| Company-Centered Perspective | Customer-Centered Perspective |
| --- | --- |
| Organizational hierarchy | Customer value hierarchy |
| Products/services | Customer value package |
| Mass production | Customerization |
| Durable goods | Enduring relationships |
| Zero defects | Zero defections |

## ADOPTING CUSTOMER-CENTERED MANAGEMENT SYSTEMS

After a company has reengineered its thinking style or mental map, the next step toward becoming customer-centered is to change its management methods. The two dominant management approaches of the past quarter century have probably been MBO (management by objectives) and TQM (total quality management). Both of these approaches have been heavily internally focused with very little consideration given to the customer's interest.

In most MBO systems, managers set performance objectives related to what they or the organization will accomplish in areas such as growth, profitability, and productivity improvement. In most TQM systems, managers work to move quality beyond the manufacturing floor and to deploy it into everything that the organization does.

TQM systems are supposed to take the customer's needs into account. However, we have found that this is frequently not the case. As Tom Peters notes, some magic, infinitely flexible elixir called TQM is not the answer to all of America's vexing business problems. In fact, TQM often looks suspiciously like the latest act in a long-running farce called "Revenge of the Number Nerds." The quantified q-word—quality—seems to be crowding out the far more important and messier c-word—customers.

Customers bleed. Customers weep. Customers hurt. Customers are capricious. Customers are testy. Customers are ridiculous. Customers don't listen. And customers, and customers alone, pay the salary that puts your kids through college.[13]

The organization that wants to succeed in the future will have to replace its internally focused MBO and TQM systems with externally oriented systems. Its success formula for the 21st century must be: MBE + TQS.

MBE stands for "management by expectations" and "management by experiences." That's what customers have. As a result, the customer-centered organizations will have a sophisticated management and measuring system for defining, operating, and tracking of those areas that are most critical to the customer.

TQS® stands for total quality service. Total quality service, as we define it, is a state of affairs in which an organization delivers superior value to its customers, employees, and stakeholders. Research has shown that those organizations that can balance and satisfy the interests of these three customer groups significantly outperform those that just concentrate on maximizing value for a single constituency.[14]

By studying the best practices of customer-centered organizations around the world, our friend and partner, Karl Albrecht, discovered that they had mastered five distinct, yet interrelated competency areas:

- **Market and customer research**—discovering the invisible truths regarding their customer's needs.
- **Strategy formulation**—creating new rules for the game by which competitors must play.
- **Education, training, and communication**—winning heads, hearts, and minds at all levels throughout the organization to maximize impact.
- **Process improvement**—doing better with less through the redesign of core organizational systems and methods.
- **Assessment, measurement, and feedback**—using the right scorecards to make the right decisions on an ongoing basis on behalf of the customer.

Karl used this discovery to develop the TQS model that he first introduced in the book, *The Only Thing That Matters: Bringing the Power of the Customer into the Center of Your Business*.[15]

The TQS model (see Figure 2–3) provides a general framework and management system for creating total customer value. However, there is no one standardized improvement approach or framework that can fit all organizations. Therefore, each organization must apply the framework to set a direction and chart a course that makes the most sense given its particular culture and conditions.

## IMPLICATIONS FOR REENGINEERING

In conclusion, the implications of the total customer value imperative are considerable and far reaching. Total customer value will ensure customer loyalty and competitive advantages into the future.

**FIGURE 2–3**
*The TQS® Model*

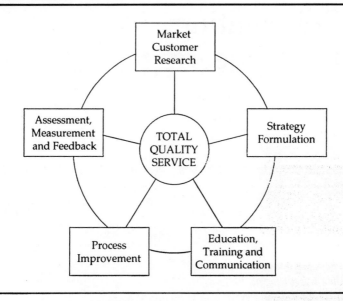

If the majority of organizations have been as insular and company-centered as we have characterized, then they will have to be willing to reinvent themselves from the outside in and the ground up in order to create customer value. They must be willing to become a customer-centered organization in which every job, every person, every department, and every process add value in order to impact the customer's experience positively.

Business process reengineering as it is normally practiced—no matter how radical—will be an insufficient response to meet these needs. What will be required instead is a much more strategic, comprehensive, and culturally integrated approach for driving and mastering change and reconstructing the way that the company does business. In order to accomplish this, we need to begin by reinventing reengineering itself.

## Chapter Three

# Reinventing Reengineering

*"We're not in the business of making cars, we're in the business of making money."*

Alfred Sloan

*I kept six honest serving men,*
*they taught me all I knew*
*their names were What and Why and When*
*and How and Where and Who.*

Rudyard Kipling

The buck stops at the top. And that is why it rarely gives you change.

## GHOSTBUSTERS

This is a lesson that we learned while interviewing the CEO of one of the largest property and casualty insurers in the country as a prelude to launching a major customer focus initiative with his company. During the course of our interview, we asked him what his top priorities were for the business.

He quickly rattled off increased market share, greater profitability, cost reduction, productivity improvement, and technical leadership. Then he paused for a moment, looked at us, remembered that we were the *customer guys,* and said proudly, "And, of course, quality and customer focus."

He thought he was following the recipe exactly—providing top management involvement, commitment, and leadership, and elevating customer focus to a major priority. However, we knew then that this particular improvement effort was in troubled waters. Why?

Because customer focus cannot survive as an equal priority. It will be set aside when push comes to shove and there's a downturn in the organization's economic fortunes or results are not achieved immediately.

The conflicting priorities issue is so pervasive that many companies never get around to becoming customer-centered. This occurs because their top executives have two lists in their heads, *hard* lists and *soft* lists. Issues on the hard list are profit, production costs, market share, shareholder return, and so on. Subjects such as customer, service, and quality are on the soft list. These managers pride themselves for keeping their *eye on the ball* and only doing the things on the hard list. Soft-list items can either be delegated or occasionally, temporarily, elevated into a priority status. Top management of some companies just never get around to the soft lists.

Why is this? Because they are victims of their company's own past and haunted by historic role models. Who are the ghosts of Corporate America past? Henry Ford, Frederick Taylor, and George Patton, to name a few.

Henry Ford—the proponent of division of labor and inventor of the modern assembly line. Efficiency and economy of scale were his watchwords, and they served him well in his day. However, in the era of mass customization and having it your way, we are still held in thrall by the precepts of the man intent on giving customers any color car they wanted "as long as it was black."

Frederick Taylor—the father of scientific management. He taught that everything that happened in a business could be broken down to its component parts and analyzed. In a very unscientific era, these concepts made great strides. However, with this as such a deep-rooted part of our corporate heritage, too many executives believe that strategic failures are due to inadequate analysis of tasks and activities rather than flawed assumptions about customers or markets or the inability to take into account the human factors.

George Patton—tank commander and the quintessential military man. His image as an exemplar of the "command and control" school of management has shaped much of our leadership behavior since World War II. For too many, the learned instinct is still to devise the grand strategy in the war room, then summon the troops, give the marching orders, and sit back at headquarters and await reports from the front. Empowerment?

## THE PARADIGM PARADOX

What do these ghosts tell us? That it's hard to break out of our dominant mindsets. The ideas, actions, and reactions that made most executives successful are hard to turn away from. By and large, Western executives are good at tactics and poor at strategy, good at fire fighting and poor at planning. Lessons learned are hard to unlearn. When executives start from these perspectives, too often they end up settling for incremental improvement, "tweaking" the system, rather than really rethinking it. They continue to develop 20th century solutions for 21st century problems.

This *company-centered* thinking contaminates the approach that most organizations take to reengineering and, as a consequence, seriously retards the nature of change and the results achieved. In their book, *Reengineering the Corporation*, Hammer and Champy define reengineering as:

> the fundamental rethinking and radical redesign of business process to achieve dramatic improvements in critical, contemporary measures of performance, such as cost, quality, and speed.[1]

This orientation represents a significant advancement in the "process improvement" arena. While few could argue with the concept, the problem is in its application.

In our experience, supported by Hammer and Champy's conclusion that as much as 70 percent of all traditional reengineering efforts fail, most companies concentrate their efforts inappropriately. They put far too great an emphasis on "business processes" and not nearly enough on truly understanding their customer's needs. This may be because, as Jim Dauner, our colleague in The TSQ Group, notes, "In too many companies, what's called reengineering is really just downsizing or cost cutting in disguise. It's a wolf in sheep's clothing."

In addition, much business process reengineering starts in the wrong place—with the company—and with the wrong tactical question, "How?" Companies should start instead with the customer and by asking the strategic questions of *who, what, why, where, and when.* These include the following:

*Strategic reengineering questions*

- Who are our key customers?
- What unmet expectations do they have?
- What current experiences are unsatisfactory?
- Where is the industry or market headed?
- What unmet market needs or opportunities exist?
- What can we do to respond to these unmet customer and market opportunities?
- In what critical business areas or units should we be investing?
- What strategies should we pursue to create industry breakpoints?
- What can we do to break away from the competition and create long-term barriers to entry?

- What competencies do we have today?
- What needs to be done to develop the differentiating competencies required to maintain a sustainable competitive edge over time?
- What changes will be required to our existing organizational structure, systems, and strategy to implement our new strategies?
- What changes will be required of our people to make this change most successfully?
- Why should they change? Why should we change?
- When is the best time to make the change to maximize its success potential?

This distinction between company-centered and customer-centered questions and answers is a critical one. It has been our experience that too many executives are quite willing to tackle the *how* without much regard to the *who, what, where,* and *why*. Therefore, the notion that reengineering is about redesigning business processes rather than first developing a clear understanding of the strategic business imperative and need for change plays right into the prevailing executive mindset and comfort zone and sets up an initiative for failure from the outset. It promotes change within the box when what is required is change outside the box. It addresses the pieces and not the whole.

Organizations can no longer afford this form of mechanistic and incremental problem-solving. They need to employ an alternative paradigm and a strategic methodology that enable them to explore and alter the fundamental manner in which they are organized and operated in response to and in satisfaction of the needs of today's and tomorrow's customers. We believe customer-centered reengineering represents such a methodology. It provides a framework for reinventing both reengineering and the organization from the outside in.

## CUSTOMER-CENTERED REENGINEERING

There are seven precepts that are central to customer-centered reengineering:

1. An organization is a complex organic system comprised of four major interdependent components—*strategy, structure, systems (processes),* and *employees*—that function together to transform inputs into outputs and accomplish goals in order to create value for customers.
2. The process of reengineering involves *remapping* and realigning of those components around the customer.
3. In order to accomplish this remapping, it is essential to have a clear and precise understanding of *customer expectations*.

4. The ultimate purpose for reengineering is to create a state of *total customer value.*

5. For reengineering to have its maximum benefit for the organization, it must be directly connected to the organization's *strategic business purpose*—its northbound train.

6. For reengineering to have the maximum long-term impact, it must be *strategically integrated* into all aspects of the organization's way of doing business: its policies, procedures, practices, and processes.

7. Reengineering is not a one-time event. It is a *continuous process of innovating* to surpass customer expectations and empowering employees to manage relationships in a manner that creates customer delight and loyalty.

Based upon these precepts, we offer the following definition of customer-centered reengineering.

---

**Customer-Centered Reengineering**

Customer-centered reengineering is reinventing the business from the outside in by remapping the organization's strategy, systems, and structure around employees so that they can create total customer value.

---

This definition is portrayed visually in the *Customer-Centered Reengineering Triangle* in Figure 3–1. As the visual depicts, the *customer* is at the center of the reengineering universe. The value creation process begins and ends there.

Employees are in the circle around the customer—the *"0"* ring if you will. They are the front-line staff, support staff, managers, and executives who, through their understanding of the customer's centrality to the enterprise and of the organization's management structure, strategy, and system, can deliver an experience and establish and manage a relationship that promotes customer delight and loyalty. They are also the ones who can recover immediately if something goes wrong.

The *strategy* is at the top of the triangle. It is a set of guiding principles that tell everyone in the organization what we are trying to accomplish on behalf of the customer, what will be done to create total customer value.

The *systems* are all the processes that affect the customer's perception of value. These include core business functions like research, engineering, design, manufacturing, marketing, distribution, and finance, and processes that cut across functions such as order fulfill-

**FIGURE 3–1**
*The Customer-Centered Reengineering Triangle*

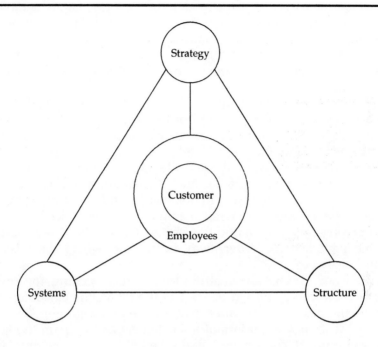

ment or product development. They also involve all other organization policies, practices, and procedures such as forms that may have to be filled out, the telephone system, the warehouse, the order desk, the signs in the waiting room—those things and activities with which customers come in contact or that affect the customer's sensibilities in the course of the entire encounter with the organization.

The *structure* deals with the way the business is organized—reporting relationships, levels of authority, centralized or decentralized—which either adds or subtracts value for the customer.

Finally, as the triangle shows, all of the components must be brought together and strategically integrated to create a framework that enables the organization to *triangulate for total customer value*.

## THE BUILDING BLOCKS OF CUSTOMER VALUE

Customer-centered reengineering starts with determining what customers value. The basic concepts of customer value are derived from the research of Karl Albrecht and from our consulting work with hundreds of clients on the issues involved in achieving and maintaining a culture of total quality service. These TQS® concepts and theories include the customer value model, the customer value hierarchy, and the customer value package. They are discussed in greater depth in the book *The Only Thing that Matters.*[2]

A *customer value model* (CVM) is the set of critical product and service factors, as perceived by the customer, that influence the perception of value.

We worked with a major national fast-food chain that had developed a fairly comprehensive CVM of its own. It had all—or almost all—the right characteristics: price, cleanliness, speedy service, friendly service, acceptably tasty food, attractive facility. Even though the elements were mostly all there, the chain was not flourishing. Through our research, we determined that high on the list was an item the chain's management had not even considered: *Getting the order right*. If a customer ordered a burger, fries, and iced tea, she would be very unhappy to find that she got Coke instead—especially after having taken the order away in her car, where the mistake couldn't easily be fixed.

Apart from finding some attributes (such as getting the order right) that the company had not put in the CVM, the customers rearranged the order of their importance. Price and a smiling "Have a nice day" were not as important to customers as the chain thought; clean environment, convenience, and speed of service were more important than expected. The customers completely revised the chain's thinking about what matters most, thereby recreating the customer value model for the company.

Any organization that wants to maintain its competitive position needs to be willing to acknowledge that it does not have all the answers: sometimes you have to ask for help. In the case of the CVM, you have to ask the customers, through *customer research* employing interviews, focus groups, surveys, or any other way you can devise. Ask the customers what is important, and what is more important and less important. Then, find out how you should weight these factors in devising your CVM.

The *customer value hierarchy* (Figure 3–2) is similar to Maslow's hierarchy of human needs. It arrays the product or service factors, each of which has some bearing on its value and its rank in the hierarchy of values for the customer.

The first step in this hierarchy is the *basic* or generic level. The attributes here are those fundamentals that generally define the product or service. At this level, an automobile, for instance, is a functioning transportation device. A restaurant meal is simply that: food that is edible and delivered as ordered to the customer by a serving person. This level of value is so basic, in fact, that it is usually not an accept-

**FIGURE 3–2**
*The Customer Value Hierarchy*

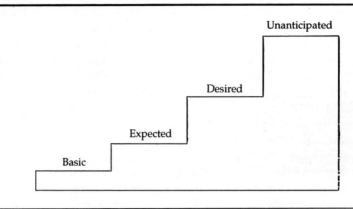

able, or positive, level at all. In most instances, if all you get is this basic level of value, you are disappointed, dissatisfied, and unlikely to buy from that vendor again.

The *expected* level of value is that which we have been conditioned to anticipate as customers. It adds to the basic level enough "grace notes" to make the basic acceptable, but not exceptional. The automobile's *expected* attributes have come to include power brakes and steering, air bags, air conditioning, AM/FM radios with cassette players, and so on. The expected level of value is in constant flux with most products that are subject to technological modification (call it *improvement*).

In services, the expected level is highly subjective and varies widely from one experience to the next. If you go to a fast-food restaurant, for example, your expectations are very different from when you visit your town's smartest—and most expensive—fine dining restaurant. In the latter, you *expect* good china and tableware, linen tablecloth and napkins, flowers on the table, discreet, liveried, attentive service, and so on, in addition to well-cooked food from an extensive menu. None of these attributes is on your list at this level when you visit one of the fast-food chains. The goods and service that have the expected attributes provide us, generally, with a *satisfactory* experience—an OK sense of having provided value for the cost. But nothing special.

When we move to the next level, we begin to exercise our wills and desires as a customer. Sure, I expect to have a good meal, but I would like to have a *really good* meal. For an automobile, desired attributes might be a "no hassle" purchase experience—not feeling as if you're locked into an adversarial fight to the death struggle for your wallet. The chocolate on your pillow at a good hotel has become pretty common, but it might still be one of the *desired* attributes, and not just expected. (What used to be at the desired level in hotels has changed over the years, just as our expectations of automobiles have changed. No longer is a kit of toiletries a pleasant surprise; it is expected. It takes a little more now to raise the hotel experience to the level of *desired* value.)

Beyond the desired lies the realm of superlatives: the *unanticipated level* of value. But maybe it's what's at this level. This is much harder to define because, as Don Mizaur, former director of the Federal Quality Institute, describes it, "We don't know what we don't know." When the fast-food restaurant puts a flower on each table (or even on each tray). When, after the purchase is finalized, the car dealer tells you that you are entitled to free maintenance on your new vehicle for its life. Or that you can return the car if you don't like it with no questions asked, within the first 30 days of ownership. When the hotel tells you, a perfect stranger, that you are invited to stay in the executive suite, at no added cost. When your insurance company calls to find out if you were happy with the repairs to your car, and actually does something about it if you are not.

What matters about this hierarchy of values, from our point of view, is this: You can define the basic and even expected level of value pretty well. You have the knowledge and experience to go on; you know what is selling and what has been selling, and how the trends are moving. But the attributes at this level are survival attributes, at best. For successful competition, you have to provide those attributes that belong to the higher levels. And those attributes are determined by the customers out there.

As a quick review and example of the customer value hierarchy concept and how one company applied it to leapfrog the competition, think about what Fred Smith did with Federal Express. Basic level— deliver letters and packages anywhere in the United States; expected level—deliver within a reasonable amount of time; desired level— deliver next day; unanticipated level—deliver absolutely, positively by 10 AM the next day.

Based on his implicit understanding of the customer value hierarchy, Fred Smith was able to reinvent and reengineer the delivery industry. This gave Federal Express a competitive advantage for a considerable period of time until the competition caught up and the customer's *expectation escalator* kicked in. Now, we have an almost level playing field again and Federal Express, UPS, and a small handful of other competitors are in a dead heat in a footrace to win the customers' hearts, minds, and checkbooks.

The customer value model and the customer value hierarchy can be used as the fundamental framework for clarifying and reengineering the organization's *customer value package* (CVP). The CVP is that combination of tangible and intangible things, experiences, and outcomes that is designed to win the approval of the customer—and which in turn earns each of us the right to survive and thrive in our marketplace.

Very few organizations have focused the design of their customer value packages squarely on the critical quality attributes of their customer value models. Indeed, probably a majority of organizations operate without any explicit customer value model at all. They do business based on historical assumptions and uneducated guesses about what the customer is really trying to buy.

As shown in Figure 3–3, the CVP can be subdivided into seven key components:

- **Environmental**—the physical setting in which the customer experiences the delivery of the product; for example, the inside of a retail store, a hotel, a post office, a hospital, the cabin of an airplane, or the slopes of a ski resort.

- **Aesthetic**—any sensory experience that affects the perception of value, such as the flavor of food, the visual appeal of a retail environment, any experience of pain or discomfort, temperature, humidity, background music, sound level, or the ambiance of a facility.

- **Interpersonal**—the customers' experience or human interaction with those who deliver what they seek; examples are telephone conversations, face-to-face encounters with salespeople, bodily contact such as in health care, and the demeanor of a person who delivers or repairs an item.

- **Deliverable**—anything of which the customer takes custody, even temporarily, such as a piece of merchandise, a food tray on an airplane, bank statements and other documents, or medications.

- **Procedural**—what a person has to go through to function as a customer, such as filling out forms, providing information, visiting various facilities, making payments, or waiting in lines.

- **Informational**—the information a person needs to function as a customer, such as signs that tell which way to go, financial figures on a statement, instructions for installing or using a piece of equipment, pricing schedules, or knowledge of what to expect during and after medical treatment.

- **Financial**—what the customer pays for the total experience, as well as the nature of the financial interaction, such as price or fee structures, billing methods, refunds or rebates, discount terms, guarantees, or collateral value such as volume bonuses.

**FIGURE 3–3**
*The Customer Value Package*

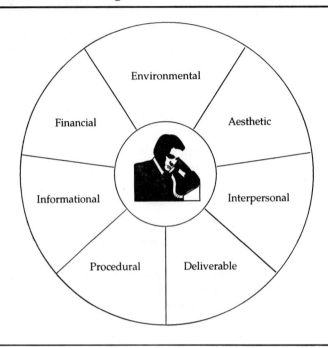

With an increasingly articulate, knowledgeable, and demanding customer out there, and with plenty of competition ready to snatch him or her up, it becomes ever more important to make the customer value package the right "size." The CVP must be distinctive. It must fit the targeted customer. In this regard, it is important to remember that you can't fit all customers or be everything to everybody. Being in the middle means losing distinction.

Take a look at the hotel industry over the past year or so. The only winners have been those that have discovered and catered to market segments that are carefully defined. Not only that, but the customers have helped to design the product.

Marriott Corporation interviewed thousands of business travelers to find out what rated high in the business travelers' customer value model. What were the features/benefits–cost trade-offs? Did this customer want exercise rooms and cocktail lounges? Two phones? Phones on the desk or beside the bed? What hotel features did the business traveler consider to have real value? As Marriott's advertising says, the Marriott Courtyards are "designed by business travelers for business travelers." And the chain is showing a profit.

Another profitable hotel segment is the upscale, luxury element, where the emphasis is on good restaurants, bigger and better towels, superb service, and the other amenities in the upper bracket customer value model. Ritz-Carlton has designed its customer value package to match this model, and as a result has captured much of the high-end business and stayed profitable.

The vast majority of hotels, remaining squarely "in the middle" and without distinguishing themselves or their CVPs, have struggled, at best, and most have suffered losses. Similarly, the big mass-marketing, middle-of-the-road airlines are also losing money left and right. Not everyone in the airline industry is losing. Through careful positioning and not losing sight of the CVP they are selling, two domestic carriers are doing very nicely, thank you.

At one end of the spectrum, Southwest Airlines is putting no-frills, low-cost travel on the map and turning a profit. Their CVP is simple: on-time departure and arrival, a smile, a Coke, a sack of peanuts, and the fairest boarding procedures in the airline industry—you are assigned a number when you arrive at the Southwest check-in counter and you board the plane in that order.

At the other end of the spectrum, tiny Midwest Express continues to rack up good numbers as a regional carrier, delivering service and amenities comparable to (maybe even better than) the first-class offerings of the majors, for all passengers, at coach-class prices. Meals are top quality, served with china and metal flatware. There are only two seats on each side of the aisle. The seats are large, comfortable, and covered in leather. Legroom is great. Ground services are comparable to those provided in the air. And Midwest flies full and at a profit.

The customer value methods are primary tools in the reengineers' tool kit. To use them correctly, the reengineer needs a blueprint for remapping the organization. Chapter Four sets out a process for developing that blueprint.

## Chapter Four

# Triangulating for Total Customer Value

*"Quality in a service or product is not what you put into it. It is what the client or customer gets out of it."*

Peter Drucker

*"In the West, the emphasis is on finding the answer to the problem; to the Japanese it is defining the problem."*

Harvey Brightman

We have seen the shape of the future, and it is triangular.

## TRIANGULATION UP TOP AND DOWN UNDER

The customer value model, the customer value hierarchy, and the customer value package are the basic building blocks for customer-centering. The customer-centered reengineering triangle provides the integrative framework for remapping the organization around the customer by *recasting strategies, redesigning systems, reshaping structure,* and *reawakening people* through a focus on the customer's expectations and experiences.

Let's take a quick look at two mini-case studies of how customer-focused triangulation has been used to turn organizations around. One case is from the private sector, relatively well-known, and from up top here in the United States. The other is from the public sector, relatively unknown, and from down under in Australia.

### IDS Financial Services: Case Study

One company already embarked on the reengineering journey is IDS Financial Services, the Minneapolis-based division of American Express Co. Known as "IDS 1994," the plan being implemented is attempting to change the core of the company's corporate culture: the reliance on more than 6,500 independent financial planners/salespeople to market IDS's financial products. Says American Express CEO Harvey Golub, "IDS represents for the whole company a very important laboratory for organizational change."[1]

The initiative was prompted by a number of converging forces: increased competition from some of the nation's largest financial service companies, like Merrill Lynch and Prudential Insurance Co.; extremely high turnover among the sales force, with 50 percent attrition in the first year among new planners and only 30 percent lasting more than four years; and a mistake-prone back-office support operation.

With the support of IDS president Jerry Stiefler, vice presidents Becky Roloff and Bill Scholz are heading a 30-person design team charged with achieving four primary objectives through the reengineering effort: achieving annual revenue growth of 18 percent, retaining 95 percent of the clients, keeping 80 percent of IDS financial planners through four years, and enhancing the company's reputation as the industry leader. Before it's completed, the initiative will have taken more than four years and cost over $1 billion. Virtually all aspects of how the company works will be touched in order to create a group of planners who work smarter, are better organized, have more access to potential clients, and are supported more effectively by the home office.

In an effort to be customer-centered, the goal of client attraction and retention, one of the four primary goals, is getting a lot of attention. Recognizing that potential customers are more and more resistant to the traditional methods of cold-calling, IDS will concentrate on working with other professionals such as lawyers and accountants to identify prospective clients. Once in the sales pipeline, the company's revamped procedures and new automation should help the planners deliver services to their customers more quickly and at a lower cost. Planners will also be assisted by tax, estate planning, and investment product experts to help design a more customized approach for each customer. One critical difference arising from the reengineering initiative: these experts will share in the commissions previously paid only to the planners.

In terms of the planners themselves, IDS will continue to spend approximately $100 million annually on training. The big difference will be that first-year *rookies* will be actively mentored by veteran planners who will be compensated for their coaching. Rookies will also be salaried during the first year. All of these efforts are aimed at reducing turnover, particularly in the crucial first year.

Early analysis of the company's systems and procedures by the IDS reengineering design team focused on interactions between the field salespeople and the headquarters staff. Following every step of a customer's experience with IDS, the team has identified many areas for streamlining and computerization, expected to cost about $150 million.

What did the design team find exactly? That about 70 out of 110 activities involved in setting up a new client account are redundant. Not only does this cumbersome process affect costs through duplication of effort, increased headcount, and downtime for planners who must help sort out the problems, but it affects client satisfaction as well. Notes consultant David Nadler, an observer of this and similar redesigns, "We've seen a movement from the materials factory to the paper factory to the knowledge factory. IDS is the natural evolution, the next step."

## Australian Department of Arts and Administrative Services: Case Study

Radical change is not just the province of the private sector. The Department of Arts and Administrative Services (DAS) is one of the major federal government agencies in Australia. DAS is comprised of approximately 20 business units and an annual budget of more than $A1 billion. DAS is presently involved in one of the most innovative experiments in the history of government worldwide: transformation from a traditional Department of State to a "commercialized" mode of public administration. It now competes with any other provider (public or private) for 90 percent of its revenue.

We discuss this transformation more fully in Chapter Twelve. However, because of the success of this "experiment," it is well worth highlighting some aspects of the transformation here.

The Australian Parliament decided to commercialize DAS because it wanted to reduce costs and achieve greater efficiency and effectiveness in the operations of government. These economies were essential given the severe recession in Australia and the fact that government accounts for such a large part of Australia's spending and GNP. In converting DAS to the commercialized mode, DAS sent a simple message to its managers and employees: You're no longer on the public purse strings. Either compete effectively, or go out of business.

How did DAS react? As Noel Tanzer, secretary and CEO of DAS at the time of the transformation puts it,

> At first, we were traumatized. I didn't know whether I was going to preside over a wake or facilitate a rebirth. I decided that I'd rather participate in the latter. And I knew that most of my mates—since their careers were on the line—felt the same way. We decided to give it a go.

Secretary Tanzer and his executive team faced a tough challenge, and they knew that only radical surgery would save the patient. They used customer-focus and a willingness to reengineer everything as the means for a dramatically successful turnaround. How did it all come about? As Tanzer says:

> We knew that it wouldn't be good enough just to change our structure or to lop off gobs of jobs here and there—to do "toe cutting" as we call it in Australia. We knew that we had to reinvent the way that we did business to survive and to succeed in the long run. We identified four major actions that we had to take. We had to change the rules and become commercial. This included giving users of DAS's service choices in who they could purchase from. We had to change the mechanics and become businesslike. This included renegotiating contracts, establishing a board of directors, and implementing new accounting and business planning procedures. We had to change the focus and become customer-centered. This included conducting customer research and developing a strategic plan for achieving a total customer focus in each key DAS business unit. Finally, we had to change the management to become servant leaders. In certain areas this meant replacing those individuals who couldn't adapt to a commercial culture. More frequently, it meant providing business and leadership training for our executives.

The most fundamental change at DAS was a complete turnaround in its strategic thinking. Tanzer says: "We committed to reengineering every one of our business units around the needs of their key customers in order to maximize the value that we offered to them. We conducted customer research and a complete operational review and assessment of each business unit. Then, we created a framework for achieving total customer focus in each business unit. In many cases, this led to the development and implementation of radically different strategies, structures, and business processes."

The results from all of this have been impressive. Four years after beginning this major change process, the commercial businesses within DAS have transformed a loss of more than $A100 million in 1989 to a modest profit of $A4 million in 1992. Profit for 1993 is estimated to be approximately $A50 million.

Other breakthroughs achieved since 1988 have included annual productivity improvements approaching 6 percent, approximately twice the average for the Australian federal public service. Costs have been reduced by more than 30 percent, resulting in savings of more than $A300 million per year. Satisfaction surveys acknowledge significant improvements in DAS's approach to understanding customer needs and in delivering services. DAS has created new business ventures and has successfully negotiated teaming arrangements, strategic alliances, and joint ventures with the private sector.

Most importantly, DAS has created an entirely new culture that should sustain this performance. To quote Tanzer again: "We knew that for DAS to change, we as the leaders had to change and that our employees had to change too. We have and they have. I'm proud of what we've accomplished. We did it as a team. And I'd rather be on a championship team than on a team of champions any day. DAS has become a championship team. And, even though I am retiring, I am confident it will stay that way."

DAS and IDS are organizations known by their initials. As these stories illustrate, they share more than that in common, however. They have achieved great success by remapping their strategies, structures, systems, and people to center on the customer. Other organizations have profited from the same perspective. Let's look at a few examples.

## RECASTING STRATEGY

Changing times require changing strategies. Nowhere is this more true than in health care. It used to be that a pharmaceutical company's sales representative ("detail man") would make his pitch to doctors, who would prescribe medicines by their "brand" names. The doctor's patient took the prescription to a drugstore, where the pharmacists would follow the instructions; if the prescription said "Brand X," you got Brand X.

Times change. Increasingly, HMOs and other group health providers will pay only for generic or less costly look-alikes, rather than the more expensive drug specified in the prescription. As a result, more often than not, it is the insurance company or the pharmacist, not the prescribing doctor, who actually decides which drug is to be used. This means the *customer* has actually changed.

We spotted the acceleration of this trend in the spring of 1992 when we were doing customer and market research for one of the country's largest pharmaceutical companies. We reported our findings to the senior management in the marketing department of the company and recommended a number of things including a radically different organizational structure, selling strategies, and staffing levels. These marketing executives chose to ignore our advice. Stuck in their paradigm, they were reluctant to move away from the industry's traditional methods for marketing and decided instead to continue their emphasis on the company's large sales force calling on physicians.

Drug giant Merck, upon recognizing these same changes in the industry, has been downsizing its sales force and looking for other ways to reach its customers. In a dramatic move, the company recently acquired Medco, a mail-order pharmaceutical company that provides a wide range of drugs to bulk users at wholesale discounts. Merck continues to function as before with its brand-name drugs and detail men making sales calls on prescribing physicians, but because it has recognized that the customer's identity has changed, it has acquired a different mechanism to reach the "new customer." Our client had the same information Merck did, possibly even earlier, yet they chose a different road. They just recently announced a substantial reduction of their sales force. Some lessons in recasting strategy are painful, and some companies never learn them.

Not so at Merck. There, rethinking strategy is serious business. As their chairman and CEO Dr. Roy Vagelos says, "It's a strategy game. You pick out the areas where you can do some good, where real innovation is possible, and put the money into them."[2]

Before the divestiture of AT&T, the old Bell system was known for its emphasis on service. After the breakup in 1984, the seven "Baby Bells" emerged, and both the companies and the customers were left without a clear set of rules, values, or direction. Neither customers nor employees were certain about where responsibilities lay—for problems with bills, changes in long distance service, fixing the phone, and so on. BellSouth was the first to get organized, according to Buddy Henry, Jr., vice president for Florida operations at Southern Bell.

The key to their success was a strategic determination to focus on customer service. The company defined a set of customer-oriented values and then ingrained them in the employee population by stressing them in employee media and by measuring and rewarding employee performance based on those values. BellSouth made total customer satisfaction a cornerstone of its strategy, and consequently outperformed the other Baby Bells from the outset.

## REDESIGNING SYSTEMS

What got you here will not necessarily get you there. Honda had captured a significant segment of the American automobile market, typified by its longtime best-selling Accord family sedan. Honda's dominance has gradually come under attack as Ford and other US automakers have responded to the Japanese challenge. The company could have sat back for some time and not reacted, but that's not the Japanese way. In its recent introduction of the 1994 model Accord, Honda embraced an entirely new design philosophy that required intensive cooperation and collaboration of marketing and manufacturing personnel from its Marysville, Ohio, plant. This breaking down of walls and closer coordination allowed the company to restructure the automobile development process, build in only those factors that were most important to the customer, and keep the cost of the new car at the same level as that of the previous model. That's creating customer value.

Taco Bell provides probably the most famous example of reengineering for customer value. They brought value pricing to the fast-food restaurant industry. They did it because they discovered that was what the customer wanted. As John E. Martin, CEO of Taco Bell puts it, "The initial research we did at Taco Bell became our declaration of independence. It helped us look at Taco Bell in an entirely different way and allowed us to turn customer value into the key element of our business proposition."[3]

This new perspective caused Taco Bell to *dramatically redesign* its operational systems. It caused them to move most of their food preparation off-site to central commissaries or other suppliers and enabled them to reconfigure the restaurants themselves.

Before 1983, Taco Bell buildings were devoted to kitchen space (70 percent) at the expense of customer space (30 percent). Their buildings are still the same size, but now 70 percent of the space is devoted to customers and 30 percent to kitchens. "The earlier configuration resulted in a peak capacity for a top unit at about $400 per hour," according to Martin, "but today our top restaurants have a peak capacity of $1,500 per hour. Moreover, our average pricing today is about 25 percent lower than it was nine years ago."

Sometimes the best systems changes are not the ones originally intended. A national oil company asked for our assistance a few years ago and said, among other things, it wanted to make its service station attendants more "customer-friendly." What kind of training or other program could we recommend to bring this about?

It turns out that most of the "service" stations are attended by one person at a time and that attendant is stationed in a booth enclosed in four inches of bulletproof Plexiglas and communicates with customers through a microphone-and-speaker system. How does this guy become customer-friendly? Forget it! Since you have removed 90 percent of the human interaction from the transaction, go the rest of the way. Our recommendation was that the routine gas transactions be completely automated, *eliminating* the attendant from some 90 to 95 percent of all the visits of customers. If you can't make the attendant customer-friendly, replace the attendant with *user*-friendly automation.

Now, a few years later, this system is in widespread use, and customers love it! Quick, convenient, and no-hassle, and you don't have to put up with an attendant in a Plexiglas booth. And for the oil companies, it means big savings on personnel costs, instant data collection on sales and inventory, and greater accuracy resulting from less opportunity for human errors or other foibles.

## RESHAPING STRUCTURE

Many organizations change their structure as part of change efforts. Most, however, do it incorrectly. They begin by looking at themselves and asking: Where can we cut costs? What positions can we consolidate to eliminate jobs? They restructure with a "function follows form" mentality and assume that they can do whatever they want to structure with little to no attention to its impact on the customer.

In contrast to this, we believe that just as in building design, organizational architecture should be restructured so that "form follows function." If the purpose of the business is to create total customer value, then its functions should be structured from the outside in so that they all maximize the value creation potential of the enterprise. They need to be *customer sized* and *customer shaped* as part of the reengineering process.

Taco Bell took this lesson to heart in its reorganizing. They eliminated entire layers of *nonvalue-added* management and completely redesigned nearly every job in their system to ensure that they were all adding value. Alberta Power and Light in Canada, based on research that we completed for them that showed the need for rapid response to customers in remote locations, decentralized their engineering function to get their engineering closer to the customer. In contrast, GTE Telephone centralized its 800 service to provide quicker and better response to its customers.

## REAWAKENING PEOPLE

Getting all of your personnel on board for customer-focused reengineering is not always easy. This process of winning "converts" can take several different forms.

Some companies have used massive, *total immersion* training programs to get the word to their people. Jan Carlzon's turnaround of SAS was made possible in part by his insistence that *every* employee get the word, through a "wall-to-wall" training effort for all employees and the distribution of a "little red book" of customer service philosophy and guidelines.

Communication, and not just lip service, is essential for getting the word to everyone. Carlzon personally took his show on the road and preached the gospel to management and supervisors, but he also demonstrated consistently that he lived the philosophy he was preaching, through simple and concrete actions.

Still flying, British Airways has made significant strides in developing high-level customer satisfaction. Part of its success is due to the fact that it has put over 35,000 employees through a training program to enhance their sensitivity to the needs of their customers.

Managers—thousands of them—have been educated in the role of supervisors and other "backstage" personnel in supporting the front-line personnel and in maintaining high-level customer service.

The interrelationship of communication and service leadership is also personified by the legendary Sam Walton, who got the word to his employees that the customer was paramount through his own habit of greeting customers and talking with them when they came into his store. Now, of course, it is standard for Wal-Mart stores to have a greeter at the entrance to each store.

## REMAPPING THE ORGANIZATION

As in any major organizational change, the process by which customer-centered reengineering will be managed is crucial to its ultimate success. As shown in Figure 4–1, the customer-centered reengineering change process model has seven major phases. We describe the phases in detail in the Implementation Guide presented as the final chapter of this book; we provide an introduction to them now.

*Organizational readiness* assesses the degree to which various parts of the organization understand the potential implications of the reengineering initiative and are prepared to support the process. While aimed at the senior management team and their involvement, it also evaluates the roles of and impact on middle management and employees.

*Planning to reengineer* encompasses the development of a comprehensive plan for implementing the initiative. This includes defining the composition of the project team, clarifying their roles and responsibilities, and completing a detailed work program for the initiative.

*Communication and training* revolves around preparing the internal project team for their roles in redesign and implementation. Because we view customer-centered reengineering as primarily an *organizationally driven,* as opposed to a *consultant-driven,* process, the skill sets of the project team are critical to the initiative. Therefore, the importance of this step should not be underestimated.

*Strategic assessment* involves an evaluation of all the major aspects of the organization, including customers, market dynamics, internal product/service delivery systems, and culture, that affect the delivery of customer value. This assessment is accomplished around the customer-centered reengineering triangle as amplified in Figure 4–2. If this step is done correctly, it will provide the basis for defining "breakpoints" and/or opportunities.

*Strategic remapping* entails developing a complete top-line plan for reengineering the entire business (unit or area) to create total customer value. It pinpoints where structural change will be required

**FIGURE 4–1**
*Customer-Centered Reengineering Change Process Model*

and which systems to target for improvement. It also pinpoints the primary human resource and culture considerations to be taken into account as part of the reengineering effort. This plan is developed through an analysis of the data compiled from the strategic assessment and is accomplished in a top down and sequential manner according to the hierarchy presented in the customer-centered reengineering pyramid in Figure 4–3. The strategic remapping plan is a "living" document. It is revised and based on the specific outcomes of the subsequent phases of the reengineering process.

*Redesigning systems* is the actual detailed analysis and revamping of the business and its core processes in the areas to be reengineered. While the ultimate degree of fundamental change may be related di-

**FIGURE 4–2**
*Customer-Centered Reengineering Strategic Assessment Framework*

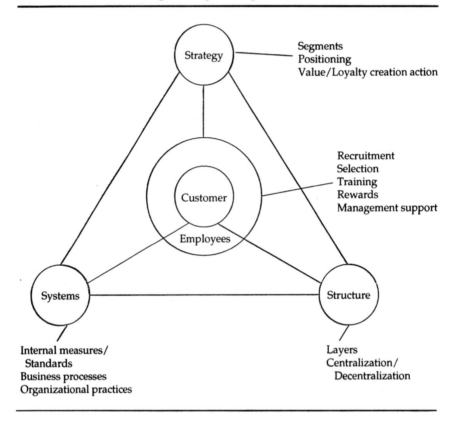

rectly to the creativity of the redesign efforts, these efforts follow the strategic decisions, not lead them.

*Implementing change* encompasses addressing the potential barriers to the successful implementation of the reengineered business processes and the development of plans for overcoming them. It includes taking the steps required to *reawaken people* and *recreate culture*. In this regard, it is important to note that the organizational structure and contextual factors, such as culture, performance management systems, human resource practices, technology, and communications methods, must be changed before the business's core processes or systems can be fully improved or modified.

**FIGURE 4–3**
*Customer-Centered Reengineering Pyramid*

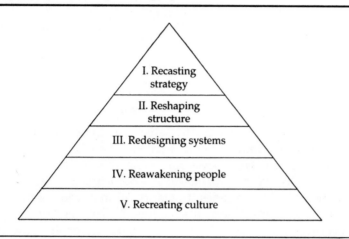

## BUILDING THE CUSTOMER-CENTERED REENGINEERING SUPERHIGHWAY

The seven phases in the customer-centered reengineering change process model provide the central path for customer-centered reengineering. If an organization was a machine that had been engineered and manufactured in the first place, rigorous adherence to these phases would ensure the desired outcomes.

However, it is not. It is a complex organic system comprised of a variety of subsystems or processes; individuals with knowledge, skills, feelings, and attitudes; and a dominant culture that has developed over time due to the organization's leadership, routines, rituals and regulations, and patterns of behavior. Consequently, any time you initiate an intervention that will disrupt the status quo, you can expect organizational resistance or *drag*.

Therefore, successful reengineering depends not only on finding the most appropriate or elegant technical solution. It also requires managing the strategic integration of that solution into the fabric of the organization in a manner that builds acceptance, support, and ongoing commitment.

To accomplish this, an organization must plan for and manage psychological and cultural considerations as part of the reengineering effort. How important is it to address these areas? Tom Peters has observed, "Most reengineering efforts will fail or fall short of the mark because of the absence of trust—meaning respect for the individual, his or her goodwill, intelligence, and naive but long-shackled curiosity."[3] We agree with Peters's assessment.

As we pointed out in Chapter One, the three critical success factors for organizational change efforts such as reengineering are:

- Executive involvement and leadership.
- Strategic customer-centered connection.
- Comprehensive change process strategy.

An organization must plan to satisfy all three of these requirements if it is to maximize the potential success of a reengineering intervention. We call the process for doing this *building the customer-centered reengineering superhighway*. As depicted in Figure 4–4, the superhighway has three lanes: transformational leadership, strategic remapping, and transition management. The customer-centered reengineering change process model builds the center lane for the highway. We need to add the other two lanes to it.

*Transformational leadership* is the ability to redirect and realign the vision, strategy, values, and critical systems of the organization and to direct their successful implementation. The transformational leader must be able to function in five key roles:

- Path finder—exploring new territory and discovering the course to be followed.
- Direction setter—charting a course and developing a vision and plan for accomplishing it.
- Change-agent—building a consensus for taking that course.
- Partner—participating actively in driving the course.
- Servant leader—acting as a role model by demonstrating the changed behaviors appropriate for the course.

*Transition management* is planning for, orchestrating, and facilitating the implementation of the individual, team, and organizational changes required to develop the new culture required in the reengineered organization. It focuses on the psychological and sociological considerations associated with change and creates a planned agenda for enlisting people's "heads, hearts, and hands" in support of the new reality.

The remainder of this book is directed to helping organizations build the superhighway. Chapter Five addresses the difficult issues associated with transition management. Chapters Six through Twelve address the pivotal interrelationships between transformational leadership and strategy in remapping an organizational "triangulation for customer value." The "Implementation Guide" at Chapter Fifteen

**FIGURE 4–4**
*Customer-Centered Reengineering Superhighway*

---

> —— Transformational leadership— (executive value map) ——

> —— Strategic remapping— (customer value map) ——

> —— Transition management— (organizational value map) ——

---

presents a suggested framework for implementing the customer-centered reengineering approach.

## CONTINUOUS INNOVATION AND KNOWLEDGE CREATION

Before we proceed, however, there is an important aside that we wish to make—that is, that we view this book and the reengineering approach that we are setting out as a work in progress. The same principles that we have espoused regarding businesses' needs to reinvent themselves continuously apply to the methodologies for reengineering.

As the world, customers, and organizations change, we should all be willing, ready, and able to reframe our definitions of reengineering and customer value. Those of us who consult to organizations in these areas must be life-long learners and committed to continuous knowledge creation and diffusion of information. We must not become victims of our dominant paradigms. We must not get stuck in a construction of reality that is solely of our own making or get locked into a static methodology that calls for continuous quality improvement or innovation, but does nothing to improve or upgrade its own methods. In a phrase, in order to help others reinvent themselves and their organizations, we must be willing and able to reinvent ourselves and our organizations.

*Chapter Five*

# The Windmills
# of the Mind

*"Man prefers to believe what he prefers to be true."*

Francis Bacon

You have to begin by reinventing yourself.

## WATT DO YOU KNOW?

There's an old joke that goes something like this:

How many psychologists does it take to change a light bulb?

Only one! But it takes a very long time and the light bulb has to be willing to change.

We're not light bulbs. We have filters instead of filaments. These filters cause us to believe, hear, and see things in certain ways and sometimes make it difficult for us to change, too.

To check out some of your own beliefs, take the opinion survey that follows, by indicating the extent to which you agree with each statement listed. Don't be afraid—there are no right or wrong answers.

If you're like most people who have completed this survey, your answers to the five statements probably ranged from "Strongly Agree" for some to "Strongly Disagree" for others. That's because we all have certain core beliefs or values that affect our attitudes and approaches to life, love, and labor. We have all been conditioned to think in certain ways and to embrace certain attitudes that influence our behavior. Our way of looking at this is that our brain is a computer that has been hardwired or a muscle that has been trained to respond reflexively to certain stimuli and cues. Indeed, recent research has shown that brain cells, like muscle tissue, become more powerful with use.[1]

**Basic Beliefs** (*Opinion Survey*)

| Statement | Degree of Agreement | | | | |
| --- | --- | --- | --- | --- | --- |
| | Strongly Agree | Agree | Neither Agree nor Disagree | Disagree | Strongly Disagree |
| Experience is the best teacher. | —— | —— | —— | —— | —— |
| If it ain't broke, don't fix it. | —— | —— | —— | —— | —— |
| What goes around, comes around. | —— | —— | —— | —— | —— |
| The more things change, the more they stay the same. | —— | —— | —— | —— | —— |
| You can't teach an old dog new tricks. | —— | —— | —— | —— | —— |

This programming is necessary and enables us to move through life efficiently and effectively and to respond successfully to most of what we encounter. However, it is less useful and helpful when we are dealing with extremely complex problems or ambiguous situations, or during times of discontinuity or accelerated change. In these times, our hardwiring makes it more difficult to consider all the relevant possibilities and to contemplate alternate viewpoints such as those that follow for the opinion survey that you took to start this chapter.

• **Experience is the best teacher.** That may be so if you're dealing with something that you've dealt with before. However, what about new situations or conditions? Our experience may not be relevant at all or, even worse, cause us to ignore important cues and signals in the environment.

• **If it ain't broke, don't fix it.** There is a book with the title, *If It Ain't Broke, Break It*. We don't know whether we agree with that. However, we would propose, as an alternative, "If It Ain't Broke, Make It Better." This is where the Japanese have excelled.

• **What goes around, comes around.** Not necessarily. Think about it. What goes around can stop or go someplace else.

• **The more things change, the more they stay the same.** This may have been so once. However, in these times, the more things change, the more things change. We used to thrive on constancy and certainty. Now, Tom Peters tells us we have to thrive on chaos. We don't know if this is accurate. At minimum, we have to accept and master change.

- **You can't teach an old dog new tricks.** We would argue that you can't teach a dog of any age anything. The prerequisite is that the dog must be willing to learn. The problem, as our partner Karl Albrecht puts it, is, "The biggest obstacle to learning anything is believing that you already know it."

What these alternative world views demonstrate is that for every basic belief, there is an equal or opposite basic belief. Success in the 90s and into the 21st century—to play on the advertising tag line—will come from "considering and mastering all the possibilities."


## THE PSYCHOLOGY OF CHANGE

The way that Tom Peters puts this is that we need to "change in a nanosecond—or never."[2] We don't agree with Tom. In fact, we're not even sure if he would really agree with himself on that statement. Can we decide to change in a nanosecond? Perhaps. Can we change? No.

Most of us have not been reared to embrace change. In fact, just the opposite is true. We grow up in a family system that is emotion-based; is oriented inward toward the security and nurturing of its members; places a high value on loyalty and protection of family members; and works to minimize change—to keep the equilibrium of the family intact. This socialization helps to form and shape who we become as individuals and our behavior within organizations.

As individuals, our natural tendency or instinct is to strive to achieve a state of *homeostasis*—a relatively stable state of equilibrium in both our personal and professional lives. We will resist strongly anything that seems likely to upset that state of equilibrium. And, if a state of disequilibrium or change occurs, we will do everything that we can to try to restore order, normalcy, and structure as quickly, as painlessly, and as permanently as possible.

There are very few among us who were born to be bungee jumpers, sky divers, or spelunkers. Is it any wonder, then, that we resist change at almost any level—even the most minuscule, or that when confronted by the need for massive change such as downsizing, restructuring, or reengineering we deny the need for it or fight like the dickens to prevent it?

In many respects, this resistance to change is natural and healthy. It is an attempt to do what is perceived to be best to protect and maintain our own self-interest. It is our effort to create certainty in an uncertain world. We know what we have under the current organizational arrangement. On the other hand, we have no, limited, or an imperfect understanding of what things will be like in our reengineered organization or whether we'll even be there. Consequently, we resist change because it is threatening.

Change threatens people in organizations on a number of levels and in a variety of ways including:

• **Loss of status.** Individuals in organizations spend years working their way up the ladder to become a supervisor or a manager. Where they are on the ladder matters. If change means the ladder is shortened or eliminated altogether, it can be terribly traumatic. As one individual said to us when we ran a meeting in a company moving to a team-based management system, "I've invested 10 years and worked extremely hard to become a supervisor. I know what that is and it means something to me. Now they tell me that I'm going to be a team leader. What the hell is that? Is this the reward that I get for my years of dedication to this company?"

• **Loss of job.** Obviously, the most fundamental threat is that of losing one's position in the organization. As an aside, one of the most interesting phenomena that we have observed over the past five years is that we have encountered several individuals who headed major organizational restructuring efforts who unwittingly "downsized or reengineered" themselves out of work.

• **Loss of security.** Security is both psychological and financial. The uncertainty associated with change challenges the individual's comfort zone in both of those domains.

• **Loss of structure.** Most of us enjoy structure and order. If there is no order, we will create it. We have a "homing" instinct. As a simple example, you go to a two-day meeting. There is no assigned seating. You take a seat at the table in the meeting room. Others take their seats. For the next two days, do you all take the same seats in which you first sat? Probably. People in organizations develop routines, rituals, and standard operating procedures. They will resist anything that changes those patterns.

• **Social disruption.** Individuals in organizations are social animals. They develop relationships, networks, and normal modes of behavior. A change can dramatically alter the social order and affiliation patterns, thus causing "disassociation" pain for those affected.

• **Group transformation.** Organizations are not just assemblages of individuals. They are comprised of teams, work units, and departments. These units develop rules and norms of behavior and performance. The more cohesive and interdependent a group is, the more strongly it will resist any change.

Because of these threats and our need for stability, individuals in organizations will sometimes consciously work to sabotage or undermine a change effort through a variety of means, including absenteeism, grievances, and reduced productivity. This resistance is understandable in that it gives the employees some small sense of control over the massive changes that are going on around them.

Resistance to change does not only occur at the conscious level, however. Frequently, even when people say that they are "getting with the program," they operate with unconscious barriers to change. These barriers exist in three areas: individual, team, and organizational. When these barriers overlap and interact as they do in Figure 5–1, they usually form a strong enough chain-link fence to reject the change effort altogether or to retard its impact significantly.

## INDIVIDUAL BARRIERS TO CHANGE: MIND GAMES

Those of us in organizations would like to think that we behave rationally and make logical decisions the majority of the time. This may be true.

It is probably true that many of us follow a "rational" problem solving sequence that goes something like this:

1. Define the problem.
2. Analyze the facts.
3. Generate alternatives.
4. Make the decision.
5. Test the solution.
6. Evaluate the results.

Following this sequence is no guarantee of "rationality," however. Two individuals applying this same logic track, looking at the same data, can come up with radically different answers.

Why is this? The answer is straightforward. Data are neutral. As human beings, we take in and process data similarly. However, the interpretation that we give to the data based on the filters through which they pass in our minds can be quite different. In this regard, there are three common types of traps that prevent us from recognizing the need for or addressing change requirements:

- The thinking trap.
- The values, attitudes, and beliefs trap.
- The feelings trap.

**FIGURE 5–1**
*Organizational Change Resistance Fence*

## *The Thinking Trap*

Thomas Gilovich has written a wonderful book entitled, *How We Know What Isn't So: The Fallibility of Human Reason in Everyday Life.* In that book, he describes in detail the "bounded rationality of human information processing" and points out the numerous errors that we all make in reasoning.[3] The most common thinking errors that we make include the order out of chaos error, snap judgment error, assumption error, similar to me error, and perception error.

**The order out of chaos error.**   This involves taking a random or short series of events and discerning a pattern that doesn't exist. As an example, review the sequence below where X = a shot made and 0 = a shot missed by a basketball player.

OXXXOXXXOXXOOOXOOXXOO

Would you say that sequence represents "streak shooting" by the player? In a study that Gilovich made, 62 percent of the subjects thought that it was. It isn't. It's perfectly random.

In business, the order out of chaos error causes us to take the results for the first two quarters and project them over the year or to compare last year's results to this year's and think that they can tell us something about what will happen next year.

**The snap judgment error.**   It's not only possible to perceive patterns that don't exist, it's also possible to reach an incorrect conclusion by ignoring all of the data or by filling in the blanks. Look at Figure 5–2. What do you see?

If you're like most people who take this test, you probably read down the vertical column, said "B" was the figure in the middle, and ignored the "13" that the majority of us find a little more difficult to perceive. Look at Figure 5–2 again. Read across the horizontal column of numbers. What figure do you see in the middle now?

**FIGURE 5–2**
*What "Is" the Figure in the Center of the Group?*

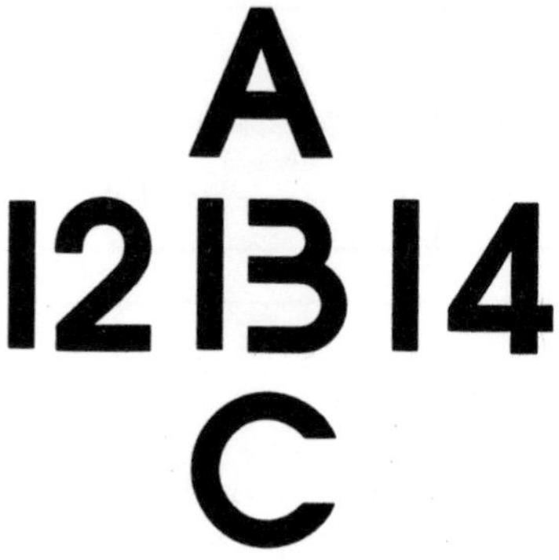

A
12 13 14
C

We can do the same thing in business. We hear about an isolated event—a failure or success—and we believe that it is representative. We ignore the numbers. As the old saying goes, "One story is worth 1,000 statistics."

**The assumption error.** This is probably the most common error. We act with insufficient or no data. We assume that we understand: for example, the customers' needs, the seriousness of the situation, or the facts. This error is made about both large and small things.

In business, IBM and NCR both assumed that few people would want a personal computer and that there would never be a real business application for the microcomputer. In the late 1970s, although the automakers in Detroit had many warnings, they chose to ignore the emerging threat of the Japanese manufacturers.

As an example of the error, on a personal level, one night we left our office at the close of business and went into the parking garage where we had parked the car. The garage has 12 floors. We pushed the button to get off at level one. A person who was on the elevator with us commented, "You must have come in very early this morning." The truth: We had arrived late in the afternoon after an all-day meeting with a client and we found a space in the garage on the first floor.

**The similar to me error.** Another common mistake is believing that others will react to stimuli in the same way that we do. To realize the folly and fallacy of this, all one has to do is to watch one segment of Gene Siskel and Roger Ebert's "At the Movies," as these two critics provide radically different reactions to and ratings for the same film.

   **The perception error.**   Many errors occur because our frame of reference is wrong. We do not have an appropriate experiential construct for reviewing the data that we receive.

   As an example of this, one of our associates in the TQS Group, Becky Glime, tells a story about her father, who every Christmas would go out and buy several albums of Christmas music. One Christmas he came home with the usual assortment of albums, including an album by Three Dog Night titled, *Joy to the World*. He asked Becky, who was a teenager, and her sister which album they would like to hear first. They of course, having a different frame of reference than their father, picked the Three Dog Night album of rock music. Needless to say, Mr. Glime was not amused by the fact that this Christmas album was not a Christmas album after all.

## *The Values, Attitudes, and Beliefs Trap*

Values, attitudes, and beliefs fall into three categories:

- **True.** Those held consciously, sincerely, and positively. They guide behavior whether or not observed by others.
- **Declared.** Those expressed for appearance's sake or conforming to norms. These declared statements don't always affect how an individual acts. But they will most likely affect "observed" or public behavior in organizational settings.
- **Obscured.** Something believed deeply that is not consciously acknowledged but that does impact behavior nonetheless.

No matter what their category, "hardened" values, attitudes, and beliefs of any type make it impossible for us to hear the other side of the argument or to accept input that is in conflict with our mindset. They cause us to go deaf.

   As a case in point, immediately following the Al Gore–Ross Perot debate on NAFTA on the "Larry King Show," CNN had a roundtable discussion with a group representing various constituencies, including labor, business, consumer action, and Mexico. As might be expected, given the deep-seated convictions and biases, each roundtable participant felt his or her side had scored the most points during the debate. Stated another way, their predispositions prevented them from reasoning.

   Along the same lines, Joe Cappo, a columnist for *Crain's Chicago Business*, wrote a column titled, "Tapping Rich Vein of Poor Reasoning." In that column, Cappo discussed the outpouring of angry letters that *Crain's* had received in response to an earlier column he had written reporting a widening gap between the rich and the poor in the United States and the Chicago area. The letter writers vehemently denied Cappo's hypothesis.

Cappo had drawn upon numerous reliable sources including the *Statistical Abstract of the United States* and reports produced by the Northeastern Illinois Planning Commission in developing his column. He had data by the bushelful to support his assertions. As Cappo noted, on the other hand, "None of my critics cited any sources to substantiate their arguments," and "several said the statistics weren't relevant."[4] What we have here is a classic case of don't confuse me with the facts—especially when they conflict with my opinions.

### The Feelings Trap

As Marlo Thomas noted in her record album for children, *Free to Be You and Me,* "feelings are such real things." Because of this and the fact that the subjective or emotional state can dominate the rational mind, many actions don't get taken that might otherwise occur in response to certain conditions. People stay trapped in toxic or abusive relationships. Managers don't demote or transfer otherwise loyal employees who have been promoted beyond their capabilities and who can no longer perform at the level required in their job. And executives are unable to make the "tough" decisions required to turn their companies around because of their affiliation with and loyalty to other executives.

Kay Whitmore, ex-CEO of Eastman Kodak, and Vaughn Bryson, ex-CEO of Eli Lilly, provide two excellent examples of executives who were squeezed in the feelings trap. Numerous articles have described the extreme difficulties that these two executives had in confronting their feelings and their business's status quo. It appears that Whitmore and Bryson are not alone, however. Eugene E. Jennings, a Michigan State University professor-emeritus, reports that in the first half of 1993, 35 percent of the 51 new CEOs hired for major corporations were selected from outside the company. This is the highest percentage of "outside" CEOs in more than 45 years.[5]

## TEAM BARRIERS TO CHANGE: WORKING ON THE CHAIN GANG

Teams are the basic building blocks of organizations. They take many forms: divisions, departments, work units, self-directed teams, quality circles, and so on. However, no matter what the form, there are three common traps that prevent any team from the productive management of change:

- Group think.
- Team myth.
- Role rigidity.

## Group Think

Over time, all groups develop their own rules and norms for what is considered to be acceptable in terms of communication, behavior, and performance. The more insular the team and the more common their socialization in terms of educational background, indoctrination, and work experience, the more likely it is that the team will evolve to a commonly shared worldview and start to think and make decisions in the same way. This leads to convergent thinking or what is commonly known as group think.

Group think is what caused the naval officers who participated in Operation Tailhook to see it as just part of business as usual or good clean fun. It's also what caused the management at Coors to think that they had all the answers and to respond to customer complaints about a newly designed can top by stating to their distributors, "We have heard that some customers have had problems opening the cans. But since we produce the best beer available, we are confident that our customers will find a way to get to it."[6]

The classic case of group think, however, is provided by the Bay of Pigs fiasco. Prior to the Bay of Pigs, the Joint Chiefs of Staff advised then President John F. Kennedy that they were certain and confident that a small strike force of soldiers could invade Cuba and foment revolution. President Kennedy bought into their construction of the future reality and ordered the invasion. The result—over 100 US soldiers were killed and America suffered one of the more embarrassing setbacks in its military history.

President Kennedy was so upset by this experience that he went to his brother Robert and said that in the future, he wanted him to be present in all major meetings with his military advisers. Robert's purpose was to be the devil's advocate, to challenge everything, and to prevent group think. The result—the successful resolution of the Cuban Missile Crisis and one of the most shining moments in American international diplomacy.

## Team Myth

Sometimes groups can't act or address serious problems because they have no common vision and can't even agree on the playbook. They're a team in name only.

It's easiest to discern failures of this type on the sporting fields where you can see a team of highly paid superstars, such as those that George Steinbrenner brought together during his original tenure as owner of the New York Yankees, who are unable to play well enough together to win a championship. This failure leads to revolving-door management and tremendous conflict.

A similar thing occurs in organizations where strong-minded and strong-willed individuals vie for authority and control of the business. Some of the most highly visible and vivid examples of this sort of internecine warfare within the business setting have been provided by family team members such as the Binghams of Louisville, Kentucky, who owned a newspaper and television empire; the Schoens, who owned U-Haul; and, more recently, the Hafts, who own Dart Drugs and Crown Books.

## Role Rigidity

In high performing teams, individuals share leadership, decision-making is decentralized, and everyone is empowered. By contrast, in traditional work teams, the leader is assumed to have all the knowledge, he makes the decisions, and the members know their place and defer to him. The consequences of doing this when the organization is treading on unfamiliar terrain can be disastrous.

We saw evidence of this potential for disaster once when we were conducting an executive development and team-building session with the top executives from a major transportation client of ours. As part of the session, we ran a group decision-making activity called the NASA Exercise. The purpose of the exercise was to demonstrate that due to "synergy," a team working well together can make better decisions than the individuals on the team.

The exercise is run as follows: Each team member is given a worksheet telling them that they are members of a space crew that has crash landed on the moon. They are asked to rank in order the 15 items listed on the worksheet in terms of their importance to survival while attempting to get to a prearranged rendezvous point on the moon. The team members first complete the worksheet individually. Then they complete the worksheet as a group by achieving a consensus on what the best ranking is.

When they have completed their ranking, they score the correctness of both their individual rankings and their group's ranking and calculate a group average score by adding their individual results together and dividing by the number of team members. The group score is almost always better than the average individual score—and frequently better than the score of the best individual in the group.

That's not what happened in this instance, however. For purposes of the exercise, we had paired up the transportation company's highly authoritarian and autocratic CEO with his six direct reports. When we calculated their results at the end of the exercise, his score was the worst in his group and their group's score after working together was worse than his. What had happened here was a case of "negative synergy." Whenever the group disagreed, they deferred to the CEO to make the decisions and his second round of decisions was even worse than his first. The result: this team stayed lost in space. How many organizations suffer the same fate?

## ORGANIZATIONAL BARRIERS TO CHANGE: KNEE DEEP IN THE BIG MUDDY

Much has been written about the importance of culture to business success. As a result, a misconception has developed that a strong culture is good and is almost a guarantee of success. Few things could be further from the truth.

A strong culture is not necessarily a sound culture. Look at IBM, Sears, and General Motors. They were all strong culture companies. However, their cultures were too internally focused, rigid, and hidebound. They did not encourage flexibility, organizational adaptation, and individuality. Rather, they, like many modern organizations, fell victim to the scientific management psychosis that if we work hard enough at systematizing our methods, stamping out corporate soldiers, and doing it our way, we can eventually convert the entire organization into a machine. And everybody knows that machines are better than people.

This *Deus ex machina* philosophy has led to a level of bureaucratization and robotization that has paralyzed many organizations and prevented them from responding to anything that isn't in the handbook. It has also fostered three of the most powerful barriers to organizational change:

- Executive wrong headedness.
- Silo management.
- Hardened arteries.

### Executive Wrong Headedness

The literature tells us a lot about how to empower individuals at the line level by giving them more discretion, latitude, and personal control over their areas of responsibility. However, it tells us very little about how to empower those individuals who, in certain instances, may be the least empowered people in the organization—that is, the top executives.

By the time the executives reach the top in many organizations, they have become sort of "idiot savants." They have been brainwashed. They know an awful lot about awful little. They have jumped so many hurdles, practiced the corporate salute so many times, and laid low so often that their ability to think independently or to perceive an emerging reality is virtually nonexistent. They have become intellectually, emotionally, and behaviorally handicapped. Because their schooling has been in organizational survival skills and not revival skills, when the time comes to lead the charge up the hill of change, they say "after you" instead of "follow me."

Most executives also are unable to shift their gaze from what they've been taught to look at—the internal false gods—the balance sheet, the income statement, the productivity report—to achieve an external focus. What they don't realize is that the employees are going to pay attention to what they pay attention to. As a result, the organization stands transfixed. As Michael Hammer puts it, "In most organizations, unfortunately, it's not the customer who is the focal point of employees; it's the boss. The axis doesn't point outward to the customer; it points due north. It's like Gothic architecture; everyone looks up."[7]

Executives don't act this way because they are evil. It's because they don't know any other way. They are victims rather than victimizers. They are products of the organization's "operant conditioning," to borrow a term from B. F. Skinner.

We personally witnessed how difficult it is for an executive to change his headset during a meeting with the CEO of a large financial service organization with which we were consulting. The executive had launched a major quality improvement initiative and had vowed to make any changes required—no matter how radical—to empower employees to satisfy the customer. The executive was well intentioned and appeared totally committed to change.

In our meeting we presented our finding from customer and employee research. We then recommended what we thought were some modest changes to corporate policies, procedures, and processes. We thought that these changes would put more control in the hands of the employees working directly with the customer and improve customer satisfaction significantly. A double victory.

The executive listened intently to us and then sat back looking thunderstruck. He reflected for a minute. Finally, he said, "I can't do that. It would be like giving the inmates the keys to the asylum." Our recommendations were not accepted. The quality initiative ground to a halt. Executive wrong headedness won again. And the customer and the organization lost.

## Silo Management

Many organizations sow the seeds of their own destruction into their organization charts. If you look at the traditional box and line charts for organizations, you can see one of the primary reasons that change is difficult.

Those charts depict a series of silos! There are the core silos: engineering, manufacturing, marketing, warehousing, distribution. And then there are the subsidiary silos: accounting, human resources, information systems, and so on. On the organization chart, these silos are bound together by solid and dotted lines that indicate how all of the silos are supposed to communicate, coordinate, and cooperate for performance purposes.

In the real world, in many organizations, each silo contains missiles pointed not at the enemy—the competitors—but at the other silos within the company. The first corporate maxim is "Be true to your silo." The second is "Protect your silo at all costs."

Organizations that operate with these territorial imperatives accomplish two things. First, they block change. Second, they assure that the territory they are defending is an ever-shrinking one.

## Hardened Arteries

If the silos don't get you, then the policies and procedures will. Most organizations put their rules, regulations, and systems into place in order to operate more professionally and to increase effectiveness and efficiency. The paradox is that these very methods become organizational straitjackets from which it is almost impossible to escape. Private and public sector organizations alike put themselves into these straitjackets. They strangle the organization and cut off its life blood.

James Heskett and John Kotter document the crippling effect that a stifling corporate culture can have on a company in their book, *Corporate Culture and Performance*. Based on their study of the performance of numerous firms over an extended period, they found that

> firms with cultures that emphasized all the key managerial constituencies (customers, stockholders, and employees) and leadership from managers at all levels outperformed firms that did not have those cultural traits by a huge margin. Over an 11–year period, the former increased revenues by an average of 682 percent versus 166 percent for the latter, expanded their work forces by 282 percent versus 36 percent, grew their stock prices by 901 percent versus 74 percent, and improved their net incomes by 756 percent versus 1 percent.

The low-performing or "unadaptive" culture companies studied by Heskett and Kotter included such well-known names as Bank America, Citicorp, Kmart, Northwest Airlines, and J.C. Penney.[8]

National research has indicated that most citizens would probably characterize the federal government as a low-performing organization also. Through his work on the National Performance Review, Vice President Al Gore, however, has discovered that there is one thing that the federal government does better than anyone else, and that is create red tape. That is why he subtitled the report that he submitted to President Bill Clinton, *Creating a Government that Works Better & Costs Less: From Red Tape to Results.*

How much red tape is there? Through his research, Vice President Gore discovered that the government's procurement process is a $200 billion a year system—$800 per American—comprised of over 900 laws and 4,500 pages of regulations. This system, administered by 142,000 people, enables the government to pay $6.43 for 25 office folders that could be bought in a Washington, DC, office supply store for $3.89; order a bulk quantity of aspirin at $107,000 more than the price proposed by the lowest bidder; and buy "designer insect repellent" as opposed to the store-bought insect spray that you and I might get.[9]

In the ultimate irony, this same log-jammed, ponderous, and inefficient procurement process is preventing the government from getting consulting assistance to make itself more customer-focused, efficient, and effective. In September 1991, the federal government issued a request for proposal (RFP) to develop a supply schedule of consultants who were qualified to consult to the government on total quality management (TQM). Over 700 firms submitted responses to the RFP in November 1991. Within nine months thereafter, the government was to have issued a new supply schedule with the selected and approved TQM consultants. Today, more than two years after the RFP was first issued, as we write this chapter, the General Services Administration is still struggling to get the new federal supply schedule established.

## BREAKING DOWN THE BARRIERS: PLEASE RELEASE ME

As the foregoing discussion illustrates, these barriers to change can be substantial. Is it any wonder, then, that most executives underestimate the rate of change in the industry, the resistance to change within their own organizations, and the extent to which they will have to change for the reengineering effort to have its greatest impact? This has caused us to formulate the following three laws of organizational change.

What should we do in response to these laws? How do we break down the barriers? First, by recognizing that, without individual change, organizational change is impossible. Second, by understand-

---

*First Law of Organizational Change*

An organization's resistance to change will be directly proportional to and a function of the need for change and the organization's past success.

---

*Second Law of Organizational Change*

All organizations will underestimate how difficult it will be to bring about meaningful change by a factor of at least 3 to 1.

---

*Third Law of Organizational Change*

The success of any organizational change effort will be directly correlated to the ability of the company's top executives to change.

---

ing that resistance to change is natural and to be expected. Third, by identifying where the primary resistance to change will come from. Fourth, by developing an explicit approach and transition management plan for confronting that resistance and converting it into power to propel the organization's reengineering efforts forward. This transition management plan needs to be as explicitly thought out as the technical process of reengineering itself.

As we have discussed, resistance to any type of change—structural, technical, or behavioral—occurs at three levels: individual, team, and organizational. Therefore, this transition management plan needs to be designed to ensure:

- **Effective leadership.** All of the company's executives need to understand their roles and responsibilities as change agents and be appropriately prepared and oriented to guide and facilitate the change effort.
- **Appropriate organizational alignment.** The organization's formal structure, systems, and methods need to be redesigned to ensure that they are congruent and compatible with the proposed change and that they reinforce the direction being taken.
- **Adequate individual involvement.** All employees who will be affected by the change need to take some ownership for and

become part of the change process. This requires an intensive education, communication, and participation process.

In the long run, it is the individuals within the organization who will enable the organization to succeed or fail. Therefore, their needs and concerns need to be dealt with and addressed as part of the transition management plan. Based on the research of Gene Hall, a professor from the University of Texas, these concerns exist at six levels:[10]

| Level of Concern | Key Question |
| --- | --- |
| Information | What is this change? |
| Impact | What does this change mean to me? |
| Implementation | How will this change be conducted? |
| Intent | Why is this change important? |
| Involvement | What can I do to help in the change process? |
| Investment | What can I do to extend the change to other areas? |

The transition management plan needs to be structured to address each of these concern levels sequentially. It also needs to be designed to be implemented in stages. This will allow for maximum employee buy-in and full integration of the reengineered changes into the business's practices.

## MANAGING THE TRANSITION: UNCHAINED MELODY

Why have we chosen to use the term *transition management* rather than change management for the process of addressing the psychological and cultural remapping associated with customer-centered reengineering? Because things can and do change quickly, but people cannot. This is why successful reengineering requires effective transition management.

A *transition* is the period between the current situation and the desired results state. It has both procedural and psychological dimensions. The procedural dimension is taking those steps specified in the reengineering plan to bring about the desired organizational or individual change. The psychological dimension is the "adjustment" process that each involved individual must go through positively in order to effectuate the full and successful implementation of the change.

Bill Bridges describes this psychological process as being comprised of three phases:[11]

| Phases | Activity |
|--------|----------|
| Ending | Letting go of the old situation and role identity. |
| Neutral zone | Existing in a sort of limbo while searching for meaning and role identity. |
| New beginning | Accepting and endorsing the organization's new vision and defining and acting on one's own new personal role identity. |

*Transition management* is the process of guiding and controlling, to the extent possible, the implementation of the transition plan through the transition period. It focuses on how things are done and addresses both procedural and psychological considerations in order to provide the environment that is most conducive to achieving desired results. It entails initiating the change plan as developed, adapting it on an ongoing basis to changing conditions, and resolving anticipated and unanticipated individual and organizational concerns and social, psychological, and emotional consequences of the transition.

## GUIDELINES FOR TRANSITION MANAGEMENT

The organization's top executives must be its *transformational leaders* and *transition managers*. To function in the role of *transition manager*, they must engage in a continuous "balancing act." They must push forward with the substantive aspects of the transition plan. At the same time, they must be sensitive to the fact that there are nonmalevolent forces at work—both within themselves and all of those affected by the transition—that could either stop change altogether or radically alter its course and intent. Recognizing this, the executives must be ready to confront themselves, proceed gradually and incrementally, listen to others, and work in collaboration to build throughout the business system acceptance and support for the necessary changes and transitions.

General actions that the executives can take to prepare to be most effective in the role of transition manager include:

1. **Accept the role and responsibility of transition manager.** Examine yourself critically. Make those personal changes and adjustments required.

2. **Understand that transitions are extremely complex.** Recognize that problems can occur in the transitions and study the requirements for a successful transition.

3. **Form a core transition management team comprised of significant individuals to assist in the transition planning and implementation process.** Educate and train them in the requirements of transition management. See the "Implementation Guide" in Chapter Fifteen for more advice on this.

4. **Write a transition management plan.** Include in it steps designed to deal with the rational and psychological aspects of the transition process.

5. **Communicate clearly the new vision espoused in the transition management plan.** Specify the underlying rationale and be specific about changes required.

6. **Provide sufficient opportunities and time for a learning and transition period.** Monitor reactions and work individually with those who have the greatest difficulty with the espoused changes. Monitor the implementation to ensure that it is accomplishing the desired organizational results and generating the individual psychological responses required to sustain the transition.

7. **Use the transition process to build an ongoing transition and transformation capability into the firm.** Create the learning organization. Design the firm for such capabilities and prepare others to repeat the transformation process on an ongoing basis to respond to the future needs of the company and its customers.

In conclusion, today's executives must not only be capable of redesigning the corporate ship through customer-centered reengineering, they must also be able to capture the spirit of the organization and use it as the wind—the invisible force—to move the ship through increasingly troubled and heavy seas.

# Chapter Six:

# Sailing the Seven C's

*"The seen is the changing, the unseen is the unchanging."*

Plato

*"Those not busy being born are busy dying."*

Bob Dylan

There's a storm out on the water.

## SINKING SHIPS

Five years ago, how many of us would have believed that three icons of American business success—General Motors, IBM, and Sears—could be in the desperate straits they're in?

Long the largest company in the United States, GM thought itself protected from competitive harm by its economies of scale. GM's historical advantage came from skills in mass production. Over time, an unspoken arrogance developed inside the company. After all, its product range and dealer network had become the envy of the industry, and consumer loyalty to GM products contributed its own dynamic.

But then, more and more customers began to change their purchasing preference to a greater perception of value being delivered by the Japanese and other foreign competitors. A series of senior GM executives couldn't even find the helm, let alone turn the ship around. Today its market value is roughly equivalent to that of youngster Microsoft, a company with only a fraction of its assets, employees, or history.

IBM, once the proudest name in computers, seems to have been left standing at the dock as the tides turned and microcomputers changed the world. Despite having been in the forefront in embracing Six Sigma quality (3.4 defects per 1 million units) and employee commitment, IBM has not demonstrated the willingness or ability to "destroy the town to save it"—to militate against the increasingly inbred vision of "the IBM way."

IBM executives did try to develop more of an entrepreneurial spirit in its employees that might result in new product ideas for their customers. "But the context in which they managed made entrepreneurship at IBM an oxymoron. That context—ever-positive and upbeat—demanded that managers demonstrate how a course of action would play out five steps into the future before they could take step one. This left managers unwilling to risk, let alone abandon, what the company had become for what it might be."[1]

Sears thought itself protected by its majestic purchasing might. After all, Sears had the best store sites and, born in 1886, it could harvest a marketing position with loyal customers who were value-processed by their families to go shopping at Sears. Yet, as new rivals, among them Wal-Mart, whom Sears failed to recognize as a primary competitor well into the 1980s, arose to challenge the company through more aggressive pricing and merchandising, and smaller specialty retailers began to slice and dice the company's traditional customer base into profitable niches, Sears was left adrift.[2]

What happened? Yesterday came not to matter. Storms of profound market change rocked these boats. Radical adaptation to these changed conditions was required, but adaptation was not delivered rapidly, decisively, and comprehensively. The result was a gradual erosion of their positions—that slow sinking into the depths that evades human perception while the daily music plays and the sailing crews merrily continue with their rituals of rank and organizational ceremony. Andrew S. Grove, chairman of Intel, summed it up best when he said, "There is at least one point in the history of any company when you have to change dramatically to rise to the next performance level. Miss the moment and you start to decline."[3]

These are extreme cases of businesses that once sailed the high seas of commerce proudly, but absent adequate maintenance or, from time to time, a complete overhaul, found themselves floundering. Most sinkings may *seem* to happen all at once, but the fact is that the seaworthiness of the business vessel was probably in decline for some period of time. And, ironically, for many an industry flagship, one can look backward in history to a proud past when few, if any, other ships could come close to its speed, grace, and beauty.

## RIDERS IN THE REIGN: CUSTOMER VALUE CHAMPIONS

The good news is that the boat does not have to sink! In the 1990s, companies survive and prosper by retaining the customers that they already have as the foundation for growth. Studies by Boston

Consulting Group and others quantitatively demonstrate that customer retention is the pathway to superior profits and growth in market share. Retention and expansion of the customer base is accomplished through reengineering for total customer value, and that means delivering the product/service/value that keeps consumers coming back for more and more and more. Companies like Home Depot, Waterhouse Securities, and Dell Computers excel at satisfying this 21st century imperative.

Home Depot's chief executive, Bernie Marcus, describes his company's service philosophy this way: "Every customer has to be treated like your mother, your father, your sister, or your brother." Cynics might be quick to snap, what is a statement like that supposed to mean? It means things like adding workers to the sales floor to improve service. It means changing work schedules so that shelf-stocking and price-tagging happen at nighttime when the aisles are empty, so that employees are free to sell during the day. It means training salespeople not to let customers overspend. Marcus says, "I love it when shoppers tell me they were prepared to spend $150 and our people have showed them how to do the job for four or five bucks."[4]

Treating every customer like a relative means taking clumsy homeowners who lack the confidence to do much more than change a light bulb and turning them into Harry and Henrietta Homeowner, unafraid to tackle the next major home improvement task. It's the long view, not the *short-term, bottom-line* view, that is causing dollars to fall to Home Depot's bottom line in both the short- and long-term.

Research and performance demonstrate that low commission rates are the most important thing to customers who are shopping for a discount broker. Waterhouse Securities delivers customer value by giving customers what they want: Their fee on a typical 100-share trade is $35, compared to the discount industry average of $47. Service, however, is not compromised. Waterhouse Securities has 41 branches and provides a full selection of financial products.

Dell Computers has grown quickly because it is responsive in delivering custom products and support services to customers. The company started in 1983, when the PC business blossomed. Founder Michael Dell had a vision—to provide custom products directly to end users with much better service and support than competitors provide, and to take the day-to-day feedback from customers and transform that feedback into better customer value. The company decided to become a consumer advocate—as opposed to a technology advocate or an advocate of a particular product, strategy, or direction. Dell states the proposition simply and directly, "We interpret the needs of the market and deliver those to customers."[5]

What could Dell possibly mean by such an outrageous statement? In his own words, "We focus not on the price of the computers we sell but on the *total value*—as defined by the product integrity, quality, service, support, brand name, ease of purchase, and all of the feelings and attitudes that come with buying the product and dealing with the company. We do not introduce technology for its own sake; we introduce technology that meets the needs of customers."

Dell Computers maintains a direct relationship with its customers, speaking with them regularly and segmenting customers by customer type. Large Dell accounts can dial Dell toll-free using a special phone number that has been assigned to the customer company, permitting direct access to the assigned Dell account team that is available to provide service 24 hours a day. This is structure to serve the needs of the customers. This is structure in hot pursuit of total customer value.

Offering value as a concept that goes far and beyond price *can* be done. But getting a company and its offering to the marketplace, to the point where the company is not caught in the ditch of price-based battling, is not easy. It requires the ability to manage organizational change—and transition—and to successfully navigate the "Seven C's."

## CHANGES AND CHANGE MANAGEMENT: THE SEVEN C's

First and foremost, customer-centered reengineering is about implementing organizational and cultural change, not just about redesigning business processes. Without guidelines for understanding the transition and change management implications involved, the best redesign efforts will fail because the organization will reject them.

Think about this for a minute. At some point in our careers, most of us have been involved with the implementation of a new computer system. How many of these system changes went smoothly, without disrupting the organization? In our experience, relatively few. This is usually due to underestimating the effect on the human factors in the organization. And implementing a new computer system is usually significantly easier than implementing a completely redesigned business process.

So what practical advice can be given to ensure that change does not become a choppy process, or a process by which nausea is induced in good instances, and apoplexy and failure in others? The answer is to be found in what we call the *Seven C's*. The Seven C's must be drawn together in a *coherent* and *congruent* manner so that the stability of the corporate ship is maintained even as the speed of its forward motion increases. Seven C's? They are:

1. **Closeness**—To all customers, external, internal, and stakeholders.
2. **Clarity**—Of vision and strategy.
3. **Courage**—To make the difficult decisions and to act.
4. **Creativity**—To think outside of the box.
5. **Competencies**—Which are distinctive, differentiating, and continually developing.
6. **Commitment**—The will to persevere.
7. **Consistency**—In words and deeds.

These Seven C's provide nothing less than the basis of reengineering for total customer value. This chapter introduces these ideas and their importance to doing business in the 21st century. In one way or another, the failures of the sunken ships and the successes of the riders in the reign can be explained by looking for the absence or the presence of these C's, respectively.

## Closeness

It often seems that people in marketing, sales, management consulting, and some executive leadership positions intuitively understand the need to get close to the customer. Furthermore, by education, training, and experience, there are people with dominant personality traits who help take companies closer to the customer and thoroughly embrace the concept.

There is a certain smugness that those *in the know* may rightfully enjoy. Regardless of the intrinsic intellectual, if not intuitive, appeal to some, however, the idea of getting close to the customer is not "natural" for all employees or all executives. This book provides repeated examples of cases in which what is intuitive—particularly with the benefit of 20–20 hindsight—may well be counterintuitive when it comes to the day-to-day conduct of business.

Consider the implications of the fact that many American corporations have CEOs who have come up through the ranks of finance. Through education, experience, and outlook, they are accustomed to counting the quantifiable results of *other* employees' closeness to the customer more than they are to getting up close and personal themselves. It is not impossible for those with the finance perspective to reengineer the company for customer value, but it may require more in the way of a change in mindset.

Getting close to the customer, achieving customer intimacy, customer care, or any variation of customer-centeredness that you want to choose—this outlook is clearly natural to Michael Dell of Dell Computers and to Bernie Marcus of Home Depot. But if it were truly natural and intuitive, IBM, Sears, and GM would have reengineered themselves by now. You may wonder how there could possibly be an alternative to this mode of thinking just as you can scarcely imagine what it would be like to relive those years when a personal computer and a cellular telephone were not at your beck and call. However, if your business is a going concern that is to remain a going concern, we can assert the following with complete confidence: Your company is not as close to its customers as it can and should be, nor is it as close as it will become in the future. Just imagining the possibilities leads to the second C.

### Clarity

Clarity of vision and strategy in conceiving new ways of getting ever closer to the customer is not optional. This clarity is required if a company is to reengineer itself for customer value. Such clarity is inextricably entwined with vision. Clarity can be defined in many ways. It's the ability to see the forest for the trees, to find the invisible truth, to read the tea leaves.

Successful reengineering efforts are built on clarity. Executives must be able to see the breakpoints and see where change is going—or, more significantly, where change can be led. They fully embrace the anticipatory aspect of transformational leadership and transition management. And, if they possess the third C of courage and can combine courage with clarity, the chemistry becomes powerful indeed.

### Courage

Courage as we use it here refers to the courage to make difficult decisions in pursuit of a vision that only a few may see clearly, if at all. Courage is that willingness to take the risk of being wrong and failing entirely. It is the "right stuff" from which progress is made. And it is the stuff of which there is a widely reported shortage.

There is no prescription drug that you can mete out to a person who needs to exercise executive leadership but who won't. You can't wrap it up in handsome paper and ship it as a gift. Why are we laboring the obvious here? We deliver nearly 100 major lecture and seminar presentations each year to a wide variety of audiences and industries. Invariably, when the klieg lights are extinguished, lingering members of the audience want to discuss the presentation. "How can these principles apply to my industry? To my company?" And then the other shoe inevitably drops and the most commonly asked question is presented, "How can you give an executive the courage that s/he needs?" The swift and direct answer is that you cannot.

If you are employed by a company that lacks executive buy-in, you need not read the remainder of this book except possibly as preparation for your next position in another company. Without executive buy-in, the company lacking a courageous executive may safely expect, but must impatiently await, a new CEO or business failure, whichever comes first. On the other hand, if you can demonstrate to the executive that the focus on the customer can and should be a driving force for increasing revenues, profitability, productivity, and quality, then you have a fighting good chance that is worthy of pursuit.

Getting closer to the customer requires exploration in unexplored territory. Such adventures do not begin and cannot continue without courage. It's just that simple. But just as clarity without courage is not enough, courage without creativity doesn't leave you with much either. Creativity is the fourth C.

### *Creativity*

In its application of the "blank sheet of paper approach" to redesign, customer-centered reengineering is fundamentally a creative, intuitive process rather than an analytical one. Creativity will achieve radical change and quantum leaps; analysis will yield incremental improvement.

What is creativity? It's the ability to *think outside of the box*. Creativity is the ability not only to think like the customer, but also to anticipate how the customer *will* think in the future. It is the ability to think in a way that is guided by the customer value hierarchy, rather than being fettered by the organizational hierarchy. It is the ability to think beyond a product, or a service, or a product/service, and to think instead about a durable relationship with the customer and how to perpetuate that relationship, adding delight to the customer's experience so that customer loyalty results.

Creativity is the process of thinking about anything with the advantage of a clean slate, unfettered by the past and its not-invented-here baggage. In corporate organizations, this means that the personal and institutional inconveniences that are occasioned by change of any kind do not worm their way into the equation, into the consideration of whether an idea has merit and will work.

Creativity requires courage and rigorous honesty. Much of what is permitted to pass for creativity in all too many organizations is merely a rearrangement of preexisting pieces at best or, more commonly, a "tinkering around the edges." The intellectually dishonest process of rearranging existing components and masquerading them as new is permitted by players and environments lacking in courage and rigorous honesty. Such rearrangement is a product of "group think," and arrangements where creativity is stifled when personal accountability and associated rewards and recognition have been erased by teamwork *in extremis.*

Creativity is stifled when left-brained "problem solving" using prescribed group thought rituals has subtly undermined the individuality that can be the mother of creativity in favor of "here's-what-we-came-up-with" collective consciousness. In such environments and with such people, the product is *innovation.* It may be an innovation, but it is not truly innovative, let alone creative.

Innovation too often is a rearrangement of the pieces. This is why we often say that *innovation is the sincerest form of conformity.* Innovation may have made America what she is today, but it won't be enough to make America what she needs to be tomorrow. Or any other country, company, or individual for that matter. It simply isn't enough.

For the 21st century, creativity is mandatory, not optional. Applying microprocessor technology to the traditional work processes of an organization so that a 10 percent productivity increase is achieved, when a trebling of productivity is needed and, in fact, available to the creative practitioner, is an example of the "innovation" we disdain.

By now the C's are beginning to accumulate: Let's assume that we are close to the customer with clarity of vision, the courage to carry it out, and the creativity that is needed to truly generate a breakpoint in the world. If something grand is to be done on a grand scale, an organization will be required for implementation, a competent organization that satisfies the fifth C of competencies.

### Competencies

Consultants and authors Richard Normann and Rafael Ramirez point out that "in an economy founded on the new logic of value, only two assets really matter: knowledge and customers. *Competencies are the technologies, specialized expertise, business processes, and techniques that a company has accumulated over time and packaged in its offerings.*"[6]

Using Normann and Ramirez' model, it is clear that they are referring to all components of our customer-centered reengineering triangle, that is, strategy, systems, structure, and employees. But their primary emphasis for competency development is in what we call the systems area, namely technologies, business processes, and techniques. To be sure, there are unique and exciting opportunities to be realized by enhancing competencies in the systems area.

Taken broadly, however, the "specialized expertise" element of competency is an even more exciting frontier. In today's global marketplace, competitiveness no longer rests exclusively on the quality of management leadership. Management leadership remains important and decisive. It is a necessary condition for success in the marketplace, but in and of itself it is not enough. The quality of the company's workforce has become more important than ever before with the end of mass production and the entrance of mass customization. Noted economist and author Lestor Thurow explains the central importance of the "knowledge worker" this way:

> If I can take your product and make it cheaper, if natural resources can be bought at competitive rates around the world, if capital can be borrowed and if technology can be copied, what are you left with? Skilled workers.[7]

Perpetual reconfiguration, instant teams, and high skill jobs require a new kind of worker. America is just beginning to deal with the enormous challenge presented when three-fourths of Americans do not complete college and when at least one in five young people drops out of high school prior to graduation. Competency was never a given in America or anywhere else. However, attainment of competency has become more rather than less difficult. Thus, it takes tremendous corporate commitment to become a *learning organization* in order to develop core competencies for the organization that are distinctive and differentiating.

### Commitment

It's not just a commitment to learning that matters. It's also commitment to following through. Commitment to eschewing nonrational impatience. Commitment to resisting the temptation to jettison the plan even before it has seen full implementation, let alone harvest.

As mentioned in the first chapter, what we call fad-based failure is a major source of frustration in business today. Clearly, one potential failure point is incorrectly applying a methodology to the wrong type of problem. Another, however, is not giving the methodology a chance to work.

Literally every company that we go into these days is full of jaded people—people who have become inured to the latest installment of "flavor of the month" management. If the executives who are running the place don't seem committed to any course of action beyond the very short term, why should the employees? It could almost be argued that in many circumstances *any* improvement methodology, applied conscientiously and consistently, would be of value. Absent evidence to the contrary, there is no reason for employees of most organizations to believe that this reengineering effort is any different than the other programs and initiatives they've seen come and go.

Mere involvement will not take the place of true commitment. If you have trouble telling the difference, just remember that when it comes time for bacon and eggs for breakfast, the chicken is involved, but the pig is committed.

## *Consistency*

Why do we act the way we do in organizations? Why do different organizations display different behaviors? The answer is culture. Norms, values, beliefs, rules, relationships, rituals, attitudes, and people's behaviors—culture is all of this and more. Culture is more because it is a feeling that each member of the organization has—a feeling that is associated with the constructive tension of high performance or the counterproductive tension of fear and loathing, or something somewhere in between. Culture is extremely important because it either facilitates the change process or is inimical to it.

The executive's role in applying culture to the reengineering effort revolves around consistency. He or she is in charge of the message machine, responsible for sending and reinforcing the right signals to the rest of the organization. We are talking about points of emphasis and punctuation in the organization. What is important and what is not. What will be rewarded and what will not. What is respected and what is not. In this way, cymbals become inextricable from symbols, from the symbolism that is imbued in the organization and its meaning. Meaning requires consistency of thought and action—talk the talk, walk the walk, and do so consistently and with perseverance. The will to persevere permits culture to develop and to become healthy, and, not surprisingly, an unhealthy culture will militate against perseverance.

Try this out: Culture is the organizational coefficient by which one predicts the level of cooperation that will be encountered in creating and implementing change. Down to earth, culture is about the degree to which people have the energy, attitudes, and beliefs that are required to work together smoothly, creatively, and confidently. A healthy culture will produce more rapid buy-in to a change strategy and process than will an unhealthy culture.

In many ways, consistency can be the most stormy of the Seven C's. Achieving a healthy culture in a time of disposable employees and heightened cynicism is not easy. What's more, companies are increasingly being viewed as disposable by many talented employees who are part of the trend toward *free agency.*

A company that chews human resources up and spits them out will, by and large, encounter higher degrees of charade and nonvalue-added theater in pursuit of new company-saving strategies. Shoddy human resource management practices will lead to a culture where employees emulate their leaders and develop a short-term bottom-line attitude that makes the executive's attitude pale by comparison. The correct answer, of course, is to build the culture of the organization from the outside in, working our way from the customer's values, needs, and preferences and meeting somewhere in the middle that is both the marketplace and the new point of *gravitas* for our organization's culture.

If there is plenty of trouble in River City, there is also plenty of trouble in many corporate cultures. These troubles obviously reflect one another because the firm does not exist in a vacuum; it exists in a society. And the firm is comprised of people who have an organizational culture. These people need to see consistency in words and deeds if the culture is to be a healthy one that incubates increases in customer value.

In conclusion, if you want growing revenue and increased profitability for your business, then you need to master the *Three Rs*, namely repeat, renewal, and referral business. As noted earlier, every new customer costs us at least five dollars, contrasted with the one dollar that we need to spend to get additional business from customers with whom we *currently* do business. To get to the Three R's, we need to master the Seven C's..

*Chapter Seven*

# The Heart of the Matter

*``The consumer is our boss, quality is our work, and value is our goal.''*

The Quality Principle of Mars, Inc.

This is a marvelous country: even aging hippies can still make money.

## GRATEFUL TO BE DEAD

The Grateful Dead have been playing rock music for more than 25 years. In 1992, they sold $29 million worth of tickets to 63 North American concerts. This placed them fourth in terms of concert revenue generated by rock stars. *The Dead*, as they are called, have survived and been remarkably successful in an industry in which fame is as fleeting as last week's number one song, and they have done it by creating the right customer value package (CVP) for their fans.

Here are some of the things the Grateful Dead have done to maintain the loyalty of their old customers from the late 60s and early 70s, and to *attract new ones:*

- Because 30- and 40-something fans are not likely to stand in line or wait a long time on the phone to get tickets, the Dead sell tickets through the mail.
- They give quantity as well as quality: Dead concerts last 3 to 3 1/2 hours, as compared to 2 to 2 1/2 hour concerts for the competition.
- Every concert in a Dead series is *different* from the others; they have a repertoire of 140 songs and seldom play a song the same way twice.
- Unlike the competition, the Dead allow their fans to tape their performances for continuing enjoyment.
- Not ignoring the price factor in the CVP, the Dead price their concerts a tad lower than other concert groups.
- They maintain—and use—a mailing list of 110,000 fans, and they keep in touch.

All this on top of the fact that they are talented musical performers who give it their best shot, every time out.

The Grateful Dead also treat their employees like customers. In an industry that provides poor pay and few benefits to the *roadies*—those who help to get the show on stage—the Dead have distinguished themselves as *employers of choice.* They provide profit sharing and medical and life insurance benefits to their nearly 50 full-time employees. They pay office staffers an average of $50,000 annually, and long-term crew members can earn over $100,000. The Dead have set up trust funds for the college-age children of long-time staffers. They do all these things because it's good business. As Dead guitarist Bob Weir says, "We do things that make sense . . . and serve the best interests of us and our fans."[1] Sounds like a pretty good formula for success, in any industry.

It's one that companies like Johnson & Johnson have been following for some time. About 40 years ago, Robert Wood Johnson, then president of Johnson & Johnson, created that company's credo, which says that permanent success is possible only when modern industry realizes that

- Service to its customers comes first.
- Service to its employees and management comes second.
- Service to the community comes third.
- Service to the stockholders, last.[2]

The Johnson & Johnson credo provides a formula for achieving *closeness* with the organization's various customer groups. You might infer that the Grateful Dead also subscribe to this customer-centered credo and that it has contributed to their success.

Oh, and by the way, does an outfit like the Dead worry about frills or fads like *vision?* Does a rock group bother itself with something so high-flown or ephemeral? Absolutely! Dead guitarist Jerry Garcia says, "The Dead are intentionally responding to the need for joy, celebration, and ritual, and they have struck a nerve." And he adds: "If it's not fun, don't do it."[3]

## SEGMENTS IN CEMENT

To a large extent, the success of the Grateful Dead can be explained by the group's ability to get close to their customers, discover the *invisible truth* regarding their customer value model (CVM), and then deliver a unique customer value package aligned with that CVM.

Unlike the Dead, many organizations will fail in their reengineering efforts because they will not hear the unbiased and unadulterated *voice* of their customers. They will not discover the invisible truth, nor will they get closer to their customers. The two major causes for this

failure will be organizational arrogance and organizational innocence.

Organizational arrogance occurs when businesses assume that
they automatically know what customers want or what's best for
them and then make changes to their customer value package based
on these assumptions. They operate with an "in loco customers" attitude. The hotel industry is notorious for this.

Over the past decade, the major hotel chains have engaged in an
ever-escalating "amenities war." From shampoos, lotions, and shoe
horns to bathrobes, health clubs, and in-room VCRs, the battle rages
on. The problem is that there is very little evidence to suggest that
any of these *frills* are very important to the customer.

Organizational innocence is the opposite side of the coin from
organizational arrogance. This occurs when an organization as-
sumes that it has a good handle on the customers' perspective because it has done some research with them. The catch here is that traditional market segmentation or research methods typically conceal
as much as they reveal about the customer. They concentrate on ag-
gregate market needs as opposed to individual customer expectations.

Much of the market research dollar is still being invested in studies
to determine whether there is a general market need or demand for a
particular type of reengineered product or service. This brand of research usually entails collecting reams and reams of data on the demographics, consumption patterns, and competition within a given
marketplace or segment. These data are ground through an elaborate
computer model comprised of complex algorithms that then spits out
the answer as to whether the reengineered product/service will be
successful. Businesses then make their decisions about whether to expand to a new market or introduce a new offering based on these
findings.

While there is a place for these demographic segmentations or
market feasibility studies, they should not be confused with customer
value research. They should also be viewed with caution and skepticism. These studies present statistics and not facts. They verify that
there may be a market need. However, they do not describe what the
nature of that need is or how to reengineer to satisfy it. They do not
answer the critical questions: What do the customers want? How satisfied are they at present? What would cause them to buy or repurchase again? What are they looking for in the experience with the
company?

In a talk to American Marketing Association executive members,
Marc Yanofsky identified 12 fatal mistakes made in traditional services marketing.[4] Believing that these errors apply across a range of

businesses and often encumber the reengineering process, we have summarized them below along with our recommended antidotes.

1. **Believing in the myth of "the" customer.** Customers are not a lumpen proletariat. You must disaggregate your customer base and develop a hierarchy of those customers that are most valuable to you. Then, you need to give them the products and services they want and not try to foist on them elements of a product or service that they don't want, or might resent.

2. **Segmenting incorrectly.** Look outward toward the customers, not inward toward yourself and your products and services for your segmentation rationale. There's more on how to do this later in this chapter.

3. **Defining the products too narrowly.** Focus broadly on the needs and expectations of the customers, not just on what you can make or do currently.

4. **Focusing on transactions rather than customers.** It's the customer who has needs the product or service can fill who should define the transaction, not the other way around.

5. **Underinvesting in retention as opposed to acquisition.** Find as many ways as you can to earn your customers' loyalty.

6. **Trying to save your way to profitability.** Cutting corners too often means reducing the value in the customer value package.

7. **Inadequate care and feeding of the brand.** Over the life of a product or service, most companies spend an enormous amount of money to develop, position, and maintain their branded image. If the competition is investing, so must you if the brand is important to the business.

8. **Trying to beat a competitor by being the competitor.** Focus on the competition is no substitute for focus on the customer.

9. **Reinforcing past mistakes by assuming that your current customers are your potential customers.** Segments shift and customer loyalty is something that can never be taken for granted. Staying in touch will help you avoid stasis and complacency.

10. **Disconnecting marketing and operations.** In Yanofsky's words, "the front line people are an integral part of marketing." Phil Wexler's phrase is that "Marketing is a philosophy, not a department."

11. **Using method-driven marketing.** Disaggregate your customer base, understand who they are, and figure out what products you ought to have for them, then determine the most effective way to communicate with them.

12. **Misunderstanding the role of quality.** "Quality by the book" is much less valued than performance that springs spontaneously from personal standards and values that are on target.

## CUSTOMER-CENTERED SEGMENTATION

Those organizations that will be successful in the 21st century will reengineer themselves around their customers rather than markets.

For years, businesspeople have talked about the importance of market segmentation. Increasingly, a number of successful businesses are adjusting their focus to customer segmentation. Writing in *Harvard Business Review*, William Davidow and Bro Uttal said, "Marketing segmentation focuses on what people and organizations need, while customer-service segmentation focuses on what they expect. . . . Only after a company has segmented its customers and chosen which ones to serve can it figure out where to substitute low touch for high, thus improving productivity without imperiling customer satisfaction."[5] The shift needs to be to the development of long-term, close relationships with individual customers, rather than processing the largest number of sales within a given period of time.

Some industries have already begun to take advantage of customer segmentation. Necessity has driven some of the banking industry in this direction. Many smaller banks, often the target of acquisition-hungry regionals and super-regionals, have prospered by focusing on customer segments whose expectations the larger banks don't address and satisfy. Some have set up personal banking services for executives. Others discourage small depositors by setting a high monthly checking account fee, waived only for high average monthly balances. Some focus on individual loans—often the kinds of loans with which big banks don't want to be bothered. One Florida bank, realizing that many of the residents in its area are 70 years and older, provides a car that goes to customers' homes to gather deposits.

Another interesting example of the application of the customer segmentation principle is provided by the investment firm of Edward D. Jones & Company. This company operates over 1,600 one-person brokerage offices spread across the United States. These offices are located in smaller rural areas. They specialize in selling low risk, conservative investments such as bonds, certificates of deposit, and annuities to older men and women in those communities.

A one-to-one relationship with each individual customer is the ideal toward which the successful business must aspire. And sometimes that can be achieved. For most businesses, however, the product, the service, and the value need to be tailored to the smallest segment you can identify and manage. An example, of course, is the credit card companies—and there are several that do this—that examine your spending pattern to determine whether you fall into the travel category, the fine dining category, or maybe department stores, menswear, or a ladies' fitness club.

*Experiential segmentation* is made possible for these operations through the existence of a vast and active database to which you contribute every time you make a credit card purchase. And it is entirely different from some of the more traditional methods, where a "market" is defined by age, for instance, or geography.

American Express regularly sends us a special offer each year, for instance, a discount coupon for a lobster dinner at a quality restaurant, based on how our spending patterns have placed us in one of their many segments. In this way, they are adding value to our *relationship* and enhancing our loyalty, which we have talked about and will continue to talk about considerably in these pages, because building customer loyalty, establishing that life-long relationship, is based in many instances on being able to recognize what segment of *our customers* you belong to.

Marriott did not need an elaborate database to know that business travelers are one of its major customer segments. But they were wise enough to understand that this segment merited an entirely new product line, and that's how the Courtyards were brought into existence.

Opportunities for customer segmentation abound. Just think of all of the customer segments that have become part of the language in the past few years. Yuppies, Buppies (Black urban professionals), Dinks (dual income, no kids), Age Quakers, Baby Boomers! These are in addition to traditional segments based solely on sex, ethnicity, race, family structure or unit, geographic region, nationality, and so on. Looking at a few of the more innovative customer segmentation approaches might prove instructive.

In *Serving the Ageless Market*, David Wolfe convincingly argues that age should not be the basis for customer segmentation. Stage of life, not age of life, has the greatest impact on customer desires, expectations, and behavior. His research has shown, however, that many people over 50 years of age tend to be motivated to buy based on very different factors than others. They have moved, as Wolfe labels it, from their *possession* experience and *catered* experience into their *being* experience years. No matter how you put it, those who will prosper in serving this market will need to reconstruct their customer value packages and reengineer themselves to operating differently.[5]

Dave Cwi, a market researcher and friend of ours, has developed a behavioral version for segmenting this *ageless* customer market. He says that these customers are either in the "go-go," "slow-go," or "no-go" segments.

Total Research Corporation, a New Jersey–based market research firm, has developed a method for customer segmentation based on perceptions of brand quality. They believe this "brand equity segmentation" approach does a better job of explaining customer preferences and market behavior than conventional market segmentation, such as those based on demographics, lifestyles, attitudes, or psychographics.

They have identified seven basic kinds of customers. These segments use obvious external cues—price, market share, and the age of a brand—as part of the process for determining which brands are worthy and which are not.

- **Intellects,** who define brand quality as intellectual, international, "new fashioned," and affluent.
- **Relief Seekers,** who associate brand quality with relaxation, simplicity, and lack of effort.
- **Sentimentals,** who favor brands that are old-fashioned, unsophisticated, feminine, sentimental, and ordinary.
- **Popularity Seekers,** who define brand quality in terms of extrinsic considerations.
- **Old-Fashioned Pragmatists,** who favor older brands and place a premium on practicality and value for the money.
- **Actives,** who prefer travel or communication-oriented brands that represent an active, healthy, and confident lifestyle.
- **Hard-Working Conformists,** who are influenced significantly by a brand's price and market share, that is, the generally accepted market leader.[6]

The logical extension of this form of expectations-based analysis is smaller and smaller segments. *Micromarketing,* or defining discrete customer segments—sometimes as small as one customer—is the wave of the future.

Note that these forms of segmentation are not based on income— they're driven by customer preference and expectations. Further, the same individual may put himself or herself in three different segments, when dealing with different purchase decisions. When you buy office supplies, you may look for the best price—a *pennypincher;* for something to eat, you may go for specialty foods or fine dining— *tailor-made;* and in clothing you may be looking for the latest fashion—a *trendy.* This tells you that you can't segment your customers based on their behavior in a *different* market, only in yours.

Just as an individual may be a part of three different customer segments at the same time, there is a shifting in segments over time. The most obvious shift, of course, is due to the fact that we all do grow older. The segment and its customer value package will change. Today's boomer market is very different from that of 5 or 10 years ago, and is sure to be different in years to come. Our friends, the Grateful Dead, have been growing old gracefully along with their customers and, as we noted, have tailored their customer value package accordingly: no long waits in line.

So, clearly, there are no cement segments. Customer segments are alive, well, and changing constantly. Therefore, the rule of thumb before starting to reengineer should be *segment, segment, segment*. This will enable you to tighten the focus of your reengineering efforts on the customer segments that will yield you the best return.

After that, the basic challenge in reengineering is to do the research and reengineer in such a way to get you *closer* to the customers to *delight* them, by delivering total customer value. As the examples that follow demonstrate, closeness can take a variety of forms. However, the end result is always the same—very satisfied and loyal customers.

## UP CLOSE AND PERSONAL

While IKEA is doing extremely well by inviting its customers to participate in value creation, Home Depot is taking an opposite tack. It creates value by adding value in a *high touch* way. At Home Depot, a do-it-yourself warehouse-type retailer, sales personnel are knowledgeable about their products and how to use them. When the average homeowner comes into Home Depot, he or she can have a sales-clerk's attention and tutoring for as long as it takes to make it perfectly clear how to do it yourself. Home Depot is selling the service of good-quality professional how-to advice. The cost of the advice is spread over the merchandise, so that you can get the same advice-value whether you are spending 79¢ or $79.

Does Home Depot's approach work? Over the past couple of years, Home Depot has moved into the Mid-Atlantic market formerly the almost-exclusive preserve of Hechinger's, a Washington, DC–based do-it-yourself pioneer in the area. Hechinger's had become a bit complacent, flaccid even, before the advent of Home Depot, and knowledgeable advice was hard to come by. Today, however, Hechinger's is racing to try to catch up. Its stores now feature project advice centers; and its help wanted ads advise that "only experienced home-building or decorating professionals need apply." By understanding the customer value model for its target customer segment, Home Depot has redefined the hardware and lumber market.

Good's Furniture, a 14–store chain headquartered in Lancaster, Pennsylvania, offers a variety of services to its customers, including free design assistance, price matching with its competition for the same item, along with free delivery and setup of new furniture, and removal of customers' old furniture. Perhaps most notable is the chain's *happiness guarantee*. If a customer isn't satisfied with the furniture he or she has purchased, for any reason and even if it was specially ordered from the manufacturer, Good's will exchange it or refund the purchase price within 15 days. Says President Richard Good, who once pulled $100 out of his pocket and gave a customer an on-the-spot refund in response to the customer's comment that he'd just seen a sofa he'd bought the previous week at Good's for $100 less at a competitor, "Our goal is to 'wow' the customer."

On the other end of the spectrum, GE Capital is numbers driven. However, they also realize that service and assistance to the big customers to help them be successful matter. They realize that they are in a sort of *partnership* with anyone to whom they loan money. As Stephen Berger, GE credit vice president, puts it, "When you lend money to a company, you'd better be ready to own it."[8]

Operating on this philosophy, GE Capital has adapted a value-added approach to asset financing. That is why GE has a team of 100 engineers who work on location at GE financed industrial projects; employs many licensed pilots and salespeople in its corporate airplane area; runs six-wheel repair shops as part of its railcar leasing operations; and does a variety of things for companies that lease vehicles from it, including getting tags and licenses and negotiating repair costs.[9]

Like Home Depot, Good's and GE practice what Michael Treacy and Fred Wiersema call *customer intimacy*. This is direct, one-on-one, *hands-on* attention to the customer. And it is highly successful.

## FROM A DISTANCE

Not all business can be done one-to-one or face-to-face, however. This is true even for retailers. In an effort to preserve a kind of *remote intimacy*, a number of businesses are using information technology combined with relationship building techniques to get and stay close to the customer.

Egghead Software, for instance, gives you a *Cue* card that confers "preferred membership" on the holder. Members get discounts and frequent notification of sales and special promotions. The wholesale grocery and merchandise chain Price Club and the Staples office supply stores have membership cards that, in the first instance, are required for admission to the store or, in the second, entitle the holder to modest discounts on most merchandise. Safeway grocery stores now feature "shopping club memberships," permitting cardholders modest discounts on some items, and occasional *freebies*.

In all of these cases, purchases are recorded in the company's database along with the cardholders' demographics—name, rank, and serial number. Special promotional mailings or offers can then be easily tailored to the buying habits of customers through simple manipulation of the database, so appeals can be directed at those who buy game software rather than business applications, or a mailing can be directed at those businesses that regularly purchase toner for copying machines, for instance.

These discounts or other modest benefits help ensure customer loyalty, while the growing database tells the companies what sells and what doesn't, to whom, and under what circumstances, permitting customer-centered refinements and reengineering in merchandising, inventory, and shelf space. Hallmark Cards has refined this approach to a high degree with its company-owned or franchised outlets. It uses real-time data on all sales to adjust existing displays and promotions, and to design forthcoming offerings.

Another way to recognize the individual characteristics of a customer was pioneered by MCI's "Friends and Family" long distance telephone package. The system looks at the record of your long distance calls, decides which numbers you call most often from your home phone, and gives you a discount on them, under certain circumstances. It's *your* pattern of phone calls that determines where the discount is. And you stay with MCI because you have a vested interest: your own discount plan. Sprint and AT&T have now followed suit, with their own plans for discounts to area codes or countries or numbers most frequently called.

As often happens in a very competitive industry, what was formerly a value advantage for one company, MCI, has become a part of all competitive customer value packages. It is now at the *expected*, or maybe even *desired*, level of the customer value hierarchy, and certainly no longer in the *unanticipated* category. The lesson, then, is to stay ahead of the pack by taking what you know about your customers and striving continually for new ways to add value for them.

## CUSTOMERS ARE PEOPLE, NOT ACCOUNTS

If you have an insurance policy with USAA, you'll likely be the beneficiary of a form of close and personal service delivered from a distance. When a USAA customer talks to a service representative on the phone, the service rep can call up visual images of the customer's entire file on the computer screen. The complete case history is available, instantly, and without shuffling from one service representative to another, without wasting time.

Other firms are increasingly assigning cradle-to-grave customer service representatives to their clients to achieve the kind of intimacy that people used to expect from, for example, *my banker*. As the services of banks have expanded in recent years, and as automation has expanded within banks' operations, service to customers has often become increasingly fragmented. It has become more and more difficult to find a bank that is able to link two or more different kinds of accounts in one customer's name. A number of progressive banks are now using technology and common sense to reassemble things, so that they deal more with "customers" and less with *accounts.*

Increasingly, financial institutions such as banks and insurance companies, as well as a number of sales offices, are moving toward a system of "case management." Under such a system, for instance, you don't get shuffled from one person to another, if you are talking about your checking account or your home equity loan. The USAA service rep mentioned above has your whole file available, and if you have two policies, say, home and auto insurance, the rep has access to them both. You are a person with a name, which is effective across all your transactions or functional areas, not a bunch of unrelated account numbers.

Contrast such an approach with the *form* letter we recently received from our bank, signed by a senior officer, which began, "Because of your outstanding banking record, I wanted to personally tell you about . . ." We didn't read the rest. You can't really be personal just by saying you are. That letter had all the up close and personal appeal of a sweepstakes envelope we received emblazoned with "MRS. TQS IS A FINALIST!!" Even with Ed McMahon's smiling visage on it, this was not a charmer, and Mrs. TQS was not a winner.

One company we have worked with on the East Coast had each *account* handled by six different people. Sales made the original contact, set terms, and took the first order; credit reviewed creditworthiness; transportation selected, scheduled, and costed the carrier; "customer service" reviewed the paperwork, checked inventory, finalized the order, and dealt with customer queries and complaints; warehouse/shipping loaded and released the shipment; and finance sent out the invoice and collected the payment.

Customers couldn't get direct answers to questions, because "customer service" didn't have the answers. Everything had to be referred to another department or office before a delivery date could be confirmed, the carrier identified, and so on. The system bred delays, inefficiencies, mistakes, dropped balls, and finger-pointing.

This system had persisted from a past when information was available on paper, or could be obtained by a phone call, but you had to be pretty expert in order to work the system. New systems have made it possible to put most of that expertise on line in such a fashion as to make it accessible, instantaneously and authoritatively, for anyone on the network. So this firm has let the computer network's expertise broaden the responsibilities of the customer service representatives.

Now, after the sales representative has made the first contact, each new customer is assigned a CSR. The new client is told, "Joan will be your personal representative; the one who will handle *all* your business in our home office." And Joan has immediate access to all the information about prices, credit ratings, shipping schedules, inventory, billing, and so on—as well as the complete history of the customer's earlier orders. Orders can be confirmed on the spot, with firm delivery dates and costs. In the few instances where a tough problem cannot be resolved this way, specialists can be called on to assist the CSR.

Not only has this change required the development of "smart" network information systems, it has meant broadening the skills of the CSRs (although they are not the experts their departmental counterparts are) and empowering them to make decisions that were previously the exclusive preserve of the specialists or supervisors. The result is a happier customer base, quicker and more efficient turnaround of transactions, and the elimination of *accounts* in favor of customers.

This example of case management also reflects a combination of *high tech* and *high touch.* As in the case of the automated gas pump described earlier, there are times when advanced technology can replace the human touch satisfactorily, to the benefit of both the customer and the company. At the same time, high tech can make possible a degree of individualized attention, in this instance through a case management approach that was previously impossible. Here *high tech* enhances, rather than replaces, *high touch.*

## WORKING THE MIDDLE

Yet another approach to responding to the needs of selected customer segments has been to acquire or develop a complementary service that adds value to your own business. It may add product depth, extend your channels of distribution, or otherwise bring the service closer to the customers.

One example is called Le Concierge. Hotel management guru Phil Wexler started the business by recruiting, training, and providing qualified concierges to hotels. This is a big service value-adder for hotels, and a service they cannot always manage cost-effectively (staffing and training) on their own. It puts the hotel on a higher service plane and closer to the needs of its clients. The original concept worked so well that Wexler has expanded his service to office buildings and apartment complexes, where developers and owners can provide a different sort of value-added service for their tenants.

Or, if there isn't someone out there with a "concession" for you to hire, you can develop your own. That's what the Jewel Food Stores chain did. It discovered a need for delivery of groceries for "big ticket" frequent shoppers who can't or don't want to spend the time and effort required for shopping in the store. So it developed a subsidiary, Pea Pod, that takes orders for Jewel's groceries by computer, packages the order, and delivers it. Customers like the convenience and time-saving aspect, and Jewel likes being able to sell groceries without even having the expense of the customer walking into the store. The resulting revenue and cost savings for Jewel are obvious, much like those involved in the banks' ATMs.

On the other hand, people may be resistant to and resentful of the impersonal nature of *some* service delivery. Pea Pod's ordering system is high tech: crank up your computer and order via modem link to the Pea Pod office—you don't even have to talk with anyone. Your billing is automatic. Delivery happens. High tech and no touch. The service is there, at a big convenience to the customer who prefers it that way.

But be careful about excluding people from your marketplace prematurely. A few years back, we researched people's reasons for standing in line for license plates, rather than ordering them through the mail. A surprising number told us they did so because they enjoyed the social contact involved in getting out and going to the license bureau! "It gets me out of the house." The moral: Some people even get some pleasure out of standing in line! Segment! Segment! Segment!

## WHY NOT EMPLOYEE SATISFACTION?

Robert Wood Johnson's hierarchy of service imperatives, cited earlier, puts the employees second only to the customer as a means for achieving *closeness*. Why not? Even if we do serious customer satisfaction research, we often fail to look closely at the employee and the employee's role in giving the customer what he or she wants.

What's the connection between employee satisfaction and customer satisfaction? What's the link between customer loyalty and employee loyalty? It's not hard to figure that loyal and dedicated employees are more likely to help you develop better products and services than a disgruntled or hostile workforce. That's the easy but not always most significant part.

Your front-line employees are the ones that directly affect customer loyalty, insofar as service plays any role at all. As the highly regarded consultant Frederick F. Reichheld points out:

> The fact is that employee retention is key to customer retention. . . . The longer employees stay with the company, the more familiar they become with the business, the more they learn, and the more valuable they can be. Those em-

ployees who deal directly with customers day after day have a powerful effect on customer loyalty. Long-term employees can serve customers better than newcomers can; after all, a customer's contact with a company is through employees, not the top executives. It is with employees that the customer builds a bond of trust and expectations, and when those people leave, the bond is broken.[10]

Increasingly, as companies tend toward a "lean and mean" staffing philosophy, as they tend toward a JIT approach toward personnel as well as hard goods in their inventories, the development of employee loyalty and satisfaction becomes both more critical and more difficult—or at least more demanding of careful attention. Few American firms now promise their employees a job for life. That end of the commitment bond is gone. Similarly, few employees expect to commit themselves for life to any company, or any position.

How can you ensure your employees' loyalty and commitment? As Reichheld points out, "All other things being equal, the best people will stay with the company that pays them most." This leads many of the shrewder firms to tie compensation to measures of employee-induced customer loyalty. Incentives, in the form of bonuses or commissions, are designed to align the employees' self-interest and that of the company. Contrast this approach with performance evaluation based on the number of phone calls handled, or customers run through the system.

We will look later at some of the approaches to human resource management that contribute strongly to employee support of a customer-centered operation. These include employee empowerment, training, and the development of a learning organization.

Flexible compensation policies that reward longevity and loyalty, based on performance in the right areas, certainly contribute to reduced turnover. Highly significant, in any case, is tying the employee's performance evaluation to measures that reflect the company's dedication to the customer, rather than to more traditional *time and motion* elements or other rituals without any real impact on the customer.

## YET ANOTHER CUSTOMER—DOING WELL BY DOING GOOD

The third category of stakeholders in Robert Wood Johnson's hierarchy of service imperatives is the community. The community in which a business exists is, of course, a customer, both in the narrow sense—the people who come in and buy—and in the broader sense, as the environment in which a company has a concern for its "reputation" as a corporate citizen, not just as a producer and seller of goods and services.

Paul Newman's line of salad dressings and spaghetti sauces enhances its appeal by informing customers that all profits from the products' sales go to charities. Another charitable focus is featured by Ben and Jerry's, the ice cream makers, with a strong flavor of ecology, in addition to their *Peace Pop* ice cream on a stick.

**Green is gold.** Ecological soundness, or *correctness*, has become widely advertised, as producers encourage recycling or proclaim their products to be ecologically sound, made of recycled goods, and so on. *Green* sells, because customers want to feel good, too. The Body Shop chain of retail health and beauty products features organic cosmetics and environmentalism.

**Citizenship.** There probably is not a hospital in the country that does not have an element in its mission statement about "contributing to the community," or something along these lines. In all too many instances, the mission statement is collecting dust. However, some hospitals do indeed "live" their mission by being heavily involved in the community in such areas as preventive education, wellness programs, and special programs for senior citizens.

## BOTTOM-LINE CUSTOMERS—SHAREHOLDERS

Clearly, the customers that are most concerned about the cash flow, the bottom-line customers, are the shareholders. Who are these shareholders, the owners of the company, and what do they really want?

Roughly 80 percent of the stock of public companies in the United States is held by institutional investors. Their principal concern, of course, is performance: return on their investment through dividends or appreciation. Additionally, some 40 percent of all investors are concerned about stability and good reputations. And some shareholder activists, of course, are interested in a cause of one sort or another. These are a very small, but often vocal, minority who can affect the kind of publicity that surrounds a company's stockholders meetings.

The shareholders, the ultimate customers, are to be satisfied through the company's performance. And that performance, ultimately, depends on the company's ability to satisfy—or excite, or delight—all its other customers, internal and external.

# GUIDELINES FOR GETTING TO THE HEART OF THE MATTER: BUILDING CLOSENESS

To win your customers' loyalty, you have to go beyond satisfaction. The value you are selling must differentiate you from your competitors, who merely provide *satisfaction*. Period.

Arnold Hiatt, chairman of Stride Rite Corporation gives credence to that notion this way: "When a mother bought a pair of Stride Rite shoes, it wasn't an act of commerce. It was an act of confidence. She expected Stride Rite to look after her children's feet in the most professional way possible. And Stride Rite took that seriously. *That's what differentiated the company from other footwear producers.* The challenge for my generation was to live up to that legacy."[11]

The basic challenge then is to reengineer in such a way that you can achieve a differentiating level of quality that carries you beyond *satisfaction,* and thus earns the loyalty of your customers. This process must begin by getting closer to your customers.

How do you go about getting closer to the customer? As this chapter demonstrates, there are a variety of approaches that will work. However, the heart of the matter is that you must believe in the *power of one,* because when it comes to creating total customer value, "one is the only number." With this in mind, we offer the following guidelines for building closeness:

1. **Be something special to *someone* in particular.** Choose your segments. Identify those customers who are most valuable to you. Target your efforts toward them.

2. **Find the *one* thing that is most important to that customer.** Build your customer value model around it.

3. **Reengineer your customer value package to do that *one* thing** much better than the competition.

4. **Expand your customer value package *one* element at a time.** Add features and benefits that will continue to delight your customer.

5. **Win customers *one* at a time.** Don't fall victim to the mass marketing mania.

6. **Reengineer your systems to manage each *one* of the customer's moments-of-truth with your organization.**

7. **Make each customer feel as if he/she is the only *one* you have.** Relationships count.

8. **Play the customer value game *one-on-one*.** Reward loyalty of customers and employees.

9. **Make *one* simple promise in your marketing.** Deliver on it.

10. **Remember: The customer's opinion is the only *one* that matters.** Listen to it. Reengineer in response to it.

## Chapter Eight

# I Can See Clearly Now

*"Every man takes the limits of his own vision as the limits for the world."*

Schopenhauer

Seeing is believing. Or sometimes believing is seeing.

## ONE MAN'S CEILING IS ANOTHER MAN'S FLOOR

The figure that follows is probably familiar to anyone who has taken a management training seminar or course in psychology in the past couple of decades. It is, nonetheless, a quick and convincing reminder that we see what we want to see, or we see what we are able to see, depending on our perspective at a given time. In one instant, a young woman. In another instant, an old woman.

Analogous to this picture is the question of whether the glass is half full or half empty. Comedian George Carlin answers that question by saying that "the glass is just too damn big." Reflecting once again in a different way, the limits of what we see are constrained by the limits of our perspective, proving that Mr. Carlin is well qualified to be a reengineer.

Our perception affects what we hear as well as what we see. This fact is illustrated by a story that Robert Marzano tells in his book, *A Different Kind of Classroom*. It seems that Mr. Marzano had to travel to Cedar Rapids on business for three weeks in a row. Each Monday morning, as he left home, he told his young daughter Ashley that he was going to Cedar Rapids, but that he would return on Friday. Finally, on the third Monday, after he had departed, Ashley went to her mother and asked quizzically, "Mommy, why is daddy always going to see Peter Rabbit?" It's all a question of perspective.[1]

## FLAWED VISION

Clearly, how we view the world shapes our approach to it. While there is no intrinsically right or wrong way to perceive anything, perception can lead to consequences that are either positive or negative. This is particularly true when it comes to creating a vision for the business and following it. If the vision is customer-centered, intent upon achieving total customer value, there is no guarantee of success. However, the odds are strong that it can succeed if the other necessary ingredients drawn from the Seven C's are also available. On the other hand, a perspective that doesn't have the customer squarely in the middle of the picture will usually lead to flawed vision and business failure.

Raytheon's Beech general aviation unit suffered a recent case of flawed vision in an attempt to introduce a revolutionary new aircraft. Made of carbon plastic, this radically designed turboprop plane, the Starship, was intended as a flashy but fuel efficient alternative to the corporate jet. Unfortunately, the customer value package was all wrong. While the company had assumed that the Starship's fuel efficiencies would attract cost-conscious buyers, this feature became less desirable as fuel cost fell during the plane's development cycle. Then the plane's relative speed disadvantage caused jet buyers to turn elsewhere. While Starship's high-tech appearance had also been viewed as a plus, it turned out that older-generation CEOs, the primary decision makers on aircraft purchases, balked at the attention-getting design. The result has been a write-off of the plane's design and development costs of approximately $500 million and an impediment to the company's diversification away from its core governmental defense business.[2]

Beech is not alone in stumbling with technology. High-flying VideOcart was once the darling of Wall Street. The company specializing in micromarketing made a video display for grocery units that displayed advertising, headline news, and supermarket information. It expanded rapidly into 15 retail chains and 200 stores nationwide. But then the bottom fell out. The system was too expensive for many stores and the advertisers who had been asked to pay upfront sponsorship of $5 million withdrew their support because of mixed results. In 1993, VideOcart withdrew from unprofitable stores, had two major clients cancel their contracts, and, in the last quarter of the year, filed for bankruptcy protection.[3]

Other flops? Try these on for size: BIC perfume, a feminine fragrance marketed like a cigarette lighter; the Cadillac Allante, introduced to the market with lots of bugs and sold at a price point that made potential buyers shudder; NeXT computer, Steven Jobs' black box designed with an optical drive that customers didn't want; and dry beer—much advertising ado about something that none of us wanted to drink in the first place.[4]

For some of these companies or products, expanding the vision was flawed. For others it was fatal. How important is vision anyway?


## THE VISION THING

When Bob Eaton began the process of turning Chrysler Motor Company around, he jolted company employees, shareholders, and everyone else who was paying attention to how he was going to take on the monumental challenge. He adamantly declared, "We don't need a vision." Then, he went about the process of spelling one out. His vision? "Chrysler needs to be 'getting a little bit better every single day.'"[5]

Similarly to Mr. Eaton, upon taking over at IBM, Lou Gerstner asserted that "the last thing that we need is a vision." Then about six months later *he* went on to spell one out: The company won't be split up, and its parts will be even more closely linked. The company will reassert its identity as the customers' primary computing resource. The company will be the dominant supplier of technology in the industry. IBM employees must waste fewer opportunities, minimize bureaucracy, and put the good of the company before their division's. The vision also provides that the PowerPC, a new micro-processor design, will be IBM's centerpiece. Built into many future computers, it will run a wide range of standard industry software, and it will steeply cut manufacturing costs.[6]

Why does the "vision thing" cause these foremost captains of American industry such unease? These utterances are reminiscent of George Bush's pained expression during his presidential campaign when his adversaries and the press (we recognize that Bush support-ers may find the terms *adversary* and *press* to be redundant) would persist in asking him to reveal his vision for America. The difference with Messrs. Eaton and Gerstner is that they lamented the need to de-velop and communicate a vision, but then just went ahead and enun-ciated them anyhow. While Mr. Bush never quite got the *vision thing*, the adage of "pay attention to what we do, not what we say" applies to business just as well as it does to politics.

The reason may be that *visioning*, as with *empowerment, resizing,* and *continuous improvement,* can be so readily viewed as a manage-ment *flavor-of-the-month*. There can be an understandable reluctance to acknowledge openly that a vision is being spun. To acknowledge vision may be to invite a flood of cynical energy that will do the orga-nization no good whatsoever. The landscape of management litera-ture is strewn with descriptions of cynical employees who wink knowingly at one another as yet another management flavor is intro-duced into the organization.

Our experience with a variety of CEOs, of companies large and small, is that there is a certain and usually unspoken fatigue with all of this. CEOs are rightfully restive about trumpeting the new vision for fear that it will trigger counterproductive responses, not only the cynical reactions of employees, but their own dark apprehensions.

Is vision yet another well-worn and outmoded tool that should be eliminated from the management tool kit? We believe that vision is far from obsolete. On the contrary, vision making is not an *option* for management, appropriate and usable in some situations but not in others. Vision making is mandatory and essential to the company's future. If a company does not have a strong vision that it can use to reenergize and reengineer itself, it will eventually succumb to Bryan's law, which is, "At some point in the life cycle of any organization, an organization's ability to succeed in spite of itself runs out."

## RUNNING THE THREE-MINUTE MILE

Vision may not be a sufficient condition for customer-centered reengineering, but it is a necessary one. Vision has power. Remember the story of English runner Roger Bannister's pursuit of the sub-four minute mile in the mid 1950s? Up until his record-breaking achievement, such a feat was deemed to be physically impossible. Within a year after Bannister broke the mark, so did numerous other milers. Did everyone just develop that much speed in such a short period of time? Or did the proven achievability of the goal spur greater levels of performance for all?

Bob Galvin, ex-CEO of Motorola, believes that expectation levels in the United States are completely insufficient. The real goal, he argues, ought to be the three-minute mile. "At Motorola we have come to the realization that if it's imaginable, it's doable. Furthermore, unless we inspire the accomplishment of the imaginable, we won't accomplish it," says Mr. Galvin.[7]

Therefore, if we don't think about running the three-minute mile, and if we don't begin to conjure up the image of the three-minute mile having already been run, then the odds are it simply won't happen. It certainly won't happen by chance. It won't happen without being preceded by a mental image. The clearer and cleaner that mental image, the more likely it is that the image will ultimately come to be realized in the material world.

In business, a vision statement has to be everything that a mission statement is not. The vision statement must have no *finish line*. It must be structured and expressed so that employees will continue to pursue it even after shorter-lived missions have been attained. The vision must set its sights high, for much the same reason. Jerry Porras of Stanford University's Graduate School of Business argues that any corporate vision worth its salt should last for at least a century.[8] If visioning *seems* to separate the visioner from his or her peers, it's because it does.

Karl Albrecht calls vision the organization's *northbound train*. He chose this metaphor because it implies "[u]nwavering commitment to a particular direction that the organization is going to follow to be successful in the future" and "conveys a strong sense of momentum, implacable movement in an unambiguous direction."

The vision needs to be communicated in a clear, compelling, and concise vision statement that is promulgated widely and incorporated into the organization's collective consciousness and behavior. As Karl emphasizes in his book, *The Northbound Train*, a vision statement

> is not a platitude. It is not a slogan. It is not an exercise in journalism; it is an exercise in careful, clear, creative, disciplined, and mature thought. It provides a critical business success premise that leaders can understand, commit to and dramatize to others.[9]

While visioning is a critical business skill, it is also something of a metaphysical skill. Most Westerners are uncomfortable with the exercise of their metaphysical faculties, with most of their exposure coming through organized religion and its rituals. We believe that the exercise of visioning as a human capability apart from approved spiritual expression is in its evolutionary infancy. Grand possibilities await the continued evolution of the human species. Visioning is a matter of breaking the mold and, as such, it is inseparable from courage.

## THE MISSING LINK

Strategy is the link between vision and action. Put another way, "Ask not what your vision can do for you, ask what you can do for your vision." A failure to ask and answer the question honestly and regularly is what can give vision the bad name that causes leaders like Messrs. Eaton and Gerstner to pretend that a vision is not a vision. What usually spells the end for vision is the lack of a well-defined, supporting strategy for action.

The classic planning structure prescribes a connectivity among vision, mission, goals, objectives, strategies, and tactics. The vision must be brought down to the ground. The train must be put on the rails. The vision must, along with all of the components of its supporting plan, *degenerate into work,* to recall Peter Drucker's famous maxim.

How do you create effective strategies for realizing the vision? Drawing upon Michael Porter's classic work, *Competitive Advantage,* we see three ways: cost leadership, differentiation, and focus.

*Cost Leadership* means the business sets the price that, in the absence of other competitive influences, competitors must follow. Obviously, in order to succeed, this implies that you are the low cost producer, otherwise lowering costs only lowers profits. Examples of companies that have pursued this course successfully include Wal-Mart, Southwest Airlines, and Hewlett Packard.

*Differentiation* means that the business creates a desired uniqueness for itself in the eyes of the market and its customers. This strategy requires you to identify performance dimensions or qualities, that is, a Customer Value Model, that are highly valued by customers and then position yourself uniquely to serve those needs. Successful performance through this strategy requires that the premium paid by the customer for the uniqueness exceeds the extra costs incurred in achieving it. Examples here include Federal Express, Disney World, and Microsoft.

*Focus* means the business positions itself to serve a specialized segment of the market or group of customers. This results in the company becoming highly specialized and efficient in serving the selected market niche. It also requires that the niche be profitable enough to stay in but not so profitable that it draws a crowd of competitors. Pizza Hut, Midwest Express, and Dell Computers are examples of successful focusing.[10]

In almost any situation, the combination of either *differentiation* or *focus* with *cost leadership* is usually a showstopper. Organizations that can reengineer themselves to achieve this combination hold two aces in a three-card-stud card game. They almost always win, and win big.

## Cost Leadership

Wal-Mart has become a "power retailer" for a myriad of reasons. However, one of its primary secrets has been to become the intermediary between the customer and the supplier. By capturing data regarding customer purchases and desires, Wal-Mart gets the supplier to produce according to its specifications, thus controlling both the nature of the product or good and its manufactured cost. This enables Wal-Mart to be the cost leader by putting the right products on the right shelf space at the right price point.

Another factor in the Wal-Mart success formula is its low distribution costs. The company has devised a distribution center network and logistics system that enables it to keep total operations costs in this area as much as 2 percent below everyone in the industry while almost never suffering out-of-stocks.

Southwest Airlines is also a cost leader. Its secret to success includes no frills, low overhead, a non-unionized workforce, and flying many direct routes rather than connecting flights that allow them to economize on fuel and baggage transfer costs.

## Differentiation

While the jury is still out on the ultimate success of the strategy, Merck's $6 billion acquisition of Medco Containment Services is a clear attempt to stay ahead of the dramatic changes in the prescription drug market and to differentiate itself from other pharmaceutical companies. According to Merck CEO P. Roy Vagelos, the goal is to create a business that is unique in the industry.

Merck's move is a direct response to the pressures from government and managed care organizations to lower the cost of drugs that threaten its margins and stock price. Medco is the largest supplier of mail-order pharmaceuticals, a lower cost niche that has created a 35 percent annual growth rate and a 26 percent share of all Americans covered by drug benefit plans.

One of Medco's competitive advantages is its sophisticated information systems that allow its pharmacists to track patient medication records. In addition to acting as a check against redundant or dangerous new prescriptions, the systems will give the combined business the ability to target its marketing efforts on the prescribing patterns of specific doctors. As managed care organizations continue their inroads, this will allow a smaller salesforce to focus with greater intensity on fewer benefit plan providers.

Says Vagelos about the potential synergies, "I've always thought there would be a better way. This is it . . . It's a chance to change the paradigm once and for all."[11]

### Focus

In 1984 as a 19-year-old college student, Michael Dell had what he thought was a pretty straightforward idea—selling computers over the phone. His $1,000 investment has since grown into a $2 billion company with over 4,500 employees operating in 18 countries. What was his secret? He had identified an emerging niche—increasingly sophisticated computer buyers who were willing to give up retail sales help for lower-priced machines. In the intervening years he's honed his original concept from selling gray-market IBM PCs to designing and assembling his own computers from purchased off-the-shelf components. In this way Dell is able to keep costs down and embrace the low-cost-producer role at the same time, although as the market for PCs has grown and fragmented, he finds himself aiming for low cost in the top tier of distributors.[12]

This strategy is also reflective of the concept of customer intimacy that has been advanced by Michael Treacy and Fred Wiersema, which means "segmenting and targeting markets precisely and then tailoring offerings to match exactly the demands of those niches."[13] It is also an example of what Treacy and Wiersema term *product leadership*, which means "offering customers leading-edge products and services that consistently enhance the customer's use or application of the product, thereby making rivals' goods obsolete." In addition to product leadership, Treacy and Wiersema also assert that *operational excellence* and *customer intimacy* are the other two "value disciplines" around which visions and strategies can be organized. Operational excellence refers to delivering reliable products/services at competitive prices and with a minimum of difficulty and inconvenience. Customer intimacy means segmenting and targeting markets precisely and then tailoring offerings to match exactly the demands of those niches.

## THE ROAD GOES ON FOREVER

The combination of vision linked with strategy can and should provide continuity for the business. The Motorola story suggests how the evolution of strategy can be done winningly. In 1981, Motorola placed an advertisement that it was going to go toe-to-toe with the

Japanese with concepts they called participative management. The company trained all of its management and employees in these quality improvement methods. Motorola then implemented a series of strategies that "moved the needle" and allowed the business units to become more competitive.

In the mid-80s Motorola unveiled its "Six Sigma" vision and associated strategies. The company moved to world-class defects control. Six Sigma, as implemented at Motorola, refers to an entire set of policies, cultural values, and organizational practices whose objective is to achieve a level of accuracy that is 99.9999998 percent. In 1989, Motorola embraced total customer satisfaction (TCS) as a driving force. This shifted the company's focus from an internal to an external focus and caused Motorola to develop better relations with its customers. The goal for Motorola's TCS initiative is "to make our customers winners by exceeding their expectations."

The message? Vision can make you more precise and more focused. In this sense, yesterday's vision becomes a stepping-stone for staying ahead of the competition today. In turn, it provides the stepping-stone for accomplishing tomorrow's vision. There is a historical continuity within the Motorola vision that is easily discernible with the advantage of 20–20 hindsight: Motorola was building on the past for the future. Sometimes evolution is appropriate, and sometimes revolution is appropriate.

*People* are often the most overlooked element in strategy. In order for the vision to be real and the strategy successful, people in the organization need to live the vision and implement the strategy. But first they need to understand and share it.

Home Depot, as previously mentioned, is but one stellar example of where vision has been communicated effectively to employees with outstanding results. Without each employee understanding and sharing the vision that he or she is expected to serve as a consultant to each customer regardless of the size of the customer's intended purchase, the Home Depot business concept would collapse like a house of cards. Microsoft and Wal-Mart have generated their respective visions and have shared these concepts with employees. The results for the customer have been outstanding and, therefore, the results for company profitability and growth have evidenced the success that comes from providing better customer value than the next competitor.

Another successful example of linking people to vision and strategy is NovaCare, the nation's largest provider of comprehensive medical rehabilitation services. Headquartered in suburban Philadelphia, the company employs approximately 7,000 people across the country, most of whom are clinical professionals in one medical rehabilitation discipline.

As part of his recent reflection on NovaCare's credo, purpose, and beliefs, CEO John Foster traveled extensively throughout the country, talking to the company's clinical employees about their views and what they believed to be special about and important to the company. As Foster notes in the company's 1993 annual report, "During 1993 we had the opportunity to reexamine and recommit ourselves to our Credo, Purpose and Beliefs. Our values are the strong foundation upon which we build our company. They are also the basis upon which we establish our reputation." As shown below, these three elements form an important part of the NovaCare culture:

*Our Credo:* Helping Make Life a Little Better.
*Our Purpose:* To effectively meet the rehabilitation needs of our patients through clinical leadership.
*Our Beliefs:*

Respect for the Individual.

Service to the Customer.

Pursuit of Excellence.

Commitment to Personal Integrity.

Foster, who invests a great deal of his time in spreading the word and *living the vision,* believes that "A company is defined by its purpose and beliefs. These form the foundation upon which the company is built. They precede goals, policies, practices and results."

## GUIDELINES FOR SEEING CLEARLY: BUILDING CLARITY

Many organizations that do reengineering develop a *mission* statement for what they want to accomplish through the effort. They define tactical objectives; for example, to lower costs, reduce waste, streamline operations. However, too few organizations that undertake reengineering consider the linkage of the reengineering to the business's strategic purpose.

This is a critical flaw. It unnecessarily limits and constrains the scope and intent of the reengineering and tends to cause a primarily internal focus. All reengineering needs to be linked to the business's vision and connected to its customer value proposition.

Vision alone is not enough, however. Remember:

- A vision without a plan is *meaningless.*
- A vision without fixed responsibilities is a *daydream.*
- A vision without total buy-in is an *illusion.*

- A vision unimplemented is a *nightmare.*
- A vision integrated strategically into the business's fabric is the *basis for business success in the future.*

Some guidelines for building vision follow.

1. **Start with the customer.** Define what you want to accomplish in terms of the end state that you are going to achieve to ensure total customer value.

2. **Keep it simple.** Flowery declarations do not make a good vision. Nor should a vision statement be motherhood and apple pie. A vision statement needs to communicate in a few powerful words—no more than 25—what you are going to do to achieve.

3. **Narrow the focus.** Concentrate people's attention on the critical few things that mean the most to the customers. Andrew Campbell, in his book, *A Sense of Mission: Defining Direction for the Larger Corporation,* reports that those organizations that do best in turning themselves around concentrate on a single issue.[14]

4. **Develop the vision as a team.** Don't go away by yourself and draft a vision statement. Make it an executive team exercise.

5. **Solicit input/build support.** Don't just communicate the vision from on high. Ask employees for their opinions and ideas. Do a reality check. See how the vision squares with the organization's current culture and core values. Determine how big a change needs to be made to achieve the vision.

6. **Link business strategies and plans to the vision.** Don't leave the vision hanging out there. Establish the clear connection between it and how the business will be operated.

7. **Reengineer to accomplish the vision.** Explain all reengineering within the context of what is to be accomplished through realization of the vision.

Finally, and most importantly, "live the vision." Based on his research, Andrew Campbell recommended that it is sometimes better to take an "actions first" approach. Don't holler the vision from the roof tops. Make the changes, achieve results, and then craft the formal vision statement to reflect the business's new operating philosophy and reality. No matter whether the vision leads or follows, the essential ingredient for change is "courage." That's the next "C."

## Chapter Nine

# Sit Down, You're Rocking the Boat

*"In management there comes a time when you have to look reality straight in the eye,*
*and to act upon it with as much speed as possible."*

Jack Welch
*CEO, General Electric*

We once worked for the seventh largest accounting and consulting firm in the world. Then on November 21, 1990, Laventhol & Horwath filed for bankruptcy.

## FORESTS AND TREES

In the 1980s, we were senior principals in the management consulting division of Laventhol & Horwath (L&H). L&H had offices in over 50 major American cities from coast to coast and boasted 4,500 employees. The firm included among its clients companies like Reebok, Hyatt Hotels, Trans World Airlines and many financial institutions, federal agencies, and state governments. In city after city, the client list read like the local who's who of real estate developers, family-owned businesses, and entrepreneurial enterprises.

L&H was a creature of the 1980s and had experienced phenomenal growth during the decade that closely paralleled the growth and prosperity of its clients. As the 80s came to an end, things began to unravel. There were too many unproductive partners, too much overhead, and too great a concentration of business in real estate and related businesses as that area of the economy went into a tailspin. Like most of the other national accounting firms, some of L&H's financial problems also stemmed from legal claims against it. Some have argued that the litigation was survivable. An inability to look reality in the eye and act on it was not.

Laventhol & Horwath needed to shift gears from the prosperity of the 80s to the new, customer-centered, value-oriented 90s. However, a succession of senior management lacked the ability to define a core set of customers and then do whatever it took to reengineer the firm around them. Despite the new realities, they were too mired in the myth of the firm as it had been, a "one-stop-shopping" center for financial advice, to imagine it in any other way.

As important, after the firm had paid out tens of millions of dollars to settle a series of lawsuits with many more pending and business in a precipitous downturn, it was unable to come to grips with the fact that the only thing that would save it was radical change. Indeed, in a conversation with the firm's last chief executive, he once stated to us, on the advice that he should take immediate steps to sell off the consulting division in order to free up enough cash to save the rest of the accounting and tax businesses, that he "was not elected Executive Partner to preside over the splitting up of L&H." Unfortunately, that's what happened when, months later, events had progressed too far to do anything else.

What can be done in circumstances like this? How do we survive situations where management doesn't confront the really tough issues?

These questions beg for an operational definition of *courage.* Ours is part of the quote from Jack Welch that opened this chapter, "the ability to look reality straight in the eye and act on it." Stated somewhat differently, courage is the characteristic that differentiates between those who will make the tough decisions and those who will not. Customer-centered reengineering is clearly about making tough decisions because it is about doing things differently.

Another expression of courage in business comes from those leaders who are strong enough, in a sense, to make themselves vulnerable. They are people who have the courage to make statements such as *I don't know, I made a mistake,* or *I changed my mind.* This element of courage, when combined with vision and consistent commitment, differentiates leadership from mere management.

## IS COURAGE ACADEMIC?

Can courage really make the difference in turning around large institutions that have existed for decades? The George Washington University in Washington, DC, is an example of an academic institution that is reinventing itself for the 1990s and beyond.

President Joel Trachtenberg has read the tea leaves. He understands that the demographic interruptions created by baby boomers who did not reproduce themselves on time and in sufficient quantity will have adverse effects on revenue *and* on the impact of his institution unless a significant reinvention is accomplished. Reinvention is thus occurring from stem to stern. For example, the School of Government and Business Administration is involved with a variety of initiatives that use the troubled city of Washington, DC, as an active laboratory. Integrating more closely with its surrounding community, The George Washington University is becoming more prominent in local public affairs as it is in national ones.

As one part of its forward-thinking initiatives, the university recently sponsored a national conference on empowerment zones—Jack Kemp called them enterprise zones in the 1980s. The conference drew 300 participants from around the nation who are interested in making a last-ditch effort to save America's troubled cities and depressed rural areas using comprehensive and concentrated approaches to economic development, tax policy, job training and social services, housing revitalization, increased law enforcement, and other applications of federal and state resources.

The university is leveraging its alumni as well as its new activism to build the value of its faculty and the degrees that it confers. Former San Antonio mayor and current Secretary of Housing and Urban Development Henry Cisneros was a keynote speaker at the Empowerment Zones Conference. Neither Dr. Cisneros nor The George Washington University made a secret of the fact that the university conferred his PhD in public administration. Everything is leverageable and should be leveraged.

The university has long offered law degrees, MBAs, and other courses of study through evening offerings that permit working Washingtonians to do all of their degree work at night. This type of flexibility for working students would be expected and does not constitute a reinvention in and of itself. However, the expanded community involvement, when coupled with convenience for the consumer as a strategy for total customer value, provides a powerful synergy.

On nonacademic fronts, The George Washington University Healthplan offers emergency child care services to its subscribers and actively promotes this benefit on radio stations that are targeted to segments that typically have school-age children.

Dr. Trachtenberg has looked reality squarely in the eye and has concluded that The George Washington University will not become an Ivy League institution; that it can only injure itself were it to pretend such status. The institution is likely to enjoy not only greater financial success but greater academic success over time because the president had the courage to make nontraditional decisions and then stick by them for implementation.

## CAPTAINS COURAGEOUS

If it takes courage to change when things are bad and you're in trouble, it may take even more courage to change when things are going well.

In 1988 when we worked with Bausch & Lomb's (B&L) International Division, the Division's then President Ron Zarrella was in just such a position. The division was doing quite well, and its subsidiaries were first or second in market share in most of the countries in which they operated. Yet, he saw the need to reinvest the profits from the company's RayBan sunglasses in the core contact lens and health care products business. The path he chose was customer-centered, articulating and leading the division's *total customer responsiveness* initiative. The results were spectacular, with the division growing so large that in 1992 it reinvented itself into three new divisions, each about the size of the old international one, and Zarrella became president of the corporation.

Jack Welch provided another example of *if it ain't broke, then break it* when he decided to reinvent General Electric. In the vernacular, GE has been described as fat, dumb, and happy. The company was a prosperous money-making machine that was not crying out for reinvention. Yet, Welch had foresight. He decided that the inertia at General Electric needed to be broken in order to prepare it for a continuously prosperous future. He analyzed the situation and decided that GE had to change.

In 1988, Donald Peterson started a process of reengineering at Ford Motor Company. He did it with quiet courage, and the net result has been the design and manufacture of automobiles that are not only among the finest in America, they are among the finest in the world.

One of our colleagues reports that he owes his life to a Ford product, the Mercury Grand Marquis. His Grand Marquis was broadsided by a motorist who ran a red light at a speed in excess of 40 mph. The strength and solidity of the Marquis permitted him and his two daughters to emerge from the wreckage virtually unscathed. The girls, aged 5 and 9, went to school the next day and didn't find the car crash worth mentioning to their teachers. Our colleague was X-rayed at the local hospital and pronounced uninjured. The next morning our colleague leased a brand new 1994 Grand Marquis virtually identical to his now-destroyed 1992 Marquis. The car was totally wrecked and the passengers were totally preserved—*that's total customer value.* To say that he is brand loyal to Ford products generally, and to the Mercury Grand Marquis specifically, would probably be an understatement.

Senior management at AT&T certainly didn't choose to reinvent their organization. After the court-mandated breakup of the Bell system, they had no choice, yet under the leadership of James Olson they began to do so. They confronted their own culture and decided that it was bureaucracy-centered and not customer-centered. Some readers may recall the 1970s-era bumper sticker that described the telephone system at that time: "They don't care because they don't have to . . ."

When AT&T began to focus on customer needs and preferences, it blazed a trail for a cornucopia of new features and resulting customer benefits from telecommunications. Indeed, under current CEO Robert Allen, AT&T has redefined itself from the "telephone company" to the telecommunications link of choice for voice and data. In August 1993, the company capped this reinvention with one of the largest deals in US business history, paying $12.6 billion for MacCaw Cellular Communications. It has demonstrated the courage of its convictions and implemented remarkable customer-centered reengineering at nearly breakneck pace.

In July 1993, Los Alamos National Laboratory announced that it was totally reorganizing, based largely on "quality management" principles. Los Alamos had long been the paragon of nuclear weapons research. Growing over the past half century to more than 11,000 workers with a $1 billion annual budget, the organization was encumbered by the layers of marbled administrative and operational fat not unlike many organizations in the private sector. Simple decisions required seven signatures at Los Alamos. Quite clearly, Los Alamos National Laboratory was bureaucracy-centered rather than customer-centered.

However, Los Alamos is now departing the fact and the mentality of *entitlement*. As the government progressively cuts back funding for a host of what have traditionally been federally funded activities, Los Alamos is attempting to transform itself to an increasingly self-sustaining organization that derives its revenue from satisfied customers.

## REARRANGING THE DECK CHAIRS

What did Sears, General Motors, IBM, and Eastman Kodak have in common? They had become experts in *rearranging the deck chairs* on ships that may well sink unless there are radical changes. Like many American businesses, they have developed a knack for the intellectual dishonesty that is inherent in pretending that a rearrangement of preexisting components somehow creates something entirely new. Indeed, such rearrangements of components without changing the fundamental direction or condition of the enterprise is precisely what is intended by the old adage about "rearranging the deck chairs on the Titanic."

In each of these cases, rigid corporate cultures severely inhibited either the recognition of and/or acting upon the fact that things were terribly wrong until it was far too late. While each of these companies has a chance to return to profitability, it can be argued that they may never return to greatness.

With the recent firing of its CEO Kay Whitmore, Kodak is the latest example of this phenomenon. Whitmore's problems, however, may have been rooted in the company's miscues over several decades, beginning in the 1970s, that stemmed from an inability to deal successfully with real and perceived challenges to its core photographic paper business. As it tried a number of new avenues, the company stumbled badly. Its bureaucratic management structure had neither the ability to deal with the entrepreneurial needs of new enterprises nor the honesty to admit its shortcomings. The result was entry into and exit from a variety of businesses, missed opportunities such as the videocassette recorder market, and millions of dollars in losses.[1]

Most of these decisions were not Whitmore's responsibility, yet as a corporate loyalist he was either unwilling or unable to undo what had been done by his predecessors. This failure to act, even at the end when dramatic downsizing was being demanded by the board of directors and his plans continued to be incremental, became his ultimate undoing.

## COURAGE—OUTSIDER STYLE

Kay Whitmore was replaced at Kodak by George Fisher, who had previously been CEO of Motorola. As we indicated in Chapter Five, the trend today is to go to outsiders to discover courage. In 1993, companies such as Westinghouse Electric, Eli Lilly, RJR Nabisco, and QVC Network, to name just a few, went to the outside to hire their CEOs.

What do outsiders bring to a situation that the individuals promoted from within the ranks do not? Usually it's a more detached objectivity, freedom from entangling personal relationships, and lack of a preestablished approach to solving the business's problems. As Michael H. Jordan, new CEO of Westinghouse Home Electric, puts it, he brings "ruthless logic" to his turnarounds that lets him "cut through emotions and people's opinions and get down to the facts." Randall L. Tobias, new CEO of Eli Lilly, mirrors Jordan's comments when he describes what he contributes to a turnaround situation, by stating, "I don't have some hidden agenda. I don't bring any emotional hang-ups."[2]

Sears, one of the companies that we cited earlier as having a history of "rearranging the deck chairs," has apparently already begun to feel some of the benefits of infusing some *outsider courage*. Sears reached out and hired Arthur C. Martinez to be chairman of its Merchandise Group on September 1, 1992. Mr. Martinez is an engineer and a Harvard Business School graduate. He has worked in a variety of industries including Exxon Corp., International Paper Co., Tally Industries, Inc., RCA, and Saks Fifth Avenue, then its parent Batus, Inc.

When Martinez came to Sears, he was given a virtual carte blanche to turn things around. He has used this authority to reengineer the entire company, including terminating Sears' famous catalog operation; reducing Sears' internal divisions from seven to three—clothes, home, and automotive; replacing large numbers of key executives; and laying off or firing 50,000 people. The net result of his action is that the Big Store has racked up 11 consecutive months of improved sales and had third quarter earnings in 1993 of $215.2 million, compared to a six-year earlier loss of $49.4 million.[3] It may be too early to tell for certain, but the Sears ship may be righted and the deck chairs may be secure for a very long time to come.

## PROFILES IN COURAGE: A SELF-TEST

So, courage can be either homegrown or imported. The real question is, how easy is it to be courageous in your organization? What kind of behavior does your culture promote and reward? Consider the following questions:

1. Do we encourage openness and honesty?
2. Do we deal in facts and not conjecture?
3. Do we encourage risk taking?
4. Do we tolerate mistakes?
5. Can we pick a direction and stick to it?

In our opinion, any *no* answer to these questions is problematic, and more than one indicates serious problems. However, based on our experience, many organizations will fall into the latter category.

As a case in point, consider the following poignant true story. One evening around 8 PM as we were working on the manuscript for this book in our office, we got a phone call from an employee of a large insurance company—a household name. She called because she said she was "going into the lion's den tomorrow" and was looking for moral support and advice.

She proceeded to explain that her company was in the worst condition she had seen in her long tenure with it—morale was terrible, nobody was being honest about current conditions, and the company was becoming more and more internally focused and bureaucratic with almost no concern for its customers. Because she cared about the company, she had called this situation to a key executive's attention in a lengthy memo. He had scheduled a meeting to discuss it, and she was now having second thoughts about her act of courage.

She had called us because she had read our book, *The Only Thing That Matters: Bringing the Power of the Customer into the Center of Your Business.* She told us that it described exactly where her company was and what it needed to do to turn around and that she had shared it with the executive. She wondered whether we had any other advice we might give her. First, we complimented her on her concern and her courage, then offered a few thoughts that we hope were helpful.

The purpose here, though, is not to discuss our suggestions or the resolution of this problem, but to call attention to the question. Why do situations like this occur? Why are there so many people in organizations with so much pain? And so few who cry out for help?

Obviously, for a variety of reasons. However, we believe a central one is that most business cultures tend to reward success, conformity, and compliance and not initiative, risk taking, and assertiveness. Yet, history has shown that most real progress is not linear. It moves in fits and starts, often stumbles and sputters, and sometimes outright fails. The flight path more resembles a butterfly's, not a jet's. The conflict between these realities induces most people in organizations to live a lie and sets our organizations up for failure.

## COURAGE IN ACTION

How do we learn to live with the courage necessary to make the tough decisions, to look reality in the eye and act?

One way is to give people the freedom they need to reinvent their own businesses, units, or departments. Wayne Calloway of PepsiCo has done this well, encouraging his people to be about the business of change—to create the breakpoints in the market so that things will never be as they once were. Says Calloway about these changes, "The market has forced it. It is a perpetual transition. And my guess is we're going to stay in transition. We'd better stay in it because if we get locked in, the world will pass us by." Calloway urges his managers to stay ahead of change, not to wait for it. "You don't wait until you're going over the cliff to change your brakes," he says.[4]

Another guiding principle for demonstrating courage can be expressed as "know when to hold them, know when to fold them." Boeing decided that it was time to fold the traditional manner in which it designed and manufactured airplanes, even though these methods had provided world-class success in the preceding decades. The company reengineered its design systems so that they could move to mass customization using CAD/CAM technology. Now the Seattle-based company can design aircraft more quickly and cheaply, be more service-oriented, and be more responsive overall to its customers' needs. Boeing reengineered for total customer value, having decided that no continuing competitive advantage could be derived from just grinding out one or at most several aircraft styles. Now, the design appearances are apparent to the customer, that is, the airlines, and to the consumer. There are different colors, seat configurations, and other features that are designed to attract and retain the airplane buying and flying public.

Another way to build courage is to *encourage* our people. This is best done by facilitating an *intrapreneurial* environment where units and subunits work to revitalize themselves because they understand that this is the cultural expectation. This encouragement and the customer-centered revitalization must be realized at the lowest logical organizational level. For revitalization to truly respond to the customer, it must happen at those levels that are, in fact, closest to the customer. While this seems obvious when expressed, all too often unit management awaits the mystical nod from higher echelons that can't realistically be expected. The top of the hierarchy may be simply too far removed from the customer.

The cultivation of courage among the people of an organization is closely related to employee empowerment. By empowerment, we mean not only enfranchising front-line employees, but mid and upper management as well. The purpose of such empowerment, as we see it, is to attain the highest and best from each employee, liberating all of his or her talents and energies in the pursuit of maximum customer satisfaction. Such empowerment, when successfully introduced, involves increases in the expectations placed on each employee according to an individual development plan that is synchronized with the individual development plans of all members of the team, regardless of organizational level. In this sense, empowerment entails the development of courage so that each employee will make decisions that he or she has not made before.

Another feature of successful empowerment is the breaking away of functional silos, increasing the velocity of the "organizational molecules" so that a more efficient and decisive structure prevails. When an empowered organization pursues a coherent strategy for creating customer value, the net result is high market impact, increased productivity and profitability, and a proliferation of ideas for product/service enhancements as well as totally new products and services. To us, empowerment should be a supercharging of the organization that accelerates movement of the company's offering to the marketplace closer, much closer to the customer.

Courage doesn't come in bottles; only false courage does. You can't buy it, nor is there a prescription medicine that provides it. It comes from within. This is a business-oriented book and not a treatise in psychology. But, by and large, business leaders either have courage or they don't. On the other hand, structures, systems, strategies, and people can be engineered to be courage-powered and courage-friendly, or they can be based on fear. The bad news is that too many organizations are based on fear rather than courage. The good news is that organizations based on fear will ultimately expire, creating fresh opportunities for companies and leadership that have the courage to get ever closer to the customer.

## GUIDELINES FOR ROCKING THE BOAT: BUILDING COURAGE

We remember some research done by the Center for Creative Leadership in Greensboro, North Carolina, with about 100 top executives in major American companies that asked them what had been their most valuable experiences in preparing them for their job. The vast majority of them, as we recall it, said it had been a situation in which they screwed up, made a mistake early in their careers, and then were supported—and in some cases rewarded—rather than reprimanded by their immediate superior.

This research frames our guidelines for building courage as it relates to reengineering:

1. **Empower employees at all levels.** Give them the authority, responsibility, and accountability to reengineer the reengineering so it makes the most sense for the customer they serve.

2. **Make change a driving force.** Make it everybody's job to challenge the status quo.

3. **Reward leaders.** Set up a system that provides open and honest feedback to management at all levels.

4. **Promote risk-taking.** Make mistakes learning events, not chances for public embarrassment or humiliation.

5. **Deal in fact, not myth or conjecture.** Look in the mirror. If you can't see clearly, get others to help you hold the mirror up to the organization for you.

**6. Listen to the front line and act on their advice.** Let them participate in reshaping the redesign of organizational structure and systems.

**7. Make sure there are no rocks to hide behind.** Don't hide behind any rocks. Restrictive policies, procedures, and practices prohibit change. Eliminate them as part of the reengineering initiative.

## Chapter Ten

# Imagine There's No . . .

*"Great ideas need landing gear as well as wings."*

Anonymous

If the right one don't get you, then the left one will.

## WHOLE BRAIN REENGINEERING

What type of activity should reengineering be? Right brain? Left brain? Or no brain, as it is practiced by some companies?

The answer is none of the above. Reengineering should be a whole brain experience. And because research indicates that each of us has a preference toward one side of the brain or the other, it should be accomplished by combining individuals with right brain and left brain preference as part of the reengineering team.

Although a bit oversimplified, the left brain/right brain distinction tells us a lot about how various people are likely to approach the reengineering task. Individuals with a left brain cognitive preference prefer linear, logical, analytical, numerical, structural, and sequential thinking. Individuals with right brain preference are disposed toward more holistic, spatial, intuitive, patterned, and emotionally referenced thinking. Because reengineering starts with a blank slate at the outset, but also includes detailed review, analysis, and design stages, the marriage of people with these two styles when accomplished successfully provides the greatest potential for producing the best results.

## HAMPERS, HARNESSES, AND HAMSTRINGS

However, all of us, whether we're left brainers or right brainers, have certain factors that impact our approach to problem-solving. As an example, look at the figure on the next page. How many squares are there? *Answer this now, before reading further.*

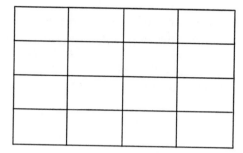

If you're like the majority of those who take the test, you probably responded "16." Then, if you stopped for a minute to reflect, you probably said 17. How many squares are there? Let's count them.

$$1 \times 1 \text{ squares} = 16$$
$$2 \times 2 \text{ squares} = \phantom{0}9$$
$$3 \times 3 \text{ squares} = \phantom{0}4$$
$$4 \times 4 \text{ squares} = \underline{\phantom{0}1}$$
$$30$$

Why do most people give the answer "16 squares" when confronted with this brain teaser? Because they fall back on a basic algorithm that they probably learned in first or second grade: $4 \times 4 = 16$. That's it! Problem solved! Next!

This form of conditioned behavior or reflex response enables us to deal productively with most of what we encounter in life. However, it is inefficient and ineffective when we are confronting complex problems or dealing with a clean slate as we are in reengineering. Then, it hampers and limits our naive curiosity and the exploratory instincts.

The same is true of attitudes we have developed over time that harness or restrain us from looking at things differently. Remember the opinion survey you took in Chapter Five; *Experience is the best teacher. If it ain't broke, don't fix it,* and so on. Our predisposition can hamstring us from open-minded inquiry and suspending judgment. Even the United States Marine Corps has found that there are benefits from breaking out of this rigid form of thinking and "going with the flow."

The Corps uses a battery of psychological tests to identify recruits who have the ability to view all situations from a fresh perspective, tolerating and deciphering ambiguity with little or no reference to previous experiences that are instructive to the challenge set before the marine. Indeed, once identified, those marines who have a high tolerance for ambiguity and who work to solve a problem with a minimum of cognitive "file-searching" for previous, similar situations are the very ones who are assigned to "reach the beach" first, clearing the way for their fellow soldiers and making *shoot from the hip* decisions just when shooting from the hip may well be the key to survival and success.

## CREATIVE CHARACTERISTICS

How do we overcome our mental restraints? How do we release the genius in the bottle? Research reveals that there is no fixed list of characteristics that predicts who will be a creative thinker and who will not. There are, however, some common traits related to personality, childhood, social habits, education, intelligence, and know-how. Here is a rough sketch of that profile.

The creative personality is generally independent, persistent, motivated, and humorous. Creative people usually had childhoods that featured diversity and unpredictability; disorder doesn't make such people anxious: it can actually make them more comfortable. The creative person is not a loner, but is more likely to be widely networked, sharing ideas with colleagues and other members of his or her learning community. An exceptionally high IQ is not required to be creative, nor is extensive graduate education at the best schools. Finally, research reveals that nearly all creativity is not innate. Those who come to be acclaimed for their creativity spent years mastering their field.[1]

Some organizations consciously hire and encourage people to be creative. Others may be inclined to screen them out or constrain them, intentionally or unintentionally. The vast majority of organizations may have no conscious policy about creativity or creative people whatsoever.

Creative organizations have characteristics, too. In their research into the effective management of innovation, academics Robert Ackersberg and Michael McGinnis have identified three components of what they call "holistic innovation management":

1. Creating an organizational climate that favors innovation.

2. Creating an innovative organization.

3. Harnessing individual innovation.[2]

Creating the appropriate organizational climate involves being open to new ideas and concepts, as well as establishing a performance gap between current and expected results. Creating an innovative organization revolves around developing core competencies (discussed in

Chapter Eleven) and focusing those skills on external challenges. Harnessing individual innovation includes recruiting innovative people to begin with, providing diverse opportunities for them, letting them function with a limited set of rules, and rewarding creativity appropriately.

In our experience, most organizations are not creative. They have developed robotic problem-solving to a high art, and the routines, rules, and repetitive behavior patterns often stand in the way of moving forward. Achieving total customer value requires creativity. Creativity requires breaking away from the hampers, harnesses, and hamstrings that limit thought and deed. We need to be willing to embrace new approaches and to see new and different stimuli if we are to break the mold. The implication here is that the full challenge of reengineering is not only to make radical changes to systems but also to change radically the underlying culture so that creativity and reengineering become the way of organizational life.

## PLAYING IN THE THREE I LEAGUE

When it comes to customer-centered reengineering, the big games are to be won in the Three I League: *imagineering, innovation,* and *inspiration.* The big games also happen to be the fun and enriching ones.

*Imagineering* is what Fred Smith did when he displayed the breakthrough thinking that resulted in Federal Express. Fred Smith and Federal Express succeeded because existing models of collection and distribution were rejected when designing the company's offering to the marketplace. Why? Traditional models could not satisfy Smith's objective of guaranteeing overnight delivery anywhere in the United States. When he decided against eliminating individual problems in the way that things had been done and instead decided to create a new model, Smith was imagineering.

Imagineering requires that we set aside "problem-solving activities" and take a clean slate approach. "By definition," says Roger Slater, "imagineering has two parts: Letting the imagination soar and engineering it back to earth. It is the absolute antithesis of piecemeal problem-solving."[3] There is a time for results-oriented thinking that imagineering permits and promotes, and there is a time for a process-oriented way of thinking that is organized around piecemeal problem-solving. All too often, large organizations only engage in process-oriented thinking rather than considering the possibility of results-oriented thinking. The fact of the matter is that business reengineering that is focused on total customer value must have elements of both, but for our money, the concepts that achieve real customer value begin with imagineering, and then downshift into engineering for specific problem debugging.

*Innovation* means throwing rule books into the trash, among other things. Earlier in the book, we denigrated innovation as the highest form of conformity. It should be emphasized that this denigration was targeted at "small i" innovation rather than "Capital I" Innovation. There is much in business today that masquerades as innovation when what is really happening is a rearrangement of the pieces of the business that existed previously. While incremental improvements may result from these rearrangements, they are hardly enough in an intensely competitive environment and certainly can't be thought of as customer-centered reengineering.

Innovation that really makes a difference is revolutionary, more in the spirit of Thomas H. Davenport's excellent text entitled *Process Innovation: Reengineering Work through Information Technology.*[4] He points out that genuine innovation in a business results in change to elements of structure, focus, measurement, ownership, and customers. We heartily agree and emphasize that the change process must begin with the customer.

*Inspiration* is the third I. Creativity consultant Roger von Oech promotes creative thinking as the "sex of our mental lives." But von Oech argues that hang-ups interfere with creativity just as they do with sex. *Follow the rules, be practical,* and *always find a right answer* will have a dampening effect on inspiration and the contribution that it can make to creativity. The inspiration to focus on results rather than rules encourages each individual to do the mental gymnastics that are involved with creativity—pulling from both the conscious and the unconscious in a way that is unbounded by normal constraints of time, space, and "but-we've-always-done-it-this-way" tradition.[5]

However, *framebreaking* and *paradigm shifting* usually fly in the face of the corporate body politic. Hal Sperlich had a spectacular career in the US auto industry. He developed the original Mustang at Ford, and he was responsible for creating the minivan at Chrysler. His warning to corporate innovators? "You're walking a very lonely road. Life in a large corporation is easier if you go with the flow and don't support major change. People who propose things that are different make more conservative people nervous, and the corporate environment just doesn't reward people for challenging the status quo. [But] if you have the ability to come up with things that are different, that create a new market, you can really ring the cash register."[6]

Inspiration for the creative individual must come from within—from the hot coals of the rocky childhood or some other of the characteristics previously mentioned—and, ideally, it must also be supported by repeated and encouraging pronouncements from the top.

# CREATIVITY IS NOT ENOUGH

We are not advocating creativity purely for creativity's sake. Creativity needs to be unleashed for the creation of customer value. Creating customer value requires talking with and listening to the customer. To an extent, it involves anticipating what the customer will think, say, and prefer next, based on a *creative extrapolation* drawn from careful listening.

Corporate creativity exists on a continuum. At one end is unbridled creativity, some critics would argue, at a level that is creativity for creativity's sake. DuPont has more patents than virtually all other companies throughout the world combined, but in the past few years has brought few new products to market successfully. AT&T has more features available for telecommunications than most of us could conceivably understand or use for the next quarter century. At the other end of the continuum, of course, is the situation where creativity is not only optional, it's probably discouraged.

To succeed at customer-centered reengineering, you need to be more toward the creative end of the continuum, but you need to be pragmatic too—to be like Rubbermaid, creating one new product or product enhancement each day, every day. This is real customer-centered creativity where multidisciplinary teams employ a creative synergy that focuses design and manufacturing talent with customer-smart marketing talent to create new products that customers actually want—whether they know it yet or not.

To many executives, this last statement may touch a nerve. After all, we've been preaching "listen to the customer," and now we're saying be willing to give them something they haven't asked for. This goes back to the concept of creative extrapolation.

If you really understand what your customers are looking for and why they do business with you, not from the perspective of particular products or service but from the value they are seeking from the experience, then you can combine this understanding with the organization's sense of what's new and possible. That's how breakthrough ideas are created. It takes the courage of the entrepreneur and the willingness to be wrong. The alternative, however, is being left in the dust by the competition. Remember, few in Detroit believed that Hal Sperlich's minivan had a market.

Pizza Hut demonstrated this kind of creativity when it decided that its food offerings need not be defined by the four walls in which it was being delivered. With this conceptual breakthrough, Pizza Hut began developing carry-out and delivery only stores where the customer provides the glassware, silverware, and dining ambiance—in the home. More than that, you now find Pizza Hut pizza in airports, hospitals, and baseball parks, plus schools at lunchtime. So long, Dominos.

In another chain restaurant example, McDonald's embraced creative innovation. It began by criticizing itself for a complacency that was causing earnings to sag. It continued by discovering and then focusing on total customer value. McDonald's reduced prices, but as we already indicated, in and of itself a price reduction won't get you much for long. Then, McDonald's focused on delivering greater customer value. It introduced the *extra value meal* to increase the average purchase per customer visit. It also introduced special promotions designed to persuade fast-food regulars to visit more often. Also, by building new restaurants in the high-density cities of countries abroad, McDonald's learned that it could do more with less space and reduced the average cost of bringing a new restaurant out of the ground to $1.2 million. McDonald's has wrapped its reinvented discovery around the central theme of flexibility that is driven by total customer value.

Andersen Consulting is overseeing its own transformation, and the growth in its revenues to an annual $3 billion with strong profitability is simply spectacular. Revenue growth has nearly tripled in less than five years.

Andersen has pursued a strategy of wrapping what it calls "business integration" around its customers. Andersen is reinventing itself as a full-service consulting organization that is adding strategic services to technological and tactical ones. The firm knows that its clients want execution, not just analysis. Certainly, execution must be based on sound analysis, but Andersen has found that there's money to be made in assisting clients to do both. Andersen Consulting also knows that the world in which any client resides is a cross-functional, multidisciplinary one. It only makes sense that practical, executable solutions to client problems will be multidisciplinary.

How does Andersen Consulting accomplish this? Largely with a cadre of young people hired right out of college. It leverages the talent of recruits by steadily increasing their assigned responsibilities and by training them long, hard, and effectively. Indeed, what Andersen Consulting does at its Center for Professional Education in St. Charles, Illinois, is beyond training. It is professional education and it is professional bonding—an *around-the-clock* immersion process. Using this approach, Andersen Consulting continues to enjoy the benefits of its famous "methodology," estimated to be 3,000 pages in length were it on paper, without creating procrustean response patterns that come to be applied whether they are appropriate to client needs or not. Andersen Consulting constitutes creativity and innovation in the cultivation and deployment of human talent. It is a triumphant human resource development and management revolution on a grand scale where the customer wins the war and the company wins the growth and profits.

## CREATIVITY IN ACTION

### Strategy

Creative strategies for creating total customer value are built to strive for the seamless customer experience. The strategy might be one of expediting transactions so that a company delivering most anything, home mortgage financing, for example, will reduce the period of uncertainty as approval is awaited, thereby strengthening competitive advantage. The strategy might also relate to passing along savings to customers and ensuring that unnecessary intermediation is streamlined out.

Another strategy can be coordinating tasks and processes and enhancing them with services that get closer to the customer as we approximate total customer value. For instance, imagine that you have an automobile accident and the car is banged up. It can't be driven, but fortunately there are no injuries. While you are waiting for the police, whom you called from your car phone, you punch up the insurance company on the same phone. After dealing with an efficient police response, a representative from your insurance company drives up and hands you the keys to a rental car and tells you she'll take it from here. She will fill out the paperwork, take your car in for repairs, and get it back to you next week. Such a scenario would be a seamless customer experience. It would be total customer value in action, and it would reflect customer value-driven strategy.

### Structure

Corporations that are structuring themselves for total customer value are about the process of creatively breaking down the functional silos that create dysfunctional tendencies: tendencies such as the sad scenario of divisions, branches, departments, or what have you competing with one another rather than focusing on customer value as a means of competing with the real competitors in the marketplace—the competitors that are outside the walls of the company.

Another dysfunctional consequence of functional silos is that too much mental energy and other resources become devoted to "coordinating" with other divisions, branches, or departments, rather than "coordinating" with the customer and the customer's needs and preferences. Related to this is the ratio of *checkers* to *creators* within the organization. A company that is reengineering for total customer value needs to examine critically the way in which it has structured and populated itself. This is not *downsizing* or *resizing* for the sake of trimming payroll. It is instead, a structural shifting of resources to those who get close to the customer and create true value through products/services that increase sales and away from those who are compensated to be the checkers, critics, or, worse yet, voyeurs.

Structurally, the reinvention should focus on making the shift from vertical dependencies to horizontal interdependencies among organizational components. The reinvention requires that old and obsolete boundaries in the organization be obliterated much as one would bulldoze a dilapidated building to make room for a new and shining edifice. It is in this way that information that is relevant to customer needs and preferences will move more quickly and with greater accuracy throughout the organization, resulting in creative action by energized personnel who are considerably more interested in getting things done than they are in "following the system."

An excellent example of creative restructuring occurred during the design and development of Chrysler's new subcompact car, the Neon. Headed by Robert Marcell, the core project team of 150 was able to produce the new model in an unheard of 42 months and at much less cost than previously experienced by any US car manufacturer. How did they do it? "If we dare to be different," Marcell believed, "we could be the reason the US auto industry survives." With this kind of attitude, the team showed an ability to look outside the company and its past ways of doing things, thereby overcoming many of the obstacles that had hampered US auto industry innovation for decades.[7]

### Systems

Reengineering systems to make them customer-centered can go a long way toward creating customer value. Unfortunately, this is often an area where organizations can be terribly uncreative, rigorously applying linear, left-brain thinking in situations where a little right-brain intuition might produce better results.

One of the most common systems we all seem to interact with as business customers these days is automated phone messages and directories. Some people love it and some hate it. From a customer perspective, the trick would seem to be letting those who love it use it as effortlessly as possible (and who hasn't been stuck in an endless menu of choices), while letting those who hate it get to a live person as quickly as possible.

Microsoft has done some interesting things in this regard, with the system it uses to field customer calls for product support of its software packages. Recognizing that getting to a live person may be difficult due to the volume of calls, and in an attempt to balance the use of its resources, it gives you the option of listening to the answers to the most frequently asked questions about the product in question. If you want to wait for a person instead, the system estimates how many minutes you'll have to be on hold. While it's not the same as getting through immediately, the added information helps the customer make more intelligent choices about the use of his time.

## *People*

The book, *Shared Minds*, describes a range of ways in which people can be linked together and stimulated to achieve the highest and best use of their individual and collective talents. Whether it be through *dueling keyboards* where employees are in synergistic interaction on the computer screen, or whether it involves tearing down the walls that separate functional silos so that people virtually *must* work together in multidisciplinary teams, the fact remains that there are tools and approaches that can be applied in the interests of human creativity. Alternately, there are still primitive in-box/out-box "here's your problem, now solve it" arrangements that abound and predominate in too many organizational environments.

Leveraging creativity in the interests of total customer value requires the empowerment of the people. Empowerment does not mean *all-or-nothing* grand schemes where the employee is cut loose without any structure, surveillance, or coaching. It means establishing a framework for change that is appropriately tuned to what employees know and don't know and what they can do and can't do. It means creating opportunities for employees to stretch their talents and their responsibilities in a *planned* manner that helps them grow and add greater value to the customer.

Another tack towards the liberation of human creativity is the recognition of the employees as individuals. This requires realizing that some people work better as individuals than as members of teams. Others work better in teams. Still others do best with a mix of individual and team involvement.

This is not about putting people in a room with a fresh piece of newsprint, a magic marker, and a Pareto diagram. Paint-by-number formulae are appropriate in some circumstances but not in others. While customer-centered reengineering requires that the employees have an appropriate degree of freedom to recreate the world on behalf of the customer, it does not require that management must accept everything that any and all employees develop. On the other hand, not all employee-inspired developments can be dismissed summarily as not being gold. The mining must be heartily encouraged and that which glints in the pan must be analyzed thoroughly. When it is the gold of total customer value, it must be appropriately celebrated with fast-paced implementation.

## GUIDELINES FOR IMAGINING: BUILDING CREATIVITY

Somewhere it is written that we need to "rediscover the child inside of us." The analog to this in organizations is that if we want to maximize our success in reengineering, we need to unshackle the individual and collective genius of the corporation.

Some guidelines for accomplishing this follow.

1. **Open the organization to new ideas and concepts.** One more time, listen to your customers—external and internal. Make this kind of interaction the root of everything you do.

2. **Establish a performance gap between existing and expected results.** Ambiguity is a key driver of innovation. When cause and effect are well understood, few new ideas are needed. When relationships are unclear and high levels of performance are expected, people are driven to innovate.

3. **Develop the organization's core competencies.** Identify what you really do well; what separates you from the competition, get even better at it and then exploit it. Don't squander your R&D resources in areas away from these competencies. There are never enough developmental dollars, so invest in and go with your strengths.

4. **Focus the organization's creative efforts on external challenges.** Find the "turbo goal," the "putting a man on the moon" objective that can energize and focus the organization.

5. **Hire the right people and give them the right combination of freedom, opportunities, tools, and rewards.** The effect of the basic hiring decision is hard to overcome in creativity. Some people can and some can't. Find the ones that can, give them projects internally that expand their worldview, especially those that link them with the customer, and expose them to other functions of the business. Let them share ideas by building opportunities for the interchange into their jobs. Reward the contributors.

6. **Seek alternative solutions to problems or opportunities.** Don't be afraid to continue the exploration a bit instead of jumping at the first idea.

7. **Be prepared.** As the old Boy Scout motto implies, creative peo-

ple and organizations are alert to things that happen around them and are able to apply tangential or lateral ideas as they find them. 3M never set out to invent Post-it™ notes; it was a serendipitous discovery by an individual in an organization that embraces innovation.

8. **Employ creative methodologies.** Don't get trapped in the lock-step, highly structured approaches. Employ helicopter thinking. Do mind mapping, brainstorming. Exercise the right side. Don't reach premature closure.

9. **Structure creative teams.** Analyze team members' thinking styles. Fill in the blanks. Achieve a balance. Create an imbalance. Push the outer edge of the envelope.

10. **Develop a creative culture.** Review your organization's values, norms, authorities, rewards, and sanctions. Modify them, as required, to tap the energy of the organization.

## Chapter Eleven

# I Could Be Centerfield

*"Each man in his time must play many parts."*

William Shakespeare

What is your organization's IQ?

## AN IQ OF 1,000,000

In a recent *Quality Digest* article, Karl Albrecht raised an interesting question. "What," he asked, "is the collective intelligence of your organization?" He then went on to suggest that a company with 100 employees, each with an average IQ of 100 points, had an IQ of 10,000.

"The critical question," he said, "is how many of these IQ points are we actually using? Bear in mind that we've already paid for them, whether we use them or not. When employees show up for work, we've already purchased their 100 IQ points, or at least we have an option on them. At the end of each day, we have either exercised the option or let it expire. That day will never come again, and we've lost the option on that day's IQ points forever."[1]

Realizing the organization's IQ potential will not be an option for those organizations that want to be successful in the future. Customer-centered reengineering will enable an organization to create total customer value. However, to *sustain* customer value in a world of continuous and discontinuous change, the organization must be able to transform itself as part of the reengineering. It must become a *learning organization*. As we will see, that's easier said than done.

## LEARNING INSTITUTIONS ARE NOT NECESSARILY LEARNING ORGANIZATIONS

Organizational learning has been a rallying cry at serious learning institutions—including those that are renowned for their business schools. We believe that Chris Argyris was one of the founding fathers of the concept in the late 60s and early 70s. We know that Peter Senge has popularized the term *learning organization* as we enter the 90s.

In spite of this academic emphasis on organizational learning, it has been of great interest to us and somewhat paradoxical that learning institutions are not always learning organizations. This may be due to a sense of complacency. Such a notion is reinforced by the chairman of the MBA program at Harvard's Business School, who said, "I refuse to see these students as customers."[2] He recanted that statement, in the face of criticism, but the perception remains that *the leading* business school is not leading at all, but resting on its laurels.

In terms of both style and content, *Business Week* graded Harvard's product this way: As for the quality of its students and faculty; Bs for leadership issues, course content, and real-world training problems; Cs for ethics instruction, diversity of students, international content in courses and case studies, and use of technology in teaching; and a flat D for a forced grading curve that discourages cooperation and teamwork. While Harvard Business School is not suffering in the marketplace, these observations may reflect a lack of desire to grow and improve its offerings on the basis of providing increased *value* to its students (customers).

Most learning institutions seem to operate on the basis of relatively static bodies of knowledge and skills. The product changes slowly; the delivery even less. There is little that is "dynamic" about imparting knowledge within those hallowed halls.

We have recently seen a few indications of some change, however. Xavier University in Cincinnati, Ohio, has recently launched an attempt to make itself customer-centered by naming Tom Hayes, head of its marketing department, to be its first ever Director of Institutional Advancement. His job? To conduct customer research to discover the expectations of all the university's customers—students, guidance counselors, parents, and so on—and then to help reposition and reengineer the university's products and services around them. That's not all. He's also got the job of ensuring useful customer satisfaction measurement so that Xavier can fine-tune and adjust itself on an ongoing basis in response to customer feedback.

We've also seen a breakthrough on the technology front. One university of which we are aware now has one lecture hall equipped with a huge-screen video monitor controlled by a computer operated by the professor/lecturer—a big leap from chalk on a blackboard. Now, in one classroom, students can be exposed to educational materials in a format and medium with which they have grown up. The professors have had to do considerable learning to bring the technology under their control, and its exploitation is still limited, but it is a beginning. (*Business Week* points out that only 5 to 10 percent of Harvard Business School's cases ever require the use of computers.)

The professors who use that lecture hall have had to develop some enhanced competence at doing what they do, and doing what they do best. And that, after all, is a large part of what a learning organization is all about.

The nonlearning qualities of our primary and secondary schools have been widely publicized as well; for the most part, our teachers are delivering their products/services/value in much the same fashion as in the past. The content has changed slightly; the methods very little. Learning institutions have not been learning organizations in the sense that many of our more successful businesses have.

Robert Marzano addresses this deficiency at the K–12 level in his book, *In a Different Kind of Classroom: Teaching with Dimensions of Learning.* He says, "We have not examined the learning process and then built instructional systems, administrative systems, indeed, entire educational systems that support what we know about the learning process. We have not built education from the bottom up, so to speak." Or from the student or customer out, in our own parlance. Marzano proceeds to describe a *learning-based model of instruction,* and posits five *dimensions* for learning in the classroom, which can be applied equally well to any business that wants to become a learning organization.[3]

**Positive attitudes and perceptions about learning.** The learner must want to learn and have positive reinforcements for his or her efforts.

**Thinking involved in acquiring and integrating knowledge.** We learn by accumulating new information and relating it to what we already know.

**Thinking involved in extending and refining knowledge.** We have to put forth the energy required to alter our views and expand our understanding. *No pain, no gain.*

**Thinking involved in using knowledge meaningfully.** Learning demands that we apply the thinking process over a period of time, independently, and directed at real (or realistic) problems or tasks.

**Productive habits of mind.** Necessary mental habits are identified as being sensitive to feedback, seeking accuracy and precision, persisting even when answers and solutions are not apparent, viewing situations in unconventional ways, and avoiding impulsiveness.

As we look at any of our organizations, we can inquire about the degree to which each of them fosters these five dimensions. Clearly, too many of our institutions—educational and otherwise—do not, either in delivering instruction to their young people or in developing their own abilities to deliver value. These organizations need to be reengineered. They need to become learning organizations.

## TEACH A MAN TO FISH

What is a learning organization? David A. Garvin offers this working definition that we would accept:

> An organization skilled at creating, acquiring, and transferring knowledge, and at modifying its behavior to reflect new knowledge and insights.[4]

We would amplify Garvin's construction with two parallel and reinforcing concepts. One is to unleash the intellectual and judgmental power that already exists among your company's employees, the IQ of 1,000,000. The second track is to build and develop even greater skills and abilities on the base of what already exists.

Unleashing the intellect is at the heart of what is now called empowerment. In one of the signal breaks with the past, some managers have come to recognize that their people, even in an assembly-line environment, are not unthinking robots, that they care about producing more and better, and that they can be responsible in exercising their judgment. Thus, we find Deming's revolutionary idea of letting the workers stop the production line at the earliest point where a defect is found. In the *good old days*, a worker would not dare interfere with the forward progress of the line, regardless of the quality he or she saw drifting by.

It's all well and good to talk of unleashing your employees, but you have to have some kind of framework to guide and even to limit their activities. That's where learning comes in. Employees have to know what *the right thing* is. Basically, successful empowerers have found that four elements need to be known (or learned) by employees for them to maximize their contributions with a minimum of constraint.

**How the company makes money.** A basic understanding of what profit and loss are all about, and the role of each individual in that process, is a necessary first step in the learning process for many firms' employees. Keeping a job and getting increasing compensation for one's work are directly linked to how the company prospers, and employee understanding of these elements is fundamental to their being able to contribute meaningfully to creative problem solving.

**What the customer values and the criticality of customer satisfaction.** If you figure out how the company makes money, it doesn't take a great deal of additional thought to realize that the customer is important. It does often take added learning, however, to interpret the criticality of the customer in terms of *my job*. How does what I do bear on the customer's satisfaction?

**What contribution do I make to fulfilling customer expectations?** How does my role relate to the customer value package?

**How to ensure that the customer gets value every time.** This third element results from combining the first two—using judgment, thinking like a customer—and enhancing the customer value package in addressing the moment of truth.

Enhanced organizational performance, therefore, combines learning and empowerment with a stake in the outcome, at all levels. John Case cites four aspects of a business's structure and operations that are critical in this form of organizational reengineering:

> 1. First, people at all levels have to be able to make decisions, and the company must be structured to encourage it.
>
> 2. Second, people need the information necessary to make intelligent decisions.
>
> 3. Third, employees need training.
>
> 4. Finally, people need a stake in the outcome of their decisions—and in the company itself.[5]

As the old adage goes: Give a man a fish and you've fed him dinner; teach a man to fish and you've taught him how to feed himself.


## REALIZING THE LEARNING ADVANTAGE: THE JOHNSONVILLE STORY

This whole thing calls for a partnership between the company and its employees. An excellent example of how these elements can be brought together is found in the now well-known story of Johnsonville Foods, Inc., a producer of quality sausages in Sheboygan, Wisconsin. Let's review how Johnsonville's CEO, Ralph Stayer, describes the way he triangulated to turn his company around, in a customer-centered way, and created a learning organization at the same time.[6]

**Rethinking strategy.** "I tried to picture what Johnsonville would have to be . . . What I saw was an organization where people took responsibility for their own work, for the product, for the company as a whole. If that happened, our product and service quality would improve, our margins would rise, and we could reduce costs and successfully enter new markets." No question about it: Stayer was making a strategic change in the way the company operated, and in the role his people played.

**Redesigning systems.**    Basically, Johnsonville continued the actual sausage production much as it had in the past. However, they reengineered their systems, nonetheless. *Quality control* was extremely important, one of the company's key competitive advantages. It had always been senior management's responsibility to check the product, for taste, color, texture. Telling them that they could live with the consequences of their own quality management, Stayer turned quality control over to the line workers, with tasting sessions on the shop floor every morning. The results, Stayer says, "were amazing. Rejects fell from 5 percent to less than 0.5 percent."

*Customer service* was also turned over, in large part, to the line workers. Customer letters were forwarded directly to the line workers, who responded to customer complaints and, when they thought it appropriate, sent them coupons for free Johnsonville products. The workers increasingly assumed responsibility for the product—call it "ownership." After all, they were the quality checkers; if there was something wrong, they should be held accountable *to the customers.*

*HR management systems* were radically altered. As Stayer's new program began to take off, people on the shop floor began to complain about some of their fellow workers whose work was still not up to standards. Stayer told his workers that *they* were the experts on production-performance, and they would have to deal with the non-performers. With help from the "pros" in setting up performance standards, the workers took this task on, shaped up some of their colleagues, and even fired some who refused to shape up.

The *compensation system* was changed from one that was longevity-based to one that rewarded performance. As workers took on added responsibilities, their compensation was increased. Further, Johnsonville worked out a profit-sharing arrangement based on a performance appraisal system designed and administered by a volunteer team of line production workers from several departments. Biannual bonds distributions are based on an appraisal form in which each employee rates himself or herself and is rated by his or her coach. After discussion, the employee and the coach agree to a score, which becomes the basis for the profit-sharing formula.

**Reawakening people.**    It should be apparent from the preceding paragraphs that Stayer had reawakened his people. Before his initiative took hold, he surveyed his employees and found that their attitudes were not very different from employees at a large, impersonal company, such as General Motors. People came to work at "a job," without enthusiasm or commitment, other than putting in their time. They considered that they had no stake in the company, and no power over their work or their futures. Stayer, after a couple of years of false starts, learned to *coach* his people, by which he meant *commu-*

*nicating a vision and then getting people to see their own behavior, harness their own frustrations and their own problems.*

We have already mentioned how the workers assumed responsibility for quality control and customer correspondence. This constitutes a major learning experience, in showing employees how quality in production affects the company's ability to make money. And the customer focus (TLC) was critical to Stayer's thinking, and to his workers' turnaround. To further enhance their own understanding, he says that "People in each section on the shop floor began to collect data about labor costs, efficiency, and yield. They posted the data and discussed it at the daily tasting meeting. Increasingly, people asked for more responsibility."

Johnsonville replaced its personnel department with a learning and personal development team, to help individual employees develop their plans for getting from here to there—*there* being their chosen destinations—and to help figure out how to get there. Each employee was allotted an education allowance, to be used in any way they saw fit. Now over 65 percent of Johnsonville's workforce is engaged in some type of formal education, most of it job-related.

As Stayer puts it, "The end state we all now envision for Johnsonville is a company that never stops learning." A similar observation was made by Jan Carlzon, chairman of SAS and an early practitioner of employee empowerment through learning: "An individual without information cannot take responsibility; an individual who is given information can't help but take responsibility."[7]

## OTHER LEARNING STARS

One of the most elaborate, and perhaps rigid, approaches to the development of a learning organization is the Xerox Corporation, which has invested heavily—and with considerable success—in systematic problem-solving.

Since 1983, Xerox has been embarked on a Leadership Through Quality program. As a part of the program, all Xerox employees have been trained in a number of activities and, most particularly, a six-step problem-solving technique. Employees are first given the fundamental principles and techniques that contribute to the problem-solving model. These are methods for generating ideas and collecting information, for reaching consensus among a group's members, for analyzing and displaying information, and for planning the actions to be taken on the basis of decisions reached. The training session, which provides employees with the opportunity to practice and develop these skills in a "safe" environment, lasts for several days. The outcome is a universe of employees using the same vocabulary and the same tools and techniques in meeting and dealing with problems.

Some of the companies in the knowledge business have succeeded very well in developing their learning potential. Among them, and high on the list, are Arthur Andersen & Co. and McKinsey & Co., Inc., both consulting firms. McKinsey CEO Fred Gluck estimates that the firm spends in excess of $50 million each year on *knowledge building*, including research, conferences, and intrafirm communication.[8] Motorola, with its Motorola University, has made human resource *development* a driving force in that company. Motorola's training program is hot enough that top managers from the Department of Energy—75 of them—have recently had training there in the TQM field.

Over the past five years, Bell Laboratories has developed a training program to turn expert engineers into *star performers*. They call it the Productivity Enhancement Group (PEG), and it provides a six-week training program of a rather remarkable sort. While Bell Labs only hires people with high levels of technical competence and intelligence to begin with, it found that star performers add nine work strategies to their basic tool chest. These strategies are hierarchically arranged, in order of importance to "starship." *Taking initiative* is the first and most important of the strategies. The second level comprises *networking, self-management, perspectives, followership, teamwork effectiveness*, and *leadership*. The third level includes *show-and-tell* and *organizational savvy*. Developing the training program focused on making these critical work strategies concrete, accessible, and learnable. To date, over 600 of Bell Labs' 5,000 engineers have participated in the PEG training, with apparent and continuing increases in productivity among the participants.[9]

There's a lot of learning going on in smaller companies, too. American Steel and Wire in Cleveland has made great strides by converting each of its employees into a *business strategist* and making the employees members of "customer value teams." The company's theory is that if the workers understand how the company makes (or loses) money and have a stake in the outcome, they will help to ensure that the outcome is positive—or even more positive. Employee-owned Springfield Remanufacturing Corp. (SRC) trains all employees to understand all the company's financial reports. Quarterly bonuses are pegged to company goals, such as return on assets. Employees hone their understanding of finances—and their success—by reviewing weekly income and cash flow statements against projected figures. The CEO of SRC says, "What they learn is how to make money, how to make a profit."[10] When this financial-based understanding is paired with an understanding of how to keep customers happy and loyal, you have an unbeatable combination.

Finally, American Brass & Iron Foundry in Oakland, California, is in a dinosaur industry—producing iron cast drains, waste and vent pipes—but it doesn't practice dinosaur methods. AB&I, which traces its origins to 1906, has thrived in a dying industry by constantly innovating, including in its human resources practices. Allan Boscacci, the third-generation son of AB&I's founder, has created a learning culture at AB&I.

As he puts it, "We believe that people are our most important asset, so we invest in them and expect them to invest in us." This value is demonstrated by the fact that since the early 1980s, Boscacci has met individually with each of the company's more than 100 employees to help set goals and has instructed shop supervisors to help the workers attain their goals. This unusual participative management style is carried over into the firm's reward structure, which includes higher wage levels than its competitors, open book accounting, and profit sharing for employees, even though AB&I is unionized.

## ORGANIZATIONAL LEARNING AND REENGINEERING

How do you establish the linkage between organizational learning and reengineering? If you use the customer-centered reengineering triangle, there is no choice. It's just part of the remapping process driven by a realization that to make customers count, you have to make people count too!

### Rethinking Strategy

Your first step must be a determination that you are going to let people provide total customer value. To do that you have to give them the tools and the freedom to do so. In other words, you must embrace the concept of a learning organization. Each of the successful examples cited earlier in this chapter has begun with a clear determination on the part of the company's leaders that employees were going to be made partners in the enterprise, were going to be given an understanding of what the business was all about, and were going to be given the latitude to perform.

And this is not a casual, passing fancy. For the first two years of his revolution at Johnsonville Sausage, Stayer headed down the wrong track and could not understand what was wrong. He had to persevere, keep working at it, and not be discouraged at an apparent lack of progress. It took some five years to bring his system to life in its full form. As *strategy* refers to longer-term, broader-scale plans, consider that the development of a learning organization devoted to total customer value is not an overnight affair, or a quick fix either.

Applied Materials, Inc., a Texas manufacturer of machines to produce computer chips, is deliberately high-tech, *smart*, and dedicated to getting smarter, as a 21st century business in the 20th. Everyone Applied Materials hires has a college degree, mostly in engineering or physics. But each employee is expected to spend 20 percent of his or her time on R&D, and the company pays up to $5,000 a year for continuing education for each employee. The strategic commitment to this kind of learning is expressed this way: "We actually want you to figure out a way to eliminate your job. We won't fire you; we'll find a better job for you to do."[11]

## *Redesigning Systems*

Because learning, knowledge, and empowerment are clearly *people* things, the systems that relate to the development of learning are those that also relate directly to people. These are systems for sharing and developing knowledge, for communicating, for exploring, and for rewarding.

The *learning systems* themselves need to be developed, encouraged, and dedicated to the improvement of the skills and cognitive base that will sustain an empowered environment that is focused on delivering value to the customer and enhancing the company's ability to deliver. Johnsonville's workers have learned quality control and customer service and have taken over those functions.

Other firms are developing on-site training programs to upgrade workers' skills in such basic and essential areas as workplace literacy and numeracy, problem-solving, and decision making to permit the operation of sophisticated high-tech machines, but also to enable workers to make critical decisions about go/no-go situations without reference to higher levels of management.

As we said at the beginning of this chapter, the learning systems must focus on how the company makes money, the criticality of customer satisfaction, and how to ensure the delivery of value to the customer, along with broadened job skills.

*Personnel management* systems, including all manner of compensation and incentives, must reinforce the company's drive to customer-centered learning. The flattened, empowered organization must be able to reward personnel who develop and use new skills to benefit the company.

As the people in the organization develop the competencies indicated here, systems are very likely to change as a result. The people at Johnsonville took on most of the responsibility for performance evaluation, hiring and firing, and coaching and training for workers who needed a little extra help.

### Reawakening People

Take as your objective *to make every employee a business strategist.* Probably the hardest and most rewarding part of the whole process is getting the people to catch fire. There is all too often the baggage of old initiatives, failed fads, lip service, coat-of-paint (read: whitewash) approaches that justify it when the employees' eyes glaze over at the mention of a new program to *improve things*. But the rewards justify the effort.

But make certain that the approach to making every employee a *business strategist* is correctly focused. It isn't just the production or sales figures that matter; what really matters is how the customers react. The more closely your employees can be attuned to hear and listen to the customers, the better they will understand the relationship between your customer value model and the bottom line. Not every business can emulate Johnsonville to the extent that products are taste-tested by people who make them, or that customer letters are answered by the shop workers—or maybe every business can, in one way or another?—but you can ensure that everyone understands the significance of building quality/value into the product at the beginning, and listening to the customer after the sale.

*Required* learning is important, but rewarded learning is better. Be sure there is an incentive, explicit or implicit, for your employees to broaden and deepen their understanding and skills. There is widespread agreement that better informed employees are better and happier employees, and the sense of personal achievement is often a strong reward and incentive in itself. Monetary rewards count, too, whether in the form of tuition paid by the company for continuing education, a bonus for completion of in-house training *on your own time*, or special compensation for the application of a broader range of skills as empowered workers take on wider responsibilities.

## GUIDELINES FOR PLAYING CENTERFIELD: BUILDING COMPETENCIES

In the most successful customer-centered organization of the 21st century, everybody will be a reengineer. Strategy, system, and structural changes will be made in real time by employees at all levels to ensure total customer value.

Here are some summary guidelines for creating the *learning organization* that will satisfy this condition.

1. **Make each employee a customer strategist.** Give them knowledge regarding the customer's expectations and experience and the ability to solve problems immediately in their areas of responsibility.

2. **Make each employee a business person.** Give them information on the business's performance and a stake in its results and future.

3. **Make each person a reengineer.** Give them the tools and training to change those systems and practices that impede customer satisfaction.

4. **Build learning methods.** Use information system technology to acquire, organize, disseminate, and track the knowledge being learned within the organization and the industry.

5. **Create a learning culture.** Demonstrate the organization's commitment to lifelong learning both for itself and its employees through its policies and procedures.

6. **Develop distinctive competencies.** Make knowledge your competitive edge by focusing learning in those critical areas that will be virtually impossible for your competitors to replicate in either the short or long term.

7. **Build learning alliances.** Reach out to those knowledge organizations most capable of helping you enhance your knowledge base. Partner with them to create new breakthroughs, knowledge, and learning technologies.

## Chapter Twelve

# Stand by Your Plan

*"An oak tree is a nut that stood its ground."*

Anonymous

*"When I step onto the court, I'm ready to play. And if you're playing against me, then you'd better be ready, too. If you're not going to compete, then I'll dominate you."*

Michael Jordan

Yogi Berra was right: If you don't know where you're going, you're liable to end up someplace else.

## LOST IN THE DESERT

One of our favorite stories involves research conducted by NASA a number of years ago around the human logistical challenges associated with landing astronauts on the moon. In preparation for the moon mission, NASA air-dropped people into the Nevada desert. What NASA then observed provides one of the most valuable lessons that any business can learn.

NASA discovered that those people who had a plan, who "knew" where they were going, doggedly marched along their chosen path and ultimately reached their pick-up destination. On the other hand, those subjects who lacked a plan, who in a real sense didn't *know* where they were going, moved more quickly, changed directions frequently, became exhausted more rapidly, and took longer to reach the pick-up point. Some even failed to get to the rendezvous spot and had to be rescued. Real life is not simulated. There's no way to rescue a business that is lost.

Therefore, as we would all readily agree, planning is an essential ingredient of any organizational change process. The tricky part involves staying with the plan through implementation as unforeseen events occur and pressure mounts to modify it, deviate from it, or junk it altogether. While these human emotions and pressures are understandable, such behavior ignores Rosabeth Moss Kantor's powerful observation that "Everything looks like a failure in the middle."

Earlier we observed that in many ways customer-centered reengineering is a creative rather than an analytical process. This is particularly true for system redesign activities. When it comes to planning, however, insight into issues and analytical thoroughness in dealing with them are key.

## MAKING CHOICES, STAYING THE COURSE

In scientific terms, time has been defined as *what the clock measures.* All too often in business, time is what the income statement measures, accounting period by accounting period. It has long been known as the *short-term, bottom-line* outlook. Simply railing against the *short-term, bottom-line* mentality without offering a constructive alternative won't do. There *is* a bottom line and it must be obliged. And there is a short term because, as John Maynard Keynes pointed out, in the long run, we are all dead. The short-term, bottom-line outlook has its rightful and powerful magnetic pull in the grand scheme of business logic. Unbridled, however, this perspective and the behaviors that flow from it generate considerable dysfunction.

One recent example of failing to stay the course involved American Airlines' value pricing program. In an attempt to gain some long-term differentiation in the market by bringing consistency and rationality to airfares, American introduced a four-tiered pricing structure that vastly simplified the morass of prices, deals, and restrictions faced by travel agents and travelers. In the face of positive customer reaction, all of the other major airlines quickly followed suit.

Because the greatest beneficiaries of this new pricing structure were the business travelers who generate the bulk of the industry's revenues, short-term cash flow declined as they were able to take advantage of the new fares. In a panic, the rest of the major airlines reverted to their old pricing structures, leaving American as the only holdout. Eventually, it too returned to the old structure.

The result? The industry as a whole lost millions of dollars and missed a chance to change the value paradigm for millions of travelers. American missed an opportunity to redefine value for its customers, and the parent corporation is currently debating whether it should stay in the airline business at all.

For those who have enjoyed Rome, it's a good thing that Rome is not being built in today's environment because the phrase *Rome wasn't built in a day* might be enough to cause many companies to abandon the project even before it was begun.

As a counterpoint to this lack-of-commitment story, consider these two excellent examples of maintaining commitment and staying the course from the sports arena. Michael Jordan recently announced his retirement from basketball after the most spectacular career in the history of the professional game. How many people know or remember that it wasn't always that way?

Jordan was cut from his high school basketball team in his junior year. He didn't give up. He committed himself to being the best. He made his team in the senior year, had a good college career, and then came to the pros. The rap on him in his early years was that he couldn't shoot the long outside jumper. What did he do? He reengineered his game through intensive practice. Result: He became one of the best three-point shooters of all time and nearly won the three-point shootout at an NBA All-Star game.

Here's where the commitment comes in. Jordan's a natural, right? He certainly has some God-given talent. But he excels because he was committed to perfecting that talent. Bob Greene, columnist for the *Chicago Tribune*, has written some exceptional columns describing how Jordan would come to the Chicago Stadium up to two hours early before a game and spend an hour shooting around by himself before his teammates got there, practicing the shots he wanted to take into the game. The best committed to get better.

The game of golf is a far cry from basketball, but it provides us with a comparable story of commitment and planning. Greg Norman from Australia is one of the superstars of the PGA tour and an exceptional athlete. However, it is reported that when he first took up the game, he had some difficulties. He was long off the tee but all over the place. His short game was erratic; his putting flawed. However, within one year he went from an 18–handicapper to a scratch golfer. When asked how he did it, he replied, "It was easy. I just practiced every day until my hands bled." The rest is history. Norman has been a dominant force on the international tour for more than a decade. But that's not all. Here's the rest of the story.

In 1991 and 1992, Norman suffered a series of major and minor physical ailments—wrist, shoulder, lower back—that threatened to tumble him from preeminence. Norman was determined not to let this happen. He committed himself to doing whatever it took to remain successful. He reengineered everything about himself to stay the course. He lost weight. He did exercises to increase his flexibility. He changed his swing off the tee. Most important he changed his mental approach and strategy for the game from one of all-out constant attack to more of a calculated, risk taking. The result? In 1993, he had one of his best years ever, winning his first US major tournament and being among the top money winners in almost every event he played in.

The accomplishments of some of the organizations that we have studied or assisted, that have stayed committed and reengineered themselves around their customers, rival—or perhaps even surpass—those of these exceptional athletes.

## TURNING THE OCEAN LINER

In the corner of the world from which Greg Norman came there is an organization that was undaunted by the enormous task it chose to undertake and one that he would be proud of. We have had the pleasure of working with the Australian Department of Arts and Administrative Services (DAS) from early in the inception of its customer-centered transformation process. As we noted in Chapter Four when we briefly described their efforts, DAS is presently involved in transforming from a traditional Department of State to a "commercialized" mode of public administration. The *strategy* it has chosen is customer-centered reengineering.

DAS is one of the major federal government agencies in Australia. It provides services to other governmental agencies and to the public. It is comprised of approximately 20 business units ranging from property development and management to printing; and from ionospheric prediction services to motor vehicle maintenance.

The economic and social climate in Australia has played a big part in creating the need for reengineering federal government in general and DAS in particular. During the past few years, Australia has been afflicted by economic recession in much the same way as other Western industrial democracies. Dwindling markets for primary products, technological change, especially in production, rising unemployment, increasing public expenditure and government intervention, and growing foreign debt are among the challenges confronting economic, political, and social life in Australia. In Australia, the public sector accounts directly for a quarter or more of Australia's economic activity. The need to boost the performance of DAS and the federal government was a major requirement for confronting the challenges that have obstructed achievement of major national goals.

### Reshaping Structure

One of the first steps taken to reengineer DAS was to reshape its structure. Currently, DAS operates its business units through a federation with a shared vision:

> To be the best in creating value for our customers, the Government, and the Australian Community.

The federation concept is central to DAS's operation because of the diversity of its business units. It implies cooperation, tolerance, and understanding among members. It also requires the *will* to make the federation concept work. The added value of a federation concept of operation is that, collectively, DAS can satisfy its diverse customer base more successfully when businesses work together rather than strictly as separate units.

By December 1992, there were 12 commercialized DAS businesses employing 7,700 persons (approximately 80 percent of all DAS staff) with consolidated operating revenue in 1991–92 of $A 1 billion. These businesses were established within a Department of State as largely self-funding businesses. Nearly 60 percent of their revenue in 1991–92 was open to competition from the private sector, and this proportion rose to nearly 90 percent by July 1993.

## Redesigning Systems

Getting commercialization started took more than just setting a new direction. It also required changing the rules. Merely changing department structure would not have been sufficient to achieve major organizational changes. Such structural changes, like the creation of DAS as a single department bringing together common service providers from several portfolios, only addressed boundary issues and modified culture at the margin.

"In general, structure should follow the needs of the customer and the organization," says Noel Tanzer, secretary and chief executive officer of DAS. "Structure should be viewed as a management tool directed more at improving responsiveness rather than promoting stability. For DAS in 1987, structural change was necessary to allow much of what followed to occur in a relatively short time slot, but it contributed little to actually initiating the change process or internalizing the reform. At best, it could be seen as complementary."

There were two basic rule changes that helped to change perspective for customers and employees alike: users pay and users choose. While not unusual in most business environments, the paradigm shift created by making the customer's interest central to DAS's mission was an enormous one in the governmental setting.

"Handing the money to customers to meet the full cost of the services consumed [users pay] placed a discipline on demand and encouraged more rational choices by consumers," says Tanzer. "It also provided better information to government, the Parliament, and the community as to the full cost of various government services."

Competition [users choose] placed a discipline on suppliers to pursue improvements in both efficiency and effectiveness. This particular rule change has been fundamental in changing the behavior of DAS's management, staff, and unions. Open information exchange and extensive involvement of staff and their representatives have been critical success factors, and it is DAS's experience that the pace at which change can be implemented is largely determined by the performance of those involved.

A second important step has been to institute a corporate or business planning process involving all levels of the organization to ensure that staff endeavors are in alignment with the department's mission and goals. In developing its corporate/business plans, DAS has been careful to base the process on solid research of its customers and staff.

## Recasting Strategy

The third element of DAS's reengineering has been to adapt a customer focus business strategy. The implementation of this strategy was driven by establishing a small team of hand-picked DAS staff, the customer focus task force, to undertake the diagnostics phase of the customer interface for each business. This work was designed to prepare the selected businesses for making the requisite changes in process, procedures, and practice demanded by the customers.

As a result, explains Ross Divett, executive general manager of a group of DAS businesses, "DAS is much better at listening to its customers. We now have a wealth of customer information developed through individual business research. Evidence of this achievement was supported by feedback from customer focus groups set up specifically to provide information on key issues for the corporate planning process. All of this data has been brought together at both the DAS corporate and business unit levels to create customer-focused business plans."

This linchpin in the DAS strategy is the federation's mission statement:

> We work together to help our customers do their job better by providing a comprehensive range of value for money services, hassle-free, Australia-wide and internationally.

Working within the context provided by that mission, each DAS business unit has developed its own mission statement, business framework, and strategies for customer focus. These strategies, some of which represented quite different directions, structures, and processes, were aimed at developing a competitive advantage for each business based on delivering total customer value.

### Reawakening People

DAS was sensitive to the need to get employee buy-in and support in reengineering its culture and mode of operation. Therefore, it launched a massive education, training, and commitment program. These included executive workshops, management training, and seminars with frontline employees, personally conducted by Noel Tanzer and Karl Albrecht, chairman of The TQS Group.

We reported the amazing results of all of these efforts in Chapter Four. Suffice it to say here that DAS has achieved a significant increase in profitability, productivity, and customer satisfaction. What made the difference? Secretary Tanzer sums it up this way, "The key to our success was our persistence in implementing the plan in spite of the ups and downs involved with all of this. This was particularly true because as a federal agency, ours is in a political environment where one is expected to change their plans as the wind shifts."

The DAS example points out a variety of valuable lessons, among them if you are turning an ocean liner, don't expect the quick response of a cigarette boat. DAS knew that it was facing a breakpoint. The breakpoint was *do or die*. This can lead to an uncommon amount of commitment. Fortunately for Australia, for DAS, and for its employees, that uncommon amount of commitment was available.

According to Karl Albrecht, chairman of The TQS Group, "Tanzer and his fellow executives accomplished the nearly impossible because they were 'fair dinkum.' That's an Australian slang term that loosely translated means that you can be counted on to be true to your word and stay the course."

## COMMITMENT TO STRATEGY

Just as it has taken time to turn DAS's ship of state, it takes time to achieve other kinds of broad, sweeping change. This is particularly true in terms of implementing global, customer-centered reengineering strategies.

In 1988, Bausch and Lomb's International Division made a strategic decision to continue the accelerated regionalization of its international business with the goals of putting resources and responsibility closer to customers in twenty-some subsidiaries around the world. By 1992, each of the regional business units (Europe, the Far East, and the Western Hemisphere) had grown large and strong enough to become divisions themselves, thereby replacing the old International Division. The nature and extent of this growth had been planned. The plan had been worked in a consistent manner for nearly four years. There had been ups and downs over the strategic planning period, but the company stayed the course and the results of persistence and consistency were unmistakably positive.

In the process of developing and executing their plans, B&L became obsessively customer-centered. The customer was at the middle of all of these plans. The goal? To become closer to the customer and to do this literally—and geographically. Good things take time. Again, Bausch and Lomb's significant accomplishment required, by most business standards, a significant amount of time.

Sometimes, in sticking with your strategy, you may not always get what you want, but you may get what you need. So discovered Bob Hall, CEO of Charter Hospital of Sugar Land, Texas, part of the Charter Hospital system, the largest chain of psychiatric hospitals in the United States.

Charter–Sugar Land launched a major customer-centered change initiative with the principal intent being to increase market share. After two years, the hospital's customer satisfaction and employee satisfaction ratings had improved, but its market share had stayed the same due to intense competition and price-cutting in the Houston market area, where Sugar Land is located. That's the bad news.

The good news is that by staying with the program and commitment to reengineering the hospital to make it completely customer-centered, Charter–Sugar Land has driven substantial costs out of its operation. As Bob Hall reports, "Using TQS concepts and the TQS change process model, we were able to reduce direct operating expenses by 21 percent ($2 million) during the last fiscal year. We flattened the organization by eliminating several layers of management; reorganized around our customers so managers, supervisors, and frontline employees had more direct customer service responsibilities; and improved high customer impact processes."

Sugar Land's reengineering was driven by its customer research. Hall continues, "We discovered that many of our traditional ways of doing business were not creating value for either our customers or our organization. We were very 'rule' rather than 'value' driven and often explained to both customers and employees that we did things the way we did because 'that's the policy.' Process improvement for us meant eliminating some processes entirely and changing others so that frontline employees were responsible for entire processes, not just a few steps, and could better manage the customer's experience. This not only required that employees have the authority to make decisions with and on behalf of our customers, but also that they were cross-trained and multicompetent to handle more tasks and jobs than they had in the past."

Sugar Land also profited by getting its employees to be the primary customer strategists. Hall explains, "We learned that most innovative ideas are not complicated and are not created out of the work of committees, task forces, and study groups. When given the authority and responsibility to improve things for the customer and the organization, front-line employees are the source of most innovative ideas."

Examples of employee-generated ideas included elimination of the tight job boundaries and numerous handoffs between employees in housekeeping, maintenance, central supply, and food services; and establishment of an employee-patient helpline using voicemail, thus creating a virtually paperless system and reduced response time for handling patient maintenance and other requests.

## COMMITMENT TO SYSTEMS

In the process of implementing a plan of far-reaching proportions, systems will require modification, replacement, or often a combination of modification and replacement at the same time. No system, be it an automated process or a series of procedures by which human beings accomplish work, is *first time final*.

All of this is to say that systems require debugging and that debugging is a time-consuming and frustrating process. Absent persistence, an organization faced with significant system-related problems can find itself wanting to *turn back* because the mission seems so foreboding, if not impossible. It is at precisely these times in the life of an organization that is reengineering for total customer value that everyone at all echelons of the company must stand by the plan.

Rosenbluth International is a fourth-generation family-owned travel management company headquartered in Philadelphia. Guided by the vision of president and CEO Hal Rosenbluth, the company has been in the forefront of customer-centered activities for years while growing to be one of the largest travel companies in the United States with revenues in excess of $1.5 billion.

Among Rosenbluth's accomplishments has been the early use of information technology on behalf of its customers, not merely for processing reservations and tickets, but for transforming these data into useful information that can subsequently be used to lower travel costs. As part of its customer-centered planning process, the company made a strategic decision in the early 1980s to pursue technological independence from the dominant airline-developed backroom processing systems. Notes Tom Peters in Hal's book *The Customer Comes Second*, "Rosenbluth has redefined a mundane business through an astonishing array of proprietary software that helps corporate clients track and manage their costs." The road, however, has not always been easy.

In 1983, Rosenbluth created a product called REACHOUT® to transmit air schedules and hotel/car information to clients' personal computers. The system flopped. "The problem," recalls Hal Rosenbluth, "was that we didn't understand the difficulty our clients had in using the product. The people who developed and tested it were accustomed to using it, but they weren't the ones we were developing it for . . . We learned our lesson, and we put a lot more listening behind the development of products today."

The upshot, however, was that by reworking the software, it "served as a platform for the development of a very powerful new product which allows our clients to send us their travel request through their electronic mail systems," says Rosenbluth.[1]

## COMMITMENT TO STRUCTURE

One key for structuring the organization so that the change inherent in a customer-centered plan is facilitated rather than hindered leverages the fact that if the organization can be structured to change behavior first, then changed attitudes can and will usually follow. Change is a personal thing. Implementing a customer-centered plan is, in many ways, easier when working with a start up or relatively new organization that has yet to fossilize structures, titles, worldviews, and procedures.

However, changing structure is not impossible at more established organizations. Hewlett-Packard provides an example of a technology business that has reengineered its structure and succeeded. As founder David Packard says, "If we didn't fix things [in 1990], we'd be in the same shape as IBM is today."

Fixing things at HP meant radical decentralization of people and power. While other companies have talked about doing it, HP has. This has meant a renewed commitment to HP's long-held belief in keeping business units small so they can stay close to customers and employees. Founders Packard and William Hewlett consistently split up any division that grew to more than 1,500 workers. Says David Kirby, retired HP manager, "Packard never wanted divisions to get so large that the people in them would lose pride in the work their division was doing."[2]

In 1990 the changes created by the founders erased a lot of the overhead, committee structures, policies, and bureaucratization that had developed over time. "Overhead is something that creeps in," says Hewlett. "It's not something that overtakes overnight."

## COMMITMENT TO PEOPLE

In order to maintain commitment to employees, organizations will have to reconcile two contemporary business themes that are apparently mutually exclusive. The first embraces the thought that empowered employees, committed to lifelong skill building, are necessary to maintain competitiveness. The other involves cost-cutting and downsizing, outsourcing, and part-timing. "Obviously these two visions of corporate utopia clash. If most of the people connected to the corporation no longer have job security, all the talk about teamwork, empowerment, investment in people and long-term orientation is a sham. . . Without a reciprocal commitment to a long-term relationship, the employee who buys into the partnership model is being romanced for a one-night stand."[3]

Even companies famous for long-standing commitments to employees, such as IBM, have had to come to grips with new realities. Alternative models of "employment" have begun to emerge and will continue to develop as organizations attempt to reconcile their needs for highly skilled talent and cost flexibility.

American Steel & Wire in Cleveland has gone a long way toward reconciling these differences by establishing a new form of reciprocity between employees and the organization. All workers are expected to purchase at least $100 worth of company stock, and managers hold regular quarterly meetings to explain the business's financial situation to employees. Approximately 20 percent of pretax profits are distributed to workers.

Tom Tyrrell, the company's president, has gone to great lengths to avoid the distinctions between managers and line employees. Everyone is salaried and has the same fringe benefits. Most important to Tyrrell, he has pledged not to lay off anyone in a business downturn, but rather to cut back everyone's hours equally. "What happens when you do that? No one's happy . . . but they all have a job, and they're all in it together, and when you come back everyone comes back together."

"I want everyone thinking that this is all there is; that the best job they can get is here and that this is a company that will take care of them. We benefit in good times, by sharing profits. In the bad times, if we hit them, well, are the workers responsible for the problems? The plant people are typically the ones that suffer, but they know they're not responsible for what the market does," he says.[4]

American Colloid has been one of the leading and best performers on the Midwest's NASDAQ stock exchange for the past few years. The company operates approximately 30 plants worldwide that provide sand and other additives to foundries. It's a fairly low-tech business, but its human resource practices are not.

Under the direction of John Hughes, president and CEO, American Colloid has implemented a partners in excellence (PIE) program. The program works like this. The company tracks quality (as measured by customer complaints) and safety performance of each plant on a monthly basis. These results are reported in American Colloid's monthly employee publication, *Quality Times*. If there are no customer complaints or serious injuries at a plant, each employee gets a piece of the PIE—one share of the company's stock.

American Colloid and American Wire & Steel are two smaller companies that are obviously committed to reengineering the traditional relationship between the organizations and its employees.

## GUIDELINES FOR STANDING BY YOUR PLAN: BUILDING COMMITMENT

Nike's *Just Do It* and Ms. Reagan's *Just Say No to Drugs* have been two of the most prevalent slogans of the past several years. It's not that simple in life, nor in customer-centered reengineering. As this chapter proves, long-term commitment is essential.

Recognizing this, it occurs to us that there is a *matching principle* for accounting that says revenue should be correlated with the expense of generating it. There is a *matching principle* for finance that admonishes us to match long-term financing with long-term requirements and short-term financing with short-range requirements. To violate these cardinal business management principles is to invite business problems and/or unemployment, depending on your personal circumstances. Oddly enough, however, there seems to be no corresponding *matching principle* for strategic commitment that requires us to grant longer amounts of time for successful implementation of the substantial change normally associated with customer-centered reengineering. We therefore offer such a matching principle and its corollary,

Major change—Long-term commitment—Maximum potential yield.

Quick fix—Short-term commitment—Modest return at best.

Our guidelines for building commitment follow.

1. **Understand the requirements.** Begin the reengineering initiative with open eyes. Educate yourself on what the level of investment of time and resources will be. Don't be misled by what others have accomplished. Focus on your own realities.

2. **Expect the change to be much more difficult than expected.** Refer to our laws of organizational change presented in Chapter Five.

3. **Expect the unexpected.** As you are well aware, the organization does not operate in a vacuum. There will be many events that can deter you from your course. Don't let them.

4. **Use your transition management team to stay the course.** As we suggested in Chapters Three and Five, you need a transition management lane to build the customer-centered reengineering superhighway, and a team to help guide you along the journey. If you started reengineering without one, now's the time to correct that oversight.

5. **Make commitment a two-way street.** Company to customer. Company to employee. Recognize and reward loyalty and contributions of each partner in the process.

*Chapter Thirteen*

# Tell It Like It Is

*"Say what you mean, and mean what you say."*

Anonymous

Actions speak louder than words. So does inaction.

## HAPPY THANKSGIVING! MERRY CHRISTMAS!

American Airlines, the country's biggest airline, is headed by Bob Crandall, a man who for years has talked of quality and service to the customers, as well as "enlightened" leadership for American's employees. Through the mid 80s to early 90s, American was ranked at or near the top as the *best* domestic carrier.

The early 90s have not been quite as kind to the company, however. American has suffered serious financial losses, and the press has reported a deterioration in employee morale and loyalty.

This was the context that existed as American began contract negotiations with its flight attendants in the fall of 1993. Because of its financial condition, the company's position was no or nominal pay increase. The flight attendants, feeling they had been abused and taken advantage of in prior negotiations, felt they deserved much more. There was an impasse.

Then, in the week before Thanksgiving 1993, traditionally the heaviest travel period of the year, American Airlines flight attendants went on strike. Bob Crandall refused to budge and enunciated a very tough line, including threatening to hire permanent replacements for the strikers. For two or three days, American's passenger flights were reduced to almost nil. As Thanksgiving drew closer, President Clinton interrupted his talk with Pacific leaders gathered in Seattle to phone Mr. Crandall and the union's leaders, urging a settlement based on binding arbitration. The union jubilantly accepted, and Crandall grudgingly agreed.

What was Crandall's message in all this? To his shareholders, he communicated huge losses during the strike, estimated at $160 million—dollars that will never be regained and something no airline can take calmly in today's market. To his employees, he communicated a tough, Theory X approach such that he alienated the workforce even further and made the union confident that an independent arbitrator would see the logic of their demands. To his customers, he demonstrated a total lack of concern and regard that he would inconvenience them by tens of thousands, disrupting or destroying their Thanksgiving travel, in order to press his point against his employees. In fact, adding insult to injury, in the early days of the strike, American representatives informed the flying public that they were doing business as usual. As a result, thousands of unwary would-be travelers came to airports such as Chicago's O'Hare only to participate in monumental traffic jams at American's check-in counters, and they never got off the ground. The long-term costs of this event for American cannot be underestimated.

Whatever happened to win-win? This was lose-lose-lose.

Given American's financial plight, the Thanksgiving message they sent to their employees and the flying public might be somewhat understandable. The message that Xerox sent to its employees, when it announced just three weeks before Christmas 1993 that it was going to cut 10,000 jobs, was probably more difficult for them to comprehend.

Xerox was floundering in the mid 1980s. However, it had turned itself around magnificently through a commitment to total quality management. It had embraced *Leadership through Quality*—a process directed at providing innovative products and services that fully satisfy customers. And it had implemented a concept called *Team Xerox* that revolved around employee involvement, teamwork, and empowering people to solve problems themselves. It has also been a leader in implementing the learning organization concept as we discussed in Chapter Twelve of this book.

Therefore, this Christmas message had to come as a shock and will strain the emotional fibers of the company. Xerox CEO Paul A. Allaire acknowledged this when he said, "When you have downsizing and you're taking people out of the business that's clearly painful. It's not the kind of thing that helps morale and helps relationships." He continued to observe, "But I think we will do this in a fair and equitable manner and we will implement any of the personnel-oriented things with compassion."[1]

We're not certain how Xerox's employees will react to the handling of those *personnel-oriented things*, but we are certain that they've already gotten the message—part of which is, while we may be committed to quality, we are not committed to you. We also believe that the difference between this message and the *quality and teamwork* message will be one that Xerox's employees will have difficulty in reconciling.

## THE VERITABLE ORGANIZATION

Everything that the top executives within an organization do or decide sends a message. This is an especially critical point to remember if you're an executive who chooses to undertake the customer-centered reengineering journey for your company.

Employees learn through observation, not conversation. They will pay attention to what you pay attention to. To think otherwise is to deny one of the fundamental realities of organizational life and culture.

Recent business literature has devoted a lot of attention to something called "the virtual organization"—a sort of synthetic business developed through joint-venturing, strategic alliances, innovative supplier-manufacturer-distributor arrangements, or other similar strategies to create a specialized expertise, economies, or other unique capabilities that a single company would not otherwise possess. In many cases, these new approaches have added considerable strength and value and have been highly successful.

The virtual organization is a concept for the 21st century. So, too, we believe is the *veritable* organization.

> **ver-i-table** (ver'i tå b'l) *adj.* being such truly or in fact; actual; having the quality of verity [truth]

The truth we are talking about here is the kind found in constancy of purpose. We are talking about being true to yourself, your customers, and your employees, as well as being true to your shareholders and the bottom line. And the best way to take care of that last category is to take care of the earlier ones.

Simply put, everybody talks a good game today of quality and customer focus. If yours is a veritable organization, it will match that talk with value and values—the quality of product and service that not only meets your claims but also responds to what the customer desires.

Being true to your employees, though, is the manager's first line of business. The previous chapter was dedicated to the concept of *commitment*: this one is *consistency*. We could have called it "Communication and Culture," because that's what it's about, too. The consistency we are referring to is making sure that your internal communications remain a consistent purveyor and reinforcer of your company's culture. In a sense, this is vertical consistency, as commitment is consistency over time.

Bob Crandall violated both precepts when he caused a shutdown of American Airlines. He violated his commitment to customers, employees, and shareholders when his message betrayed American's stated culture.

The culture of the Disney theme parks is constantly supported and reinforced by deliberate manipulation of communication. Disney World and Disneyland are show biz. There is no personnel department: *Central casting* hires and trains its people. The people work *on stage*, often in costume. They are trained to *act* as hosts and part of the big show. People who pay to visit the parks are *guests*, rather than tourists or even customers. The language is part of the consistency, but it is not all of it.

This installation and distillation of culture is always a top-down thing. SAS's Jan Carlzon put it this way, when asked how he convinced his managers to adopt his style of management: "I'm not sure I have *convinced* so many people. If they think I'm acting in a specific way, well, you know and I know that every manager wants to copy the chief executive—especially if the company is successful. If I wear a jacket and trousers, managers will do so. If I play golf, more people will play golf. And so forth. It is natural for people to copy me if my way is successful. If it is bad, I think they will find other ways." Carlzon's message, in effect, is that when you play "show and tell," what you show speaks louder than what you tell.[2]

Speaking of her ex-boss, Tenneco's supersuccessful turnaround CEO Mike Walsh, Roberta McDonald says he was very clear, and very consistent, about his expectations. "He put it out there and said, 'This is what I believe in: things like quality, creativity, cost control. No surprises. No excuses.' And he has always been open to criticism. You walk the walk as well as talk the talk. You structure the environment to foster the changes."[3]

In 1991, *Fortune* magazine lamented the decline of morale among middle managers across the country. Partly as a result of the era of megamergers, hostile takeovers, and other major corporate upheavals, middle managers consistently complained they did not know what was going on until it was too late. And, as *Fortune* put it, "Like lieutenants in the army, these are the people who translate the generals' commands, squad by squad, into movement on the ground."[4] As middle managers became increasingly disenchanted, they passed on to their workers their sense of disenfranchisement and cynicism. This cultural malaise, across companies, is the kind of sickness that can affect any company internally, and even fatally. What *Fortune* reported here underscores the way cultural essence will be communicated in an organization (downward, of course) and the vital importance of keeping the message, the right message, on track at all levels, to maintain the *verity* of your organization.

We mentioned the credo of Robert Wood Johnson in Chapter Seven, with its profound dedication to customers, employees and management, community, and stockholders. J&J managers recently challenged the validity of that credo, in today's world. Did it, they wondered, still reflect the values of J&J? Or was it an empty and meaningless sentiment, devaluing the integrity of the company? So they "took it down off the wall" and went on a management retreat. They examined the credo critically and concluded that it does indeed make a perfectly valid statement of their values today. They put it back up on the wall and let all their employees know that it had been reaffirmed. In effect, "these are words we still live by." There can be consistency over time, and it can be the real force in a company's culture.

## CREATING MEANING

The defining moment that put furniture manufacturer Herman Miller on the path to becoming one of the most admired and written about companies occurred in the 1930s, when a key blue-collar worker died at work one day, and company owner D. J. DePree visited the widow and learned that the worker was also a talented poet. A *poet!* DePree was stunned. Had he been employing a worker who wrote poetry, or a poet who made his living working on the shop floor? In one of the best-known instantaneous transformations, DePree altered his view of his workforce—and his own role—on the spot. Herman Miller has continued for the last 60 years to be regarded, not just as a highly successful manufacturing business, but as one of the best places to work, one with extremely high employee loyalty and extremely low turnover.

What has the company done to deserve this reputation? The most unusual thing is its compensation system, which links executive pay directly to that of factory workers. For example, the CEO's cash compensation is limited to 20 times the pay of the average worker. Contrast this to the typical Fortune 500 CEO who earns about 110 times more than his employees. Says Chairman Max DePree, "People have to think about the common good." And the workforce agrees. "This is a fair and equitable way to pay them [the executives]," concludes factory veteran John VanWieren. "If they tried to revoke it, people would speak out."[5]

Creating meaning. What's the point? People search for meaning in life, and most of us spend more of our life at work than in any other waking activity. It has been said that Dad goes to work every day for

two reasons: Christmas and summer vacation. But the monetary rewards that were such a strong driving force for employees in the
sweatshop era, while still plenty significant, are not the differentiating forces that generate loyalty to an employer. As companies no
longer promise a job for life, employees no longer commit for life, or
for a paycheck alone.

We have spoken before of the trend toward "free agency" among
American workers. Many now phrase DePree's question about his
poet-worker this way: "I am not an employee of Company X, where I
am an engineer; I am an engineer currently employed by Company
X." Only if Company X makes the job *meaningful* does the company
gain any supremacy over any other possibility that comes along. This
is part of the reengineering challenge.

To help inculcate this thought into the business's continuing operations, Herman Miller's training for managers is based on the notion
that employees are *volunteers*. They could get good employment making office furniture anywhere. We need them as much as they need
us—or more. So Herman Miller managers focus on two things: making money and making the company a great place to work.

But beyond keeping the good employees because of their loyalty,
the idea of creating meaning for people relates to their sense of participation and accomplishment in something worthwhile, something of
a higher order. For instance, this well-known parable: Three stonema-
sons are hard at work, carving gargoyles to adorn a place of worship,
and each is asked what he is doing. "I hit the chisel with the hammer,
and make the stone into a different shape," says the first. The second
says, simply, "I am carving a gargoyle." And the third replies, "I am
building a cathedral."

Creating meaning means turning chisel-pounders into cathedral
builders.

Creating meaning means giving *purpose* to the hours people spend
working for you, beyond the paycheck. And this is how you can still
be successful in today's labor market. Just as it costs much more to
gain a new customer than it does to keep an existing one, the cost of
employee turnover is generally considered to be one to two times the
employee's annual salary. Just as important, we mentioned earlier
that customer loyalty is often closely tied to the stability of a workforce. What are the secrets of fostering the meaning that keeps employees loyal and dedicated to producing more and better value for
customers?

Strong leaders do it. They do it because of their confidence in their
own strength and ability. They do it by displaying their confidence
and their competence, and by respecting the limits of their own ability and the unlimited abilities of their employees. Jan Carlzon calls it
managing by love. Yes, love. He says,

In my experience, there are two great motivators in life. One is fear. The other is love. You can manage an organization by fear, but if you do you will ensure that people don't perform up to their real capabilities. A person who is afraid doesn't dare perform to the limits of his or her capabilities. People are not willing to take risks when they feel afraid or threatened. But if you manage people by love—that is, if you show them respect and trust—they start to perform up to their real capabilities. In that kind of atmosphere, they dare to take risks. They can even make mistakes. Nothing can hurt.[6]

There *is* purpose in work. Work is constructive, creative, rewarding. But if a manager is to be a leader, the task is to provide direction, to illuminate the purpose, to underscore the meaning.

## MANAGING MESSAGES

About 20 years ago, Marshall McLuhan created a snappy phrase relating to advertising, but of much wider application. It certainly fits here: The medium is the message. What you *do* is what you say.

We were engaged by an East Coast wholesaler to help improve its customer service operations. The company was also in its second year of a TQM program. As a result of some earlier downsizing, the receptionist's position at the headquarters office had been eliminated, and the lobby counter sported a sign, hand lettered in black crayon on brown cardboard: "For Service, Ring Bell." Every customer service employee we interviewed lamented the sign. "Not in keeping with the company's professed concern for customers." "Bad enough we can't afford a receptionist, but that sign is too much." We also found eyes rolling upwards when we asked about the TQM program. "Oh, yeah. We all have to be on teams and things. It hasn't made much difference."

Because customers had also been commenting negatively about the sign, we agreed with the employees, and our report to management recommended spending $15 or $20 for a more respectable sign. The general manager was astonished and annoyed that we mentioned "such a tiny, insignificant thing," along with matters of substance. At least three months later, the cardboard sign was still in place. But a TQM committee was looking at getting it replaced.

We think of it as crashing cymbals and clashing symbols.

Here's another tragic but true case of mixed messages. After a speech we had given, a well-dressed 50–something business executive came up to us and related the following story. He had been the executive vice president of marketing and part of a six-person top management team at a large manufacturing company. These six executives, including the CEO, had decided to explore the *total quality* religion. They went off as an intact team to a well-known quality college. They came back to their company converted and decided to implement a full quality program immediately. The CEO went to inform the chairman of this decision. Surprisingly, the chairman came down hard and told the CEO that he wanted nothing to do with the *TQM BS* and to cease and desist at once. The chagrined CEO returned to his team and told them to stop. He thought that that was the end of it.

Not! The other five executives didn't want to give up. They continued to work on the weekends and in the evenings to put together a total quality plan for their company that they felt would save the business millions of dollars and increase customer satisfaction. With some pride and a strong sense of accomplishment, they put the plan into a three-ring binder and presented it to the CEO.

He acknowledged their hard work and promised to take the plan with him to discuss it with the chairman after a meeting they were going to in Florida. The CEO came back three days later to tell his team that he never got to discuss the plan with the chairman because he had lost the three-ring binder during the plane flight down to Florida. Within six months, all of the members of this executive team, except the CEO, had left the company for other positions.

Enough horror stories? How about one that does work? Look again at Stride Rite, in the words of Chairman Hiatt:

> It always surprises me that what Stride Rite has done is considered innovative because we see ourselves as a very traditional company. We are not in the fashion business, and we're not interested in setting trends. Our strength lies in building on classics, on knowing who we are. That is how we have succeeded as a company.
>
> And the same quality lies behind the social programs [including one of the first company-provided day care centers for employees] and policies we've introduced over the years. They are conservative in the best sense of the word because they restore something that was in danger of being lost—extended families, a healthy work environment. Moreover, they reflect the same values and business principles that have driven Stride Rite's evolution and growth as a company.[7]

Language contributes strongly to culture, and part of changing the culture is changing the language. And consistency includes repetition of the words and phrases that are to be the culture. The pattern of our language helps create our culture.

To manage the message, first the words must be consistent over time and up and down the line. But the actions that speak louder must also convey the same message. Too often the betrayal of words by actions creates the cognitive dissonance that puts people out of commission. If there is truly a value set, a vision that guides the organization, it is not difficult to know how to align behavior in accord with the words. But when push comes to shove, as in the case of the American Airlines strike of Thanksgiving 1993, the values break down, and dissonant words take over.

Normally, however, the message is made up of less dramatic events—like the cardboard sign in the entrance lobby. It is *patterns* of behavior, as well as speech, that create culture. Culture, after all, is caught, not taught. If we say our watchwords are "quality" and "service," but spend our time watching the company's financial reports, it quickly becomes apparent which is dominant.

Research says less than one-half of employees believe management is aware of (much less sympathetic to) the problems they face; only one-third think their companies listen to them. Why? Management's actions tell employees what to believe.

## THE THREE R's REVISITED

Just as there are three R's for customer focus, there are three R's for culture, too. They are routines, rites, and religion. The routines are the daily meta-messages that are conveyed by our actions, as well as our words. Day in, day out, we repeat our emphasis on what really counts.

Rites are celebrations, special occasions, messages of congratulations or appreciation, announcements of good news. If they are meaningful, however, they are never routine. When employee-of-the-month becomes routine, it is no longer a celebration. The routine "Have a nice day" is a ritual, not a rite. Rituals are those acts that are repeated constantly, to the point that they lose meaning and serve only to fill the void in an accustomed manner—the stuff that causes eyes to glaze over, going through the motions. Rites are special indications of what you think are special events or people. They signal a recognition of value in the workplace.

Religion is what underpins the rites and routines. Consultant-author Jack Hawley writes, "The key questions for today's managers are no longer issues of task and structure, but questions of spirit."[8] Religion is the corpus of the company's beliefs and values. Max DePree of Herman Miller actually calls his relationship with his employees "covenantal," not legal or contractual, and the term "evangelical" crops up in discussions of the training environment at Herman Miller (which is dedicated to furthering DePree's business philosophy). Ultimately, the rites and routines will reflect the ultimate religion of the company.

It is the executive leader who must shape and implement the routines, rites, and religion in any organization. So it is incumbent on the leader to have a clear understanding of and dedication to their meaning. In the words of Karl Albrecht, "Clarity of meaning and direction throughout the organization can never be any greater than it is at the top."[9]

Several years ago, we worked with a midwestern state government agency with literally millions of customer encounters annually that wanted to improve its service quality. They were about 18 months into an agencywide quality improvement effort when we did employee research that revealed the following:

|  | Agree (%) | Disagree (%) | Neither Agree nor Disagree |
|---|---|---|---|
| The concept of what constitutes quality customer service is well defined and communicated in our office. | 71 | 5 | 24 |
| People in my section know our standards and strategy for quality customer service. | 79 | 5 | 16 |
| Our goals for quality service are clearly stated. | 76 | 5 | 19 |
| *But . . .* |  |  |  |
| Delivering quality service to customers is rewarded with compensation increases. | 14 | 76 | 10 |
| Relationship between compensation and performance related to customer service is strong. | 12 | 73 | 15 |
| Delivering quality service results in promotions within our agency. | 8 | 77 | 15 |
| The organization provides opportunities for individual growth and development based on providing quality service to our customers. | 7 | 60 | 33 |

Management really did want to improve its customer service. The religion was being preached. But the routines and the rites were missing. The package was not whole.

## CREATING CULTURE

Do you know what your company's culture is? Here's how to find out. At the close of business today, stop five people on their way out of work and ask each of them, *What are the four things that are most im-*

*portant to our company.* Mentally tally the answers. What you get is what you've got: a description of your company's culture. How does it look? Did they mention customer/quality/value? Are you on your way or on your way out? Do you have a long way to go? How can you make that culture conform with what you believe are—or should be—your company's real values?

Basically, any company's culture is derived from its organizational structure, system, business goals, personnel policies, and practices. This is why this must be the stuff of customer-centered reengineering. An organization is also shaped by its environment and physical surroundings. Many things influence an organizational culture, but the *determinants* are the factors noted here.

Too often we underestimate the dominance of structural forces and how they communicate and shape a culture. Look at what the *Minneapolis-St. Paul Star Tribune* did. The Twin Cities' largest daily newspaper undertook a substantial reorganization, beginning with self-managed workteams in operations relating to home delivery. About a third of the affected staff were phased out—mostly front-line supervisors who were transferred or took early retirement. Supervisors, now "team leaders," set policy for their teams' operations. Cultural impact: Turf battles virtually disappeared, strong service improvements occurred, teams moved from a competitive stance with one another to a collaborative one.

*Flattened* organizations, with fewer levels of supervision, review, and buck-passing, tend to create and reflect a different culture from those that are rigidly hierarchical and bureaucratic. Decision making is often done at the lowest possible level; accountability is high, and so are trust and respect for people's professional abilities, regardless of title or hierarchical standing. Organizations that favor matrix management and team operations tend to have a life of spirit, innovation, and cooperation. Structure is important and contributes mightily to the shape of your culture.

But don't expect just to be able to reorganize your way out of trouble. Carlzon did not reorganize SAS; fundamentally he didn't change its structure—but he did eliminate the executive dining room, and he and his managers now eat in the employees' cafeteria. He revolutionized the company within its existing structure, by his "culture of loving."

Similarly, you'll find that your organizational structure can facilitate the development of a positive cultural change only if there is a consistency of that structure with your business goals, human resources practices, and the values that the company holds. So structural change must reinforce, and be reinforced by, those other culture-shaping factors.

## CONSISTENCY IN ACTION

A cultural shift must be a strategic determination. It takes time and effort: the *commitment* we spoke of in the previous chapter. It must be renewed and reviewed to be realized. You must know and understand who you are, in a corporate as well as a personal sense. And you must constantly and consistently align your actions with the strategy.

A chief operating officer we know had assembled his executive staff for a meeting. After a few minutes, he was summoned "upstairs" for another meeting. His staff was obliged to sit and wait until he returned. *We're customers, too,* they felt, and the boss's actions betrayed his professed devotion to the idea that he was to serve his employees as customers.

Look at your human resources practices. Do they reward the right things? Are your people evaluated on the basis of the true, professed values of the company? Or are they rewarded on some other basis, often meaningless and contradictory, that makes a lie of the professed values? We were interviewing a mid-level manager one day and her phone rang twice. She picked up the phone and immediately dropped it back in the cradle. We were stunned and asked her why she did that. She replied, "We've got a customer service standard that you have to answer the phone within two rings. I'm evaluated on it."

Similarly, our friend Phil Wexler tells of asking a hotel reservationist to state what her job is. "I answer the phone," she said. "I'm evaluated on the number of phone calls I handle in a day." Her objective, then, was clearly to get callers off the line as quickly as possible, rather than give them a courteous sales pitch or otherwise treat them like something better than cattle. "Head 'em up and move 'em out" was what the real culture told the reservationist.

The Herman Miller training department rarely uses any outsiders. The training director says he hasn't found any external sources that capture and reflect the Herman Miller philosophy. Reflecting that philosophy, however, much of their job training and problem-solving is accomplished by employee teams, guided by a workteam leader. The training department is called for help only if needed. The philosophy says that the company's people are as competent in their profession as anyone, and they can teach and learn together. The training focuses on two things: making money and making the company a great place to work. The training is totally consistent with the company's professed culture.

While training can be an important conveyor of the organization's culture, it cannot be the only creator of it. People become a part of culture, or participate in the culture's change, only when immersed in a 360–degree environment. "Some of the least effective organizations

I've seen," says Sallie Taggart, corporate director of training and development at NovaCare, "use training as a crutch. They try and cure weaknesses in management behavior or structure by running people through training like it was a car wash and expect it to have a long-term effect."

Stanford business professor Jeffrey Pfeffer says the way to get people on board is through policies that are consistent with a strategy that seeks advantage *through* the workforce. "Neither false heroes, ideology, or inadequate theoretical conceptions of the employment relationship will withstand confrontation with empirical reality."[10]

Teambuilding among employees can be done. In a recent retreat we were running, we asked the participants to describe the attributes of a "Dream Team." The first respondent said, "I can do that, because I worked on a Dream Team. There were too many of us in a room that was too small, with no walls between us. We were all driven against a tight deadline toward a goal we all knew and shared. The physical environment alone ensured that there were no secrets: communication was about as close to perfect as you can get. In very short order, we came to know each other's strengths and weaknesses, and we were able to exploit them in maximum fashion toward our common goal. It was chaos. And it worked beautifully; we met our objective. And we made some friendships, too." The common thread for many successful teambuilding endeavors is *surviving adversity together*. This group did just that, and also shared the benefits of totally open communication.

Two of the strongest cultures we know can be found at relatively young organizations. The first is Rosenbluth International, the Philadelphia-based travel management company. Even though it's a fourth-generation family business, the vast majority of the company's growth has come in the last eight years. In 1985, we worked with CEO Hal Rosenbluth and his executive team on their first strategic plan, one that helped chart the course that they have sailed so successfully. In the process, Hal Rosenbluth has gone to great, some would say extraordinary, lengths to create an environment where the employees feel like they come first and that they are truly expected to do the right thing for the customer. He's written a wonderful book about this, controversially titled *The Customer Comes Second*.[11]

One of the most interesting rites of Rosenbluth's culture occurs during a new hire's first two days, when they come from all over the country to Philadelphia for the company's new associate orientation program. This program emphasizes the company's philosophy, values, and concept of "elegant service." The culmination of the two days is afternoon high tea served by the senior management team. Says Hal Rosenbluth, "There's a service message behind the choice of tea for the activity. A cup of tea can come from a vending machine, it can be tossed to you in a diner, or it can be elegantly served to you at high tea. The tea is just the product; the service surrounding it makes all the difference in the world. By serving our new associates, we're showing them that we're happy they're part of the team, they're important to us and our people come first."

The second organization is Microsoft. All of the Redmond, Washington–based software company's messages are about technology and the primacy of microcomputers. The workforce is young, educated, energetic, and committed. It comes as close as any can at this stage of the PC evolution to having grown up with them. Computers and how we use them are part of their fiber, and everywhere you go on the campus you see them. At last count, there were approximately two PCs for each employee.

For those of us used to the obligatory tour of a client's main computer facility, Microsoft's is an eye-opener. Instead of one or two enormous mainframes there are row after row of custom-racked microcomputers that the business uses to run its worldwide information systems network. Major customers from around the globe come to Redmond to see for themselves how Microsoft is using technology in groundbreaking ways to run its business.

Useful technology is the Microsoft mantra, and the company lives it. All employees, even the chairman Bill Gates, are part of the corporate e-mail system. They can and do communicate with anyone in the organization, including the chairman. It helps to create a culture where intelligence, breadth of ideas, and speed of response are prized. The hours are long, but the challenges are exciting and the rewards, including the fulfillment that comes from doing leading-edge work as well as the widespread use of stock options, are meaningful, and the organization pursues them vigorously.

## GUIDELINES FOR TELLING IT LIKE IT IS: BUILDING CONSISTENCY

Jeffrey Pfeffer asserts that many organizations continue to mismanage their most valuable resources because they still worship or employ outmoded concepts.

- **Wrong heroes.** Guys like Frank Lorenzo, ex-CEO of Eastern Airlines. It is amazing to us that *Fortune* magazine, in this *Age of Enlightenment*, can still run an annual feature article on "America's Toughest Bosses" and describe behavior that makes your skin crawl because of how these neanderthal bosses make their employees crawl.
- **Wrong theories.** They believe that the workforce is lazy, incompetent, or both.

- **Wrong language.** Much management language is still strewn with and promotes negative concentrations and adversarial overtures. Consider boss, conflict, control, disputes. Compare that to the *caring* language of Herman Miller and SAS.[12]

As you contemplate a reengineering journey, who are your organization's heroes? What are its dominant theories? What words matter? The answers will tell you a lot about what the organization is today and what it needs to become. Here are some guidelines for ensuring consistency in action.

1. **Check it out.** Answer the questions above. What are the core values of the organization? What is done to create it then? What are its primary messages?

2. **Change it.** Decide what you need to do to match meaning and messages in such a way that consistency is ensured.

3. **Live it.** Ask for feedback on how well your own behavior matches the espoused organizational goals. This can be accomplished through personal or survey feedback.

4. **Consider the consequences** of anything that you are going to do that you believe is inconsistent with the new culture.

5. **Celebrate it.** Develop the rites and routines that advance the religion.

## Chapter Fourteen

# Taking It to the Streets

*"You must be what you would like to see happen."*

Mahatma Ghandi

"I started as a player, then became a player-coach, then a coach, and then a scorekeeper."

## DON'T BE A SCOREKEEPER

These are the words of Terry McDermott, the ex-president of Cahners Publishing Co., an $800 million publishing empire, as reported in *The Boston Globe*. McDermott continued on to say that he had left his position with Cahners, one of the best in the industry, because, "I didn't want to be a scorekeeper."

What is a scorekeeper? It's someone to whom the numbers are everything. Forget about customers, forget about products, forget about people—just give me the numbers. From our personal experience, it has been both surprising and saddening how many talented executives end up in this role.

How do we avoid falling into the scorekeeping trap? By concentrating on continually creating value in both our organizational roles and our individual ones. It's hard to stay in touch with the organization's value-adding activities if we don't add any of our own. Sure, any business needs some scorekeepers, but you can't win with a whole teamful. Player, coach, or scorekeeper—that's the choice.

If you're a senior executive in your organization, to a large measure, how you choose will determine the direction your reengineering efforts will take. Or, indeed, whether you undertake customer-centered reengineering at all.

In Chapter Three of this book we said that to maximize the potential success of a reengineering initiative, you have to build the *cus-*

*tomer-centered reengineering superhighway.* As a reminder, that high-way has three lanes as shown below:

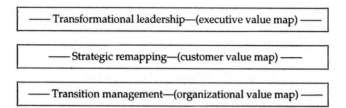

—— Transformational leadership—(executive value map) ——

—— Strategic remapping—(customer value map) ——

—— Transition management—(organizational value map) ——

We want to use this chapter of the book to give you some final advice that we hope will prove helpful to you both in building the highway and throughout your journey on it.

## THE SOUL OF A REENGINEER

In the movie *Dances with Wolves,* Kevin Costner plays a cavalry officer who is reassigned from his post in the East to be in charge of a frontier outpost fort. When he arrives at the fort, he finds it completely deserted. Being the good soldier, Costner immediately goes about trying to restore order and to operate in the proper military manner. He also discovers that he does have one companion—a single gray wolf.

The wolf symbolizes the spirit—of the western frontier, of the Indian, of a culture, and of a belief system that is totally contrary to Costner's consciousness. Costner is initially uncomfortable and understandably afraid of the wolf and the Indians whom he encounters a little later in the film.

However, over time he starts to let go of his fears, preconceptions, and inhibitions. In one of the most striking scenes in the film, he gets up and dances by the campfire with the wolf as the sparks fly into the evening sky. The movie viewer can almost visualize the spirit of the wolf entering Costner. Later, Costner becomes friends with the Indians, learns their ways, and adopts their customs. The Indians accept him into their tribe and give him the name "He Who Dances with Wolves."

This name has both a literal and figurative meaning. Literally, it describes something that Costner has done. Figuratively, and more significantly, it acknowledges what he has become. He has not only accepted a spirit that was foreign to or hidden deep within him. He has become imbued with it. He has transformed himself. He has revised his values, attitudes, and beliefs and modified his behavior in response to what he has learned about himself.

A similar challenge or opportunity confronts each and every person in those organizations that are truly committed to customer-centered reengineering. They must be able to reject those thinking styles, role stereotypes, and behavior patterns that are not customer-centered and replace them with ones that are. In order to do the right thing for the customer, they must tap their own service spirit and learn to trust themselves and others in the organization.

They must rediscover their innocence and spontaneity—what Kevin Costner referred to as "boyish enthusiasm" when he accepted the Academy Award for the best picture for *Dances with Wolves*. They must recapture their imaginations. They must let go. In the words of the popular country song, they must "learn to dance like nobody's watching."

This will be more difficult for some individuals than for others. It may be impossible for many. Based upon our experience and exposure to a large number of organizations, it will probably be most difficult for those individuals who are closer to the top of the traditional corporate hierarchy—its executives and middle managers.

## DEVELOPING THE REMAPPING PLAN

Assuming you've made the personal commitment to making the organization customer-centered, where should you start? How difficult will it be for your organization to undertake customer-centered reengineering successfully? We've developed the following diagnostic questionnaire around the components of the customer-centered reengineering triangle to help you answer this question by identifying degrees of difficulty and areas to address. After you've completed it, total the points in each subsection.

|  | Strongly Agree | Agree | Neutral | Disagree | Strongly Disagree |
|---|---|---|---|---|---|
| *Customers* | | | | | |
| 1. We have a thorough understanding of our customers' value premises and can anticipate their unmet needs. | 5 | 4 | 3 | 2 | 1 |
| 2. We know who our "best" customers are and do everything we can to ensure their loyalty. | 5 | 4 | 3 | 2 | 1 |

|  | Strongly Agree | Agree | Neutral | Disagree | Strongly Disagree |
|---|---|---|---|---|---|
| 3. We understand the environmental forces that affect our industry and can anticipate changes that will affect our relationships with our customers. | 5 | 4 | 3 | 2 | 1 |
| 4. Our customers consistently give us superior ratings for delivering total customer value. | 5 | 4 | 3 | 2 | 1 |

*Customer score* _____

*Strategy*

|  | Strongly Agree | Agree | Neutral | Disagree | Strongly Disagree |
|---|---|---|---|---|---|
| 5. We have a compelling and articulated vision that provides our "Northbound Train." | 5 | 4 | 3 | 2 | 1 |
| 6. We have a strategy clearly focused on creating total customer value. | 5 | 4 | 3 | 2 | 1 |
| 7. We have historically been first or second in our industry. | 5 | 4 | 3 | 2 | 1 |
| 8. We understand the critical success factors in each of our businesses and have developed distinctive competencies for achieving them. | 5 | 4 | 3 | 2 | 1 |

*Strategy score* _____

*Systems*

|  | Strongly Agree | Agree | Neutral | Disagree | Strongly Disagree |
|---|---|---|---|---|---|
| 9. Our delivery systems and core business processes are designed to give us a competitive advantage. | 5 | 4 | 3 | 2 | 1 |
| 10. We are leaders in applying technology in our industry. | 5 | 4 | 3 | 2 | 1 |
| 11. We have information systems that help us share learning and experiences across organizational boundaries. | 5 | 4 | 3 | 2 | 1 |
| 12. We have human resource practices that promote superior teamwork and decisions. | 5 | 4 | 3 | 2 | 1 |

*Systems score* _____

*Structure*

|  | Strongly Agree | Agree | Neutral | Disagree | Strongly Disagree |
|---|---|---|---|---|---|
| 13. Work is always done closest to the customer. | 5 | 4 | 3 | 2 | 1 |

| | Strongly Agree | Agree | Neutral | Disagree | Strongly Disagree |
|---|---|---|---|---|---|
| 14. Our organizational structure has as few levels as possible. | 5 | 4 | 3 | 2 | 1 |
| 15. We are willing to experiment with alternative organizational arrangements. | 5 | 4 | 3 | 2 | 1 |
| 16. Our concept of "structure" extends beyond traditional boundaries to include customers and suppliers. | 5 | 4 | 3 | 2 | 1 |

*Structure score* _____

*Employees*

| | Strongly Agree | Agree | Neutral | Disagree | Strongly Disagree |
|---|---|---|---|---|---|
| 17. We are able to attract and grow people who exploit and extend our competitive advantages. | 5 | 4 | 3 | 2 | 1 |
| 18. Our people feel valued, and we rarely lose people we want to keep. | 5 | 4 | 3 | 2 | 1 |
| 19. Our executives are excellent leaders, with vision, courage, and commitment. | 5 | 4 | 3 | 2 | 1 |
| 20. Our culture will help achieve a reinvention of our business. | 5 | 4 | 3 | 2 | 1 |

*Employee score* _____

Take a look at the results, then rank how you scored in each subsection from highest to lowest. Evaluate each subsection along the following dimensions:

**16–20 points.** You're doing great (if you were really honest). You are set to begin customer-centered reengineering. Or, if you're at 18–20, you may not need any reengineering initiatives at all in this area.

**12–15 points.** Some potential for concern, but can be addressed as part of the overall reengineering effort.

**8–11 points.** Significant problems in this area. Depending on which questions caused the low score, give special attention to these issues as part of your planning for reengineering.

**4–7 points.** Extreme problems in this area. Don't attempt any reengineering effort without first addressing the reasons why.

## SECRETS TO SUCCESS ON THE CUSTOMER-CENTERED REENGINEERING SUPERHIGHWAY

We've also developed some guidelines for your remapping journey, ones that we think of as the Seven Maxims for Remapping, which summarize in a more pithy fashion much of what we've been saying throughout this book.

**Tools are for fools.**   It's not enough just to find a methodology and to try it on for size. Tools won't work if what you need is an entirely new blueprint for success.

**Inside out is out.**   The dominant improvement techniques of the past decade or more—downsizing, cost cutting, productivity improvement, total quality management—and, yes, even most reengineering efforts have been almost entirely internally or company-focused. This myopia eventually leads to blindness.

**It's the customer, stupid.**   It's the customer, stupid. It's the customer, stupid. See Chapter Two.

**You need a northbound train.**   As Karl Albrecht so eloquently puts it, the northbound train is the driving force that creates meaning and focuses everyone's efforts on a common cause.

**Strategy integration is the secret weapon.**   Success requires more than a shared vision and good planning. It demands a well thought-out approach for implementing and integrating that strategy into the day-to-day policies, practices, procedures, and processes of the business.

**The nerve to serve.**   Effective leaders must be willing to be both servants and debtors. They must remember that they are both the message and the messenger.

**Change is strange.**   To quote Jack Welch, "Change has no constituency. People like the status quo. They like the way it was." If Welch is right, and we believe he is, then organizations need a transition management plan to help people confront change and to function productively as strangers in the changeland.

# LAND MINES ON THE CUSTOMER-CENTERED REENGINEERING SUPERHIGHWAY

Like any new journey, the customer-centered reengineering super-highway is fraught with danger. Land mines await the unsuspecting or the unwary at every turn. Here are seven that we can identify for you.

**Long on tactics, short on strategy.**   The surest path to failure in a reengineering initiative is to pick the wrong thing to reengineer, to miss the northbound train. Focus on unmet customer needs as a starting point.

**Long on content, short on context.**  Choosing the right value-adding activities is only one lane on the superhighway. Understanding the changes that implementing these activities will make necessary and the organizational context in which they will take place is crucial.

**Long on information technology, short on customer logic.** Let's be clear: reengineering *is not* just about designing new information systems, no matter how good they may be. Technology might be the means, but it is never the end.

**Long on cost consciousness, short on customer value.** Certainly, figuring out how to do something using fewer resources is important and can often contribute to enhancing value for customers. However, the actual enhancement usually only occurs when *adding value* is the goal, not just cutting costs.

**Long on "NIH" (not invented here), short on "what if?"** The organization needs to break away from its old perspectives and old habits, even if it's painful. Focus on the potential that comes from new ways of looking at customers, supplier relationships, product/service delivery, and support activities.

**Long on function, short on process.**   You can't reengineer functions because most processes are cross-functional. If you start in only one corner of the organization, not only will you miss opportunities for improvement, you may miss the point entirely.

**Long on delegation, short on leadership.**   The decisions necessary on a journey like this can't be delegated to middle managers. Transformational leadership is the third lane on the superhighway.

## TAKING THE JOURNEY: FISSION OR FUSION

As we completed this chapter, we heard a report that a group of Princeton scientists had achieved nuclear fusion. For those of you who don't remember your physics, and we have to admit that we had to look this up, nuclear energy can be created in one of two ways—through either fission or fusion.

Nuclear fission creates a *large* amount of energy by breaking atomic molecules apart. Nuclear fusion, on the other hand, creates *enormous* amounts of energy through the emission of light elements generated by uniting atomic nuclei to form heavier nuclei. Fission has the potential for terrible side effects—nuclear meltdown, threats to the environment, and potential loss of human life. Fusion has none of these side effects.

As a result, fusion, because of its greater power and safety, will be the preferred source for energy creation in the 21st century. However, scientists tell us that we're still 25 to 30 years away from making the conversion from fission to fusion.

It struck us that we are faced with the same choice—fission or fusion—when we do reengineering. Fortunately, we don't have to wait 25 to 30 years to exercise the fusion option.

We believe that most reengineering that is being done today is of the fission type. It breaks the organization apart, destroys jobs, and causes tremendous negative fallout. In contrast, we believe that customer-centered reengineering is of the fusion type. It brings the power of the customer into the center of the organization to generate an even greater power by adding value for the customer, the employees, and the shareholders. This joint value creation should promote growth, opportunity, and even greater potential for successful organizations in the 21st century based on continuous expansion, enhancement, and redefinition rather than retraction and reduction.

Fission or fusion. The choice is yours. Choose wisely.

## Chapter Fifteen

# Implementation Guide
*The Map for Remapping*

*"Would you tell me, please which way I go from here?"*
*"That depends a good deal on where you want to*
*get to," said the Cat.*
*"I don't much care where," said Alice.*
*"Then it doesn't matter which way you go," said the Cat.*

Lewis Carroll
*Alice in Wonderland*

*"Two roads diverged in a wood, and I—*
*I took the one less traveled by,*
*And that has made all the difference."*

Robert Frost

Many are called. But few are chosen.

## THE CUSTOMER MANTRA

Consider the evidence: Customer care, customer focus, customer driven. *Customer* has become the mantra of the 90s. Given ad campaigns, annual reports, and proclamations of corporate executives, it seems that there isn't an organization in the United States, or perhaps the world, that has not rededicated itself to or launched some program directed at the customer over the past several years.

In spite of this, the research suggests that, in general, the consuming public is becoming increasingly less satisfied with many of the products and services that it receives. More significantly, many organizations that have attempted to become more customer-oriented have already abandoned their programs or let them fade quietly away as failures.

We have pinpointed reasons for these failures throughout this book and have provided suggestions for success in building the three lanes of the customer-centered reengineering superhighway as a pathway for avoiding or overcoming them.

### *Customer-Centered Reengineering Superhighway*

| |
|---|
| ——— Transformational leadership—(executive value map) ——— |

| |
|---|
| ——— Strategic remapping—(customer value map) ——— |

| |
|---|
| ——— Transition management—(organizational value map) ——— |

In this Chapter, we concentrate our attention on the center lane of the highway and address the "how to" of developing and implementing the organization's map for remapping. Specifically, we outline a *recommended* methodology for applying the customer-centered reengineering change process model that we introduced in Chapter Four. We have evolved this methodology based on our own consulting experience and research into the "best practices" that maximize the potential of a reengineering intervention.

We present this methodology with a caveat, however. Each organization is unique in terms of its present customer focus, corporate culture, and competitive situation. As a result, this methodology needs to be fine-tuned and adjusted to respond to the organization's particular needs and circumstances. As such, it should be seen not as a classical score with the notes to be played exactly as composed but as a jazz piece that sets out general parameters and then requires individualization, improvisation, and imagination for performance.

## CUSTOMER-CENTERING PRECEPTS AND PERSPECTIVE

Regardless of what form the final process for reengineering takes, there are seven precepts and one unifying operational definition and concept that are central to customer-centered reengineering. We introduced these first in Chapter Three. They warrant review here as the essential underpinnings for implementing the customer-centered reengineering change process model.

The precepts are

1. An organization is a complex organic system comprised of four major interdependent components: *strategy, structure, systems (processes)*, and *employees* that function together to transform inputs into outputs and accomplish goals in order to create value for customers. The components as presently constituted comprise the organization's current *customer value map.*

2. The process of reengineering involves *remapping* and realigning those components around the customer.

3. In order to accomplish this remapping, it is essential to have a clear and precise understanding of *customer expectations.*

4. The ultimate purpose for reengineering is to create a state of *total customer value.*

5. For reengineering to have its maximum benefit for the organization, it must be directly connected to the organization's *strategic business purpose*—its northbound train.

6. For reengineering to have the maximum long-term impact, it must be *strategically integrated* into all aspects of the organization's way of doing business: its policies, procedures, practices, and processes.

7. Reengineering is not a one-time event. It is a *continuous process of innovating* to surpass customer expectations and empowering employees to manage relationships in a manner that creates customer delight and loyalty.

These precepts lead to the following operationalization of customer-centered reengineering.

---

Customer-centered reengineering is reinventing the business from the outside in by remapping the organization's strategy, systems, and structure around employees so they can create total customer value.

---

This definition is portrayed visually in the *customer-centered reengineering triangle* below.

## THE PROCESS FOR REMAPPING

The customer-centered reengineering change process model provides the framework for putting customer-centered reengineering into action.

As the model implies, there is a design and flow logic that can be employed to guide the entire reengineering initiative. In addition, there is a design and flow logic and core process for each phase that

*The Customer-Centered Reengineering Triangle*

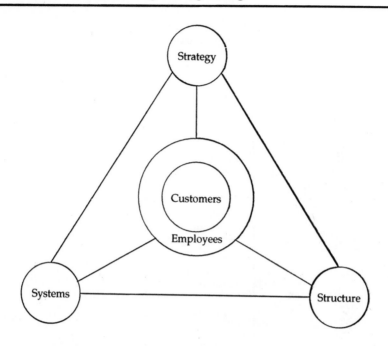

can be followed to facilitate progress to the next phase. We describe our recommended general approach and process for each phase in the remainder of this section.

### Phase I: Organizational Readiness

Well begun is half done. So goes the old maxim. It stands true for customer-centered reengineering.

The impetus for considering reengineering and implementing a customer focus usually comes from somewhere near the top of the organization. However, that does not mean that there is universal agreement among the organization's leaders about the need for or direction of change. That is why the organizational readiness phase is so critical. It provides the opportunity for building a shared understanding and commitment to initiating the reengineering process.

**Purpose.** The basic purpose of this phase is to determine whether customer-centered reengineering makes sense for the organization and to decide how and whether to proceed.

## Customer-Centered Reengineering Change Process Model

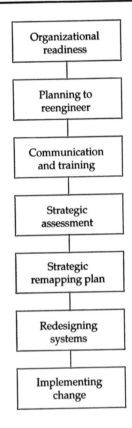

**Process.**  The firm's senior management is the primary audience for this phase. There are a variety of ways to secure their involvement. However, we have found the executive retreat to be an extremely useful and efficient technique for developing executive awareness and facilitating decision making and *buy in*.

The readiness retreat should be held off-site so that the executives are removed from the day-to-day humdrum and are more open and receptive to exploring new ideas and options. Depending on the complexity and sensitivity of the business's situation, the retreat can take anywhere from one to three days.

Topics and issues to be addressed in the retreat include

- Core customer centering concepts.
- Why reengineer?
- Reengineering: what it is, what it is not.

- Characteristics of a reengineered process.
- Changes in how work is done.
- Description of the reengineering change process model.
- Role of top management.
- Role/involvement of middle management.
- Role of staff.
- Critical success and failure factors.
- Case study examples.

Prior to the retreat, it is helpful to have the executives complete a customer-centered reengineering readiness questionnaire similar to that presented in Chapter Fourteen of this book and to summarize all relevant organizational research, such as customer satisfaction measurement and competitive analysis findings. These data can then be reviewed as part of the executives' analysis and decision-making process.

**Product.** There are three primary outputs from this phase.

*Go/No go decision.* We should emphasize that "no go" is an acceptable option here. This is especially true if

- The executives do not feel that an exceptional customer focus will give them a competitive advantage.
- Other priorities preclude the executives from devoting the attention to this initiative that it will demand.
- There is any question regarding top management's (CEO/COO) commitment to this effort.

*Agreement on approach.* A preliminary definition of the scope of this initiative and the next step to be taken to implement it are developed.

*Appointment of a reengineering "champion."* A senior manager is selected to be the leader within the organization who will be charged with overseeing the overall implementation of the initiative. Because of the organizationwide effect of this process, this person is usually the CEO, COO, or someone with a comparable stature within the organization.

## Phase II: Planning to Reengineer

Dwight Eisenhower once noted, "The plan is nothing. Planning is everything."

Translated to reengineering, this means that the quality of the job that is done in organizing for reengineering will have a significant impact on implementation and the results achieved through the initiative.

**Purpose.**   Recognizing this, the purpose of this phase is to establish the overall framework for successful implementation of the reengineering initiative.

**Process.**   There are four areas that have to be addressed in the planning to reengineer phase:

1. Establishment of reengineering project management architecture.
2. Definition of key roles and responsibilities.
3. Selection of the customer value strategic remapping team.
4. Development of work program.

*Establishment of customer-centered reengineering project management architecture.*   Because the reengineering effort cuts across the organization, it is imperative, at the outset, to establish the appropriate project management architecture for it. Again, the nature of this architecture will vary substantially depending on the size and nature of the organization. A typical organizational structure for a reengineering initiative is portrayed below.

**Customer-Centered Reengineering Typical Project Management Architecture**

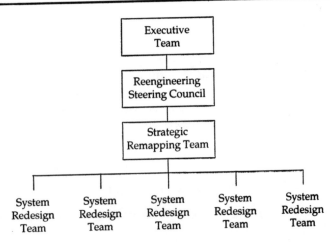

*Definition of key roles and responsibilities.* The organization's executive team must take the lead in the sponsorship of the customer-centered reengineering initiative if it is to make a difference for the entire company. They must be the facilitators, supporters, role models, and cheerleaders.

The steering council should be selected by the executive team to direct and coordinate the reengineering initiative organizationwide. The council is usually comprised of 6 to 10 individuals (key executives, senior managers, significant opinion leaders) representing the major divisions, departments, or functions within the company. In smaller organizations, the full executive team normally acts as the steering council.

The reengineering steering council should be headed by the organization's reengineering "champion" or by a senior vice president who has credibility both with the executive team and throughout the organization. The steering council head is the communication link between the executive team and the strategic remapping team. The head of the council is frequently assisted by a coordinator who handles the administrative burden and provides assistance in areas such as meeting preparation, report preparation, and development of executive and employee presentations.

Key responsibilities of the steering council include

- Finalizing the strategic remapping plan for approval by the executive team.
- Defining the priority system innovation projects to be pursued as part of the reengineering initiative.
- Ensuring the appropriate training, direction, and support for the strategic remapping team and the system redesign teams.
- Monitoring the implementation of the reengineering initiative over its lifetime.
- Suggesting changes to the strategic remapping plan as required.

The strategic remapping team is the group that has the responsibility for conducting the strategic assessment of the organization and developing the recommendations for the strategic remapping of the organization for submission to the steering council and final approval by the executive team. The strategic remapping team is a cross-functional team of mid-level and/or senior managers and subject matter experts/specialists drawn from across the organization. This team is headed by a team leader who should be a senior manager or opinion leader who has the appropriate level of clout and credibility with the reengineering steering council and executive team members.

The system redesign teams are the groups that are given the specific charge to redesign those organizational processes and practices that are targeted for reengineering as part of the strategic remapping plan. Each system redesign team should be comprised of a team leader and six to eight team members. Each redesign team addresses a discrete cross-cutting business process or system, such as order fulfillment or product development and delivery.

*Selection of the strategic remapping team.* The steering council should select the members of the strategic remapping team. The composition of this team is especially critical.

As noted, the team should be cross-functional. However, as important, it should be constructed to secure a blend of organizational experience, talents, and perspectives. It should include both "rational analytical" and "perceptive intuitive" thinking styles. This will help to create the appropriate chemistry and satisfy some of the preconditions for developing a high performing team.

*Development of work program.* The final area to be addressed in this phase is developing a work program for the reengineering initiative. That program can be prepared in any of the classic project management formats. At a minimum, it should spell out

- Mission statement/rationale for the initiative.
- Primary goals to be accomplished/tasks to be performed.
- Situational assessment priorities (critical areas to be examined).
- Role definitions for team leaders and team members.
- Time frames for performance.

**Product.**   To summarize, the output from this phase is

- Well-defined reengineering project management architecture.
- Clearly articulated reengineering roles and responsibilities.
- Reengineering steering council members appointed.
- Strategic reengineering team selected.
- Detailed work program in place.

## Phase III: Communication and Training

This phase is dedicated to preparing the strategic remapping team to conduct the strategic assessment of the business. However, because the assessment involves exploring all aspects of the organization's operations, it is inevitable that the employee population will learn of the reengineering initiative as it is being conducted. It is also probable by this time that the organization's informal channels of communication or rumor mill will have begun to transmit messages regarding the proposed reengineering initiative. Therefore, as another facet of this phase, and as part of the firm's transition management plan, the executive team should communicate the purpose and intent of the reengineering initiative to the entire organization, if this has not already been done.

**Purpose.** The purpose of the communication and training phase is twofold:

- To develop the skills and orientation required of the strategic remapping team members.
- To communicate the "reengineering message" to the entire organization in a positive and forthright manner.

**Process.** The principal vehicle for accomplishing this phase is a reengineering and action planning workshop. This workshop can take anywhere from three to five days, depending on factors such as availability of existing data for analysis purposes, the extent and sophistication of the proposed strategic assessment, and the individual development required.

This workshop should be designed to enable the strategic remapping team members to complete the *technical* aspects of the reengineering assessment in a rigorous manner and to manage the *process* aspects of the assessment by working together well as team members.

Therefore, issues to be addressed in the workshop include

- Introduction to core customer value concepts (customer value model, customer value hierarchy, etc.).
- What is reengineering?
- Reengineering as a technical process.
- Reengineering as a creative process.
- Review of the strategic assessment framework (see discussion of the next phase).
- Review of assessment case study material.
- Reengineering project architecture.
- Roles and responsibilities of the strategic remapping team.
- Requirements for high performing teams.
- Team development and goal setting.

At the end of the workshop, the strategic remapping team members organize themselves, divide up responsibilities, establish their organizational structure, and develop a time-phased assessment action plan and work schedule for the strategic assessment phase.

**Product.**    The primary outputs of this phase are

- Communication to the entire organization regarding the reengineering initiative.
- Trained and competent strategic remapping team.
- Strategic remapping team organization and reporting structure.
- Time-phased assessment action plan.

## Phase IV: Strategic Assessment

There is an old organizational maxim that goes, "Where you stand depends on where you sit." It explains why it's so difficult to get individuals to change opinions, attitudes, and viewpoints once they've locked into their positions on the organization chart.

Corollaries to this maxim that apply to a strategic assessment are

What you see depends on where you look.

What you hear depends on whom you talk with.

These maxims emphasize how important it is to make the strategic assessment as comprehensive and focused in scope and nature as possible. Sound strategic assessment is at the heart of remapping.

**Purpose.**    The purpose of the assessment phase is to assess the major components of the organization and to identify the principal targets of opportunity for innovation that will enhance customer value and lead to increased customer satisfaction and loyalty.

**Process.**    As noted in Chapter Four, the strategic assessment is accomplished around the customer-centered reengineering triangle presented below.

To repeat, this triangle represents the organization's current customer value map. To add value, it must be remapped. The strategic assessment provides the baseline data for that remapping.

Key questions that need to be answered as part of this assessment include the following:

*Customer*

- What are the key drivers of customer value (customer value factors)?
- What is the relative importance of those factors?
- How well are we performing on these factors, compared to the relevant competition?
- What breakaway opportunities exist to create a competitive advantage?

*Strategy*

- Who are our key customer segments?
- Do we have a unique selling proposition or reason for them to do business with us?
- What are we doing to
  Add value to our product/services?
  Enhance customer delight?
  Create customer loyalty?

*Structure*

- Is our customer value package the right one for our customers?
- Is our organization streamlined?
- Do we have too many layers of review?
- Do all positions add value for the customer?
- Are we too centralized? Decentralized?

## Customer-Centered Reengineering Strategic Assessment Framework

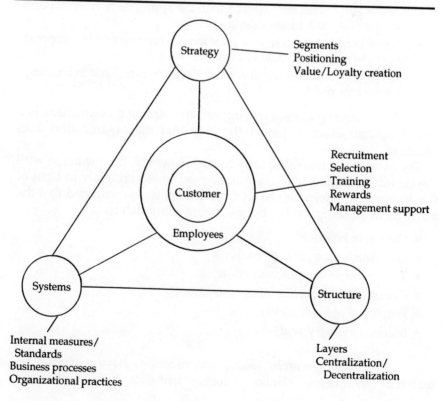

Strategy — Segments
Positioning
Value/Loyalty creation

Customer
Employees

Recruitment
Selection
Training
Rewards
Management support

Systems

Structure

Internal measures/
Standards
Business processes
Organizational practices

Layers
Centralization/
Decentralization

*Systems*

- Are our business processes designed to make it easy for the customer to do business with us?
- Are our business processes designed to expedite and accelerate decisionmaking or action on behalf of the customer?
- Are our business processes designed to minimize cost and deliver the greatest value to the customer?
- Do our business processes enable us to get "close" to our customers?
- Are our internal control measures and standards the right ones? Do they connect to the external measures of customer value?
- Are our organizational policies, practices, and procedures externally focused and customer friendly, or do they focus internally on our needs?

*Employees*

- Are our employees recruited and selected based on their ability or potential for delivering customer value?
- Are our employees trained in the core competencies required to maximize customer value?
- Are our employees empowered with the appropriate authority and responsibility to address customer needs?
- Does management make customer focus a top priority and support employee's efforts to deliver customer value?
- Are employees rewarded and recognized for excellence in creating customer value?

As the foregoing questions suggest, the strategic assessment is a top to bottom examination of the way that the organization does business.

The assessment can take many forms. However, it must begin with the customer and all findings must be examined critically in light of the customer's requirements. At a minimum, we recommend that the assessment be comprised of the following components:

- Customer research.
- Customer value package analysis.
- Top-line business process review.
- Organizational performance assessment.
- Employee opinion survey.
- Market/industry analysis.

**Customer research.** Many organizations have customer research or customer satisfaction measurement data. If this is the case, these data can be massaged to answer the customer questions posed earlier. If this is not the case, we recommend that these data be gathered through a two-step process. Step 1 would be conducted using *qualitative* focus groups and/or personal interviews to determine what factors are of importance or value to the customer. Step 2 would be a *quantitative* study to define the relative importance of those customer value factors to identify the "key drivers" of customer satisfaction and to assess the organization's performance on them compared to its primary competition.

*Customer value package analysis.* After the customer research has identified the customer's key drivers, the strategic remapping team should evaluate the construction of each of the seven elements of the organization's existing customer value package, as listed below, to identify priority areas for innovation.

- **Environmental**—the physical surroundings.
- **Aesthetic**—impact on the five senses.
- **Deliverable**—tangible items provided to the customer.
- **Procedural**—what we ask the customer to do, to transact business with us.
- **Interpersonal**—how we interact one-to-one with the customer.
- **Informational**—what data we share and how we communicate with the customer.
- **Financial**—what the customer pays and the terms and conditions of purchase.

*Top-Line Business Process Review.* As part of the strategic analysis, the strategic remapping team should also do a macro-level business process flowchart or map of the way that the business is organized and operated today to deliver value for each of its key customer impacting processes, such as order fulfillment, product development and delivery, sales, and service. This top-line view of these processes will enable the team to identify those work flows that are most problematic.

*Organizational performance assessment.* The organizational performance assessment is an operational review of the business along the following dimensions to identify performance problems in customer impacting areas and their probable causes.

- *Organizational structure*—deficiencies in design in terms of management, supervision, allocation of authorities and responsibilities, division of work, and work flow.

- *Policies and procedures*—deficiencies in systems and methods or operational techniques for accomplishing the task or controlling the work.
- *Technology*—deficiencies in the types, quantity, or quality of equipment available and utilized.
- *Resources*—deficiencies in the nature or level of resources such as finances, personal contacts, access to information available, and information utilized.
- *Human factors*—deficiencies in the knowledge, skills, abilities, or attitudes of individual performers or personnel in a group.
- *Management and supervision*—deficiencies in the style or methods used to direct and coordinate work within units.
- *Rewards and recognition*—deficiencies in the manner of compensating or motivating performers.

*Employee opinion survey.*   An employee opinion survey can be an especially useful tool in the strategic assessment process. This is not a typical employee attitude or "climate" survey but one that is directly focused on obtaining employee input into the remapping effort by securing their assessment of customer expectations and experiences and an evaluation of the business processes, policies, and practices to determine which add or create value for the customer and which don't.

*Market/Industry analysis.*   The market/industry analysis consists of looking at where the industry and the business are in terms of the life cycle for key products/services. This can be accomplished using any of the "classic" tools that have been developed by academics or consulting firms such as the Boston Consulting Group for such purposes.

After the assessment activities are completed, the data from all of the forms of inquiry are reviewed and analyzed against the customer value findings to reach conclusions and to make recommendations.

The strategic assessment usually takes anywhere from four to six months to complete, with the team members committing 50 to 100 percent of their time to the assessment during that time period.

**Product.**   The output of this phase is a strategic remapping assessment report. At a minimum, that document spells out

- The key drivers of customer value.
- The organization's performance on those drivers.
- Recommended changes to the organization's customer value map: strategy, structure, system, and employee practices.

- The "critical few" business processes/systems to be redesigned.
- Potential breakaway or breakthrough opportunities.
- Rationale for recommendations.
- Projected costs and benefits.

## Phase V: Strategic Remapping Plan

The strategic assessment report provides the basis for strategic remapping of the organization. As we noted in Chapter Four:

> *Strategic remapping* entails developing a complete top-line plan for reengineering the entire business (unit or area) to create total customer value. It pinpoints where structural change will be required and which systems to target for improvement. It also pinpoints the primary human resource and culture considerations to be taken into account as part of the reengineering effort. This plan is developed through an analysis of the data compiled from the strategic assessment and is accomplished in a top down and sequential manner according to the hierarchy presented in the customer-centered reengineering pyramid [below]. The strategic remapping plan is a "living" document. It is revised and updated based on the specific outcomes of the subsequent phases of the reengineering process.

### Customer-Centered Reengineering Pyramid

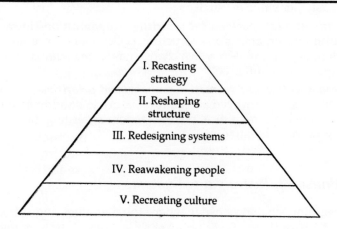

I. Recasting strategy

II. Reshaping structure

III. Redesigning systems

IV. Reawakening people

V. Recreating culture

**Purpose.** The purpose of this phase is to produce the guidance document or blueprint for framing the organization's entire reengineering initiative.

**Process.**   The elements of the strategic remapping plan are defined by the organization's steering council or executive team. There are numerous approaches that can be employed to create the organization's plan. However, as in the organizational readiness phase, we have found the executive retreat to be an excellent vehicle for developing the plan.

In advance of the retreat, the executives are sent the assessment report for review. At the retreat itself, the strategic remapping team or representatives from the team make a presentation of their findings and recommendations. Then the executives review the data together to achieve a shared consensus on the organization's current situation and the course of action to be pursued to achieve a competitive advantage based on customer-centered reengineering.

**Product.**   The typical output from a retreat is a written document that details the following:

- *Vision*—desired end state to be realized through the customer-centered reengineering initiative.
- *Strategic goals*—the key results to be achieved through the initiative expressed in measurable terms.
- *Critical processes/systems for redesign*—the business processes targeted for innovation in order to create total customer value.
- *Customer value package enhancements*—major alterations to be made to the organization's core products or services in response to the customer value research.
- *Organizational development priorities*—organizationwide areas—for example, organizational structure, policies and procedures, and personnel practices—in which change has to be initiated to support the remapping initiative.
- *Communication and transition management priorities*—major messages to be conveyed and cultural issues to be addressed in companywide communications and actions regarding the reengineering initiative.

## Phase VI: Redesigning Systems

The redesigning system phase is where the reengineering rubber hits the road. To paraphrase Peter Drucker, it is where "strategy degenerates into work."

What kind of work is it? It's work that requires a combination of inspiration and perspiration. It's work that says to those employees fortunate enough to be involved, "You have been liberated. You can take off the blinders. You can take off the handcuffs. You have the singular opportunity to forge a new reality." It's work on the cutting and creative edge. It is the work of the artisan that reconnects the organization's employees to its customers and the contribution they make to producing customer value and thus creates personal pride and pleasure.

**Purpose.**    The purpose of this phase is to redesign the most customer critical system/processes of the organization to ensure that they deliver total customer value.

**Process.**    There are probably as many ways of doing systems or business process redesign as there are firms and individuals doing reengineering. The approach that we recommend has four key stages:

1. Team establishment and selection.
2. Team training and preparation.
3. Customer value cycle remapping.
4. Review and approval.

*Team establishment and selection.*    A separate system redesign team should be established for each major work process that has been selected to be a target for innovation and remapping.

The first step in establishing these teams is selecting a team *sponsor*. The sponsor is not a member of the team but an influential executive or middle manager from the process area that is targeted for redesign. The sponsor has the responsibility to ensure that the system is redesigned in such a way that it results in the desired breakthrough in terms of performance. The system redesign team is selected by and reports to the sponsor. The sponsor selects all the members of the team with assistance as required, and the team reports to him/her. As noted earlier, each team should be composed of six to eight members. These teams should be structured to

Be cross-functional in composition.

Include individuals familiar with the process being redesigned and those inexperienced with it.

Have one person with a sound information technology/systems development background.

Include a variety of personality and communicating types.

Some consultants suggest that the reengineering team operate as a leaderless group. As noted earlier, we advocate that, while leadership functions can be shared and rotated, there be one individual who is the formal team leader. Our experience is that having a team leader accelerates the process of group development and facilitates completion of the redesign process. This person can be appointed or selected by the team itself depending on the culture of the organization in which the reengineering is being done.

*Team training and preparation.* The training and preparation of the system redesign team members usually takes four to five days and is accomplished in workshop format. Some of the content of this workshop is similar to that covered in the workshop for the strategic remapping team. The major difference is that this workshop stresses the mechanics of *redesign* as opposed to *assessment* and provides the opportunity for a hands-on application of the tools and methods to be employed as part of the system redesign process.

Among the material covered in the workshop are

- **The philosophy of reengineering,** which include
  Customerize: better, faster, cheaper, closer.
  Blank sheet planning.
  Radical breakthroughs.
  Improvement versus innovation.
  Process thinking versus functional thinking.
  Customer value cycle versus customer value chain.
  Customer value maps versus organizational charts.

- **The principles of reengineering,** which include
  Creating a single continuous process flow from beginning to end.
  Combining functions.
  Eliminating handoffs.
  Avoiding redundancies.
  Creating a single point of control or management for a customer or group of customers.
  Empowering employees to make decisions and choices.
  Minimizing controls and review.
  Centralizing for efficiency/decentralizing for effectiveness.

- **The process of system redesign,** which spells out the steps to be taken to redesign the customer value map for an organizational process: research, diagnosis, design, testing, and finalizing. (See the discussion that follows later under the heading "Customer value cycle remapping" for a description of these steps.)

- **The practice of reengineering,** which orients the workshop participants to the key tools of reengineering including block and line diagramming, work flow process charting, service blueprinting, value analysis, and relational diagrams.

- **The power of reengineering,** which covers how to use techniques and tools such as information technology, benchmarking, outsourcing, and strategic alliances as part of the redesign efforts to realize the full power of reengineering.
- **The problems of reengineering,** which, in addition to the overriding issues of leadership and transition management, include

Ignoring the customer's needs.

Focusing on a process that is too small.

Focusing on a process that is too big.

Changing *what is* rather than creating *what should be.*

Focusing only on the mechanics of the process and not on the other elements of the customer value map.

Ignoring the relation and impact of the system changes on the larger organization.

- **The planning for redesign,** which prepares the participants to plan and manage their redesign activities.

At the conclusion of the workshop, each team develops its time-phased system redesign work plan.

*Customer value cycle remapping.*   The centerpiece of system redesign is remapping the organization's *customer value cycle,* the complete sequence of workflow activities by which value is delivered, for the targeted area and set of functions. However, for the redesign to be sufficient to enable true change, it must address and remap all of those critical organizational components that impact the customer's perception of value. Therefore, the framework and backdrop for customer value remapping is the customer-centered reengineering triangle.

Working within this framework, we recommend a five-step process for customer value remapping: research, diagnosis, design, testing, and finalizing.

1. *Research.* The research step is *externally* focused on the customer and the customer's requirements. It is a step that is sometimes ignored or given short shrift in reengineering efforts. We cannot overemphasize the importance of this step. The better the job that is done in reaching out and bringing the voice of the customer into the heart of the redesign activities and making it the driver for decisions, the more likely that it will result in breakthroughs and provide the source for a competitive advantage.

The system redesign team may have some customer research or satisfaction measurement data available to it when it begins its process. Our recommendation though is that even if good quantitative data exist, the design team personally *interview* selected customers to gain a better understanding of what the customer is looking for (key attributes) and how the customer sees or experiences the organization's product or service. In addition to interviews, it is also extremely useful for the redesign team members to *observe* the product or service in use and, if possible, to *participate* in its application.

Being a participant-observer gives the redesign team member a depth of knowledge and an appreciation that could never be gained just by reviewing statistics or conducting interviews.

2. *Diagnosis*. The diagnosis step is *internally* focused on the organization's existing system. There is a fair amount of debate in the literature and among reengineering practitioners about how much time and what level of attention should be given to studying the organization's existing process. Some reengineers argue that virtually no attention should be given to it and that you should just start whole cloth. Others argue that you should flowchart and system diagram the process in intricate detail.

We fall somewhere in the middle. We believe the system redesign team needs an understanding of the realities/problems of the current system to work away from and avoid them. We also believe that this understanding can be used to construct a new design that has the highest potential for breakthrough change, ease of conversion or installation, and organizational acceptance and support.

Given this perspective, the process that we recommend for diagnosis is

- Develop a "top-line" work flowchart or blueprint to document the existing system that includes points of contact or interface with the customer during the process as part of the chart.
- Examine the existing customer value package to identify features, benefits or attributes that are unnecessary, do not exist, or do not maximize value.
- Use relational diagrams to identify other aspects of the organization that impact significantly the workflow or input or output from this process that have to be considered as part of the remapping.

3. *Design*. After the system redesign team has completed its analytical work, it is time to move on to the creative or "design" step. Note that this step is "design" and not redesign.

One of the common errors that we see at this stage in reengineering is that the team will simply try to improve the existing process rather than to innovate and create an entirely new system. The process that we recommend to ensure that the process under consideration is designed "from the ground up" is

- **Define the strategy for this process.** What is the vision or desired performance endstate and characteristics for this process expressed in customer satisfaction terms?
- **Brainstorm the new desired customer value cycle.** Use a white board, flipchart, Post-it™ notes, and the walls of the meeting room to visualize the entire top-line flow of the process, then add the detail. If there is no one clearly best cycle, generate alternative constructions.
- **Brainstorm the new desired customer value package.** Employ creativity techniques such as mindmapping, piggybacking, hitchhiking, and helicopter thinking to ensure that this process involves "whole brain thinking." Again, if there is no one best package, generate alternative constructions.
- **Compare the brainstormed desired cycle and package to the existing cycle and package.** Identify any gaps that might exist in the new design that need to be addressed in the remapping.
- **Conduct a value analysis of the steps in the new cycle and the elements of the new package.** Review each step/element critically to test whether it adds value for the customer.
- **Develop performance measures or standards.** Specify customer-centered internal and external measures. As part of this process, ensure that each internal measure is clearly linked to an external measure to ensure that the things that are being measured matter to the customer and not just to ourselves.
- **Identify key structure, employee, and system changes required to support the new value cycle/package.** For example, rewards and recognition, job consolidation, and revised policies and practices.
- **Identify relational implications of the new system.** Pinpoint major actions that have to be undertaken in organizational areas, such as information systems, accounting, and human resources, to support the implementation of the new system.
- **Develop a preliminary process redesign.** Integrate all of the design activities to create a new proposed *customer value map* for this process area. If there are options, create maps for each of these, too.

4. *Testing.* In this step, the redesigns are tested prior to presentation to the organization and implementation. Depending on the nature of the process being redesigned, this testing can take a variety of forms, including

Computer modeling.

Concept or prototype testing.

Pilot testing within a geographic area.

Controlled experiments using different process innovation approaches in different areas and comparing results to evolve the best system.

One technique that is especially useful in this step is taking the system redesign(s) back to customers affected by and employees working in the process area for their critical review and feedback. This can be accomplished through review in focus group settings.

5. *Finalizing.* The results of the testing are used to finalize the process redesign and new customer value map. This information is presented in a system redesign report that highlights both *process changes* and the *system change requirements* that will be necessary for the redesign to be implemented fully, such as

A revised mission statement/organizational chart.

New position descriptions.

New internal controls and performance measures.

Training and development in new core competencies and critical capabilities.

Recruitment and selection of new staff.

Outplacement of selected staff.

Revised reward and recognition systems.

In addition, this report defines as precisely as possible the costs of implementing the redesigned system and the benefits of the redesigned system not only in financial payback terms but also in customer value terms such as increased customer loyalty, retention, and referral.

Finally, the system redesign report pinpoints implementation recommendations, including actions to be taken to overcome potential organizational barriers and sources of employee resistance to the change process.

*Review and approval.*   When the system redesign report is prepared, it is presented by the team and its sponsor to the organization's steering council for review and approval. The system redesign team makes changes required based on council feedback, and the report is submitted through the council to the executive team for approval and implementation planning.

A system redesign project can take anywhere from three months to more than a year to complete depending on the breadth and complexity of the process being worked on and the extent of organizational change required for the remapping. During this time period, the members of the system redesign team should be prepared to commit 50 to 100 percent of their time to the project.

**Product.** The final output from this process is a new customer value map and a fully redesigned system ready for implementation.

## Phase VII: Implementing Change

The implementing change phase includes taking the steps required to *reawaken people* and *recreate culture*. In this regard, it is important to note that the organizational infrastructure and contextual factors, such as culture, performance management systems, human resource practices, technology, and communications methods, must be changed before its core processes or systems can be fully improved or modified.

**Purpose.** This book provides numerous guidelines and examples for addressing the process of organizational change in all three lanes of the customer-centered reengineering superhighway: transformational leadership, strategic remapping, and transition management. Our final recommendation on what should be done in this phase for each lane follows.

*Transformational leadership.* It is critical that the members of the executive team embrace and endorse the strategic remapping plan and the resultant system redesigns. The key steps that the executive team should take to facilitate implementation of the remapping plan are

1. Develop a clear statement of what each individual executive is going to do to introduce, support, and reinforce the plan.
2. Build this into the executive's job description.
3. Monitor the results achieved through the plan.
4. Survey employees and customers to ascertain the degree to which each executive is perceived to be a "champion" for change.
5. Relate executive performance bonuses to results achieved and employee survey results.

*Strategic remapping.* The remapping plan specifies the technical steps to be taken in this area. Additional points to keep in mind here follow:

1. A phased rollout should be considered.
2. Regular review checkpoints need to be built into the implementation process to ensure that the system is having the desired impact with both customers and employees.

3. It may frequently be necessary to operate two systems in parallel or tandem as you make the migration or transition from one system to another.

4. After the new system is on-line and fully operational, the results achieved need to be measured and corrective actions taken immediately to address any problems.

5. The environment needs to be scanned routinely and the organization needs to be prepared to respond immediately to dramatic changes in customer needs and expectations or competitive pressures by reengineering again.

*Transition management.* We present general guidelines for transition management in Chapter Five. The specific steps we recommend to manage the transition in its early stages are

1. Create a communication plan that makes the executives the necessary bearers and spokespeople for how this change process will be rolled out.

2. Make all necessary changes to the organizational infrastructure (e.g., human resource policies, information system, etc.) as soon as possible so there is an appropriate alignment between the redesigned system and the organization's body so it does not reject the new system.

3. Solicit employee reactions and feedback to the changes and deal openly and honestly with their concerns.

4. Use an employee survey to measure progress toward the desired state.

5. Make cultural adjustments as required.

**Product.** The initial output of this phase should be a three-part implementation plan. The end result should be realization of the organization's vision.

## CONCLUSION

As we reviewed this implementation guide chapter and thought about what to say in closing this book we were reminded of *The Wizard of Oz* and the yellow brick road.

Unfortunately, there is no yellow brick road upon which to take the reengineering journey. Each organization must build its own reengineering superhighway. We hope that this book serves as a resource and enhances the ability of those organizations that are willing to do that highway construction which is demanded for successful travel into the 21st century.

# Endnotes

## Chapter 1 There's Something Happening Here . . .

1. Emshwiller, John, "Corruption in Bankruptcy System Injures Firms in Need," *The Wall Street Journal*, December 3, 1993, p. B1.
2. Grenier, Larry, "Evolution and Revolution as Businesses Grow," *Harvard Business Review*, July–August 1972.
3. Strebel, Paul, *Breakpoints* (Boston: Harvard Business School Press, 1992).
4. Murray, Chuck, "Supercomputing Giant Cray Moves to Extend Its Dominance," *Chicago Tribune*, September 28, 1993, Section 3, p. 1.
5. Tomasako, Robert, *Rethinking the Corporation* (New York: AMACOM, 1993).
6. Fuchsberg, Gilbert, "Total Quality Is Termed Only Partial Success," *The Wall Street Journal*, December 8, 1992, p. B1.
7. "Making Quality More Than a Fad," *Fortune*, May 18, 1992; pp. 12–13.
8. Barlow, Stephanie, "No Weak Links," *Entrepreneur*, 1992, p. 49.
9. Champy, James and Hammer, Michael, *Reengineering the Corporation* (New York: Harper Business, 1993), p. 200.
10. Bleakley, Fred, "Many Companies Try Management Fads Only to See Them Flop," *The Wall Street Journal*, July 5, 1993, p. 1.
11. The TQS Group, "The State of American Quality Programs: 1991 Quality Survey," (TQS Group, 1992).

## Chapter 2 It's The Customer, Stupid!

1. Woods, Wilson, "Can John Akers Save IBM," *Fortune*, July 15, 1991.
2. Loomis, Carol, "Dinosaurs," *Fortune*, May 3, 1993, p. 39.
3. "Lou Gerstner's First 30 Days," *Fortune*, May 31, 1993, p. 58.
4. Buzzell, Robert and Gale, Bradley, *The PIMS Principles* (New York: The Free Press, 1987).
5. Technical Assistance Research Programs Institute, *Consumer Complaint Handling in America: An Update Study, Part III* (Washington, D.C.: Consumer Affairs Council, March 31, 1986).
6. Lash, Linda, "Trying Harder: Profiting from Total Quality," (New York: The Conference Board, 1993), pp. 9–10.
7. Reichheld, Frederick, "Loyalty-Based Management," *Harvard Business Review*, March–April 1993.
8. Drucker, Peter, *Management* (New York: Harper & Row, 1979), p. 83.
9. "New Study Shows Americans Changing Need for Satisfaction," *Service Marketing Today:* September/October 1992, p. 1.
10. Norman, Richard and Ramirez, Rafael, "From Value Chain to Value Constellation: Designing Interactive Strategy," *Harvard Business Review*, July–August 1993.
11. Treacy, Michael and Wiersma, Fred, "Customer Intimacy and Other Value Disciplines," *Harvard Business Review*, January–February 1993.
12. Pine, Joseph et al., "Making Mass Customization Work," *HarvardBusiness Review*, September–October 1993.

13. Peters, Tom, "TQM Isn't Panacea for Business Woes," *San Antonio Light,* September 17, 1991.
14. Heskett, James and Kotter, John, *Corporate Culture and Performance* (New York: The Free Press, 1992).
15. Albrecht, Karl with The TQS Group, *The Only Thing That Matters: Bringing the Power of the Customer into the Center of Your Business* (New York: Harper Business, 1992).

## Chapter 3 Reinventing Reengineering

1. Champy, James, and Hammer, Michael, *Reengineering the Corporation* (New York: Harper Business, 1993).
2. Albrecht, Karl with The TQS Group, *The Only Thing That Matters: Bringing the Power of the Customer into the Center of Your Business* (New York: Harper Business 1992).

## Chapter 4 Triangulating for Total Customer Value

1. "Rethinking IDS from the Bottom-Up," *Business Week,* February 8,1993.
2. "Merck & Company: Sheer Energy," *Business Month,* December 1988.
3. Champy, James and Hammer Michael, *Reengineering the Corporation* (New York: Harper Business, 1993).
4. Peters, Tom, "Out of the Ordinary," *Quality Digest,* September 1993, p. 16.

## CHAPTER 5 The Windmills of The Mind

1. Krantz, Lee, *Facts that Matter* (Price, Stern, Sloan, 1993).
2. Peters, Tom, "Change in a Nanosecond—or Never," *Chicago Tribune,* November 15, 1993, Section 8, p. 4.
3. Gilovich, Thomas, *How We Know What Isn't So: The Fallibility of Human Reason in Everyday Life* (New York: The Free Press, 1991).
4. Cappo, Joe, "Tapping Rich Vein of Poor Reasoning," *Crain's Chicago Business,* August 23, 1993, p. 10.
5. Wackerle, Frederick, "Beyond the Fisher Move, Why Outside CEO's Are In," *Crain's Chicago Business,* November 22, 1993, p. 11.
6. Kotter, John A. and Heskett, James L., *Corporate Culture and Performance* (New York: The Free Press, 1992), p. 71.
7. Hammer, Michael, as quoted in *Speakers Idea File,* November 1993, p. 3.
8. Heskett and Kotter, *Corporate Culture,* p. 11.
9. Locin, Mitchell, "Gore Plays Let's Not Make a Deal," *Chicago Tribune,* September 9, 1993, Section 1, p. 4.
10. Blanchard, Ken, "Seven Dynamics of Change," *Executive Excellence,* June 1992, p. 5.
11. Bridges, Bill, "Managing Organizational Transitions," *Organizational Dynamics,* 1986.

## Chapter 6 Sailing The Seven C's

1. Gross, Tracy; Pascale, Richard; and Athos, Anthony, "Risking the Present for a Powerful Future," *Harvard Business Review,* November—December 1993.
2. Loomis, J. Carol, "Dinosaurs," *Fortune,* May 3, 1993, p. 36.
3. Ibid.
4. Sellers, Patricia, "Companies That Serve You Best," *Fortune,* May 31, 1993, p. 74.
5. "The Education of Michael Dell," *Business Week,* March 22, 1993, p. 82.
6. Norman, Richard and Ramirez, Rafael, "From Value Chain to Value

*Constellation: Designing Interactive Strategy," Harvard Business Review,* July–August 1993.

7. Thurow, Lester, *Speakers Idea File,* November 1993, p. 3.

## Chapter 7 The Heart of The Matter

1. Donahue, Deidre, "Magazines," *USA Today,* October 5, 1993, p. 80.
2. Senge, Peter, "The Leaders' New Work: Building Learning Organizations," *Sloan Management Review,* Fall 1990.
3. Donahue, Deidre, "Magazines," *USA Today,* October 5, 1993, p. 80.
4. Yanofsky, Marc, "Twelve Fatal Mistakes of Service Marketing," as quoted in *Interface,* p. 7.
5. Davidow, William and Utal, Bro, *Harvard Business Review,* July–August 1989.
6. Wolfe, David, *Serving the Ageless Market* (New York: McGraw-Hill, 1992).
7. Total Research Corporation, *Brand Equity Segmentation* (Princeton: Total Research Corporation, 1990).
8. "GE's Money Machine," *Business Week,* March 8, 1993, pp. 66–67.
9. Ibid.
10. Reichheld, Frederick F., "Loyalty-Based Management," *Harvard Business Review,* March–April 1993.
11. Stone, Nan, "Building Corporation Character: An Interview with Stride Rite Chairman Arnold Hiatt," *Harvard Business Review,* March–April 1992.

## Chapter 8 I Can See Clearly Now

1. Marzano, Robert, *A Different Kind of Classroom* (Alexandria, VA: Association for Supervisor and Curriculum Development, 1992), p. 7.
2. Wilke, John, "Beech's Sleekly Styled Starship Fails to Take Off with Corporate Customer," *The Wall Street Journal,* September 29, 1993, p. B1.
3. Ryan, Nancy, "Ailing Videocart Loses Two Big Supermarket Clients, *Chicago Tribune,* November 13, 1993, Section 2, p. 12.
4. "Flops," *Business Week,* August 16, 1993, pp. 76–82.
5. Lavin, Douglas, "Robert Eaton Thinks 'Vision' Is Overrated," *The Wall Street Journal,* October 4, 1993, p. 1.
6. Kirkpatrick, David, "Gerstner's New Vision for IBM," *Fortune,* November 15, 1993.
7. McKana, Joseph F., "Bob Galvin: Life after Perfection," *Industry Week,* January 2, 1991.
8. "The Vision Thing," *The Economist,* November 9, 1991, p. 81.
9. Albrecht, Karl, *The Northbound Train* (New York: AMACOM, 1994), draft manuscript, pp. 29–30.
10. Crego, Edwin T., Jr.; Deaton, Brian; Gunn, Ronald; and Schiffrin, Peter D., *Strategic Planning for the Entrepreneurial Business* (New York: American Management Association, 1988), p. 131.
11. "Why Merck Married the Enemy," *Fortune,* September 20, 1993, p. 60.
12. "The Education of Michael Dell," *Business Week,* March 22, 1993, p. 83.
13. Treacy, Michael and Wiersma, Fred, "Customer Intimacy and Other Value Disciplines," *Harvard Business Review,* January–February 1993.
14. Campbell, Andrew, *A Sense of Mission: Defining Direction for the Larger Corporation* (Addison-Wesley 1993).

## Chapter 9 Sit Down, You're Rocking The Boat

1. "Chakravarty, Subrata and Feldman, Amy, "The Road Not

Taken," *Forbes*, August 30, 1993, p. 40.

2. "CEOs with the Outside Edge," *Business Week*, pp. 60–62.

3. Veverke, Mark, "The Man behind Sears' Comeback," *Crain's Chicago Business*, November 29–December 5, 1993, pp. 48–49.

4. Lubove, Seth, "We Have a Big Pond to Play In," *Forbes*, September 13, 1993, p. 218.

## Chapter 10 Imagine There's No . . .

1. "Are You Creative?" *Business Week*, September 30, 1985, p. 81.

2. Ackersberg, Robert and McGinnis, Michael, "Effective Innovation Management: Missing Link in Strategic Planning," *The Journal of Business Strategy*, Summer 1983.

3. Slater, Roger, "Integrated Process Management: A Quality Model," *Quality Progress*, May 1991.

4. Davenport, Thomas H., *Process Innovation: Reengineering Work through Information Technology* (Boston: Harvard Business School Press, 1993).

5. "Are You Creative?" *Op. Cit.*, p. 81.

6. Huey, John, "Nothing Is Impossible," *Fortune*, September 23, 1991, p. 135.

7. "Chrysler's Neon," *Business Week*, May 3, 1993, p. 116.

## Chapter 11 I Could Be Centerfield

1. Albrecht, Karl, "An IQ of 1,000,000," *Quality Digest*, September 1993.

2. "Harvard Business School," *Business Week*, July 19, 1993.

3. Marzano, Robert, *A Different Kind of Classroom* (Alexandria, VA: Association for Curriculum Development, 1992), pp. 1-17.

4. Garvin, David, "Building a Learning Organization," *Harvard Business Review*, July–August 1993, p. 80.

5. Case, John, "A Company of Businesspeople," INC, April 1993, p. 79.

6. Stayer, Ralph, "How I Learned to Let My Workers Lead," *Harvard Business Review*, November–December 1990.

7. Albrecht, Karl, *The Only Thing That Matters*, op. cit., p. 143.

8. Huey, John, "How McKinsey Does It," *Fortune*, November 1, 1993, p. 62.

9. Kelley, Robert and Caplan, Janet, "How Bell Labs Creates Star Performers," *Harvard Business Review*, July–August 1993.

10. Case, John, "A Company of Businesspeople."

11. "Retrained for What?", *Time*, November 22, 1993, p. 38.

## Chapter 12 Stand by Your Plan

1. Rosenbluth, Hal F. and Peters, Dianne McFerrin, *The Customer Comes Second* (New York: William Morrow, 1992).

2. Pitta, Julie, "It Had to Be Done and We Did It," *Forbes*, April 26, 1993, p. 148.

3. Kuttner, Robert, "Talking Marriage and Thinking One-Night Stand," *Business Week*, October 18, 1993.

4. Case, John, *From the Ground Up: The Resurgence of American Entrepreneurship* (New York: Simon & Schuster, 1992), pp. 211–212.

## Chapter 13 Tell It Like It Is

1. Lowe, Stephen, "Xerox Layoffs Pose Quality Questions," *Chicago Sun-Times*, December 13, 1993, p.43.

2. "The Art of Loving," *Inc.*, May 1989, pp. 35–41.

3. Huey, John, "Managing in the

Midst of Chaos," *Fortune*, April 5, 1993.

4. Fisher, Anne, "Morale Crisis," *Fortune*, November 18, 1991, pp. 70–80.

5. *The Wall Street Journal*, May 7, 1992, p. B1.

6. "The Art of Loving," *Inc.*, May 1989, p. 35.

7. Stone, Nan, "Building Corporate Character: An Interview with Stride Rite Chairman Arnold Hiatt, *Harvard Business Review*, March–April 1992.

8. Hawley, Jack, *Reawakening the Spirit in Work*, (Berrett-Koehler Publishers, 1993).

9. Albrecht, Karl, *The Northbound Train* (New York: AMACOM, 1994), typed manuscript.

10. Pfeffer, Jeffery, *Competitive Advantage through People: Unleashing the Power of the Workforce*, (Boston: Harvard Business School Press, Spring 1994).

11. Rosenbluth, Hal F. and Peters, Diane McFerrin, *The Customer Comes Second* (William Morrow and Company, 1992).

12. Pfeffer, *Competitive Advantage through People*.

# Index

Thank you for choosing Irwin Professional Publishing for your business information needs. If you are part of a corporation, professional association, or government agency, consider our newest option: Irwin Professional Custom Publishing. This allows you to create customized books, manuals, and other materials from your organization's resources, select chapters of our books, or both.

Irwin Professional Publishing books are also excellent resources for training/educational programs, premiums, and incentives. For information on volume discounts or Custom Publishing, call 1-800-634-3966.

Other books of interest to you from Irwin Professional Publishing . . .

Added Value Negotiating
The Breakthrough Method for Building Balanced Deals
Karl Albrecht and Steve Albrecht

A breakthrough method for negotiating that eliminates many of the problems of conventional negotiating approaches. The authors offer you a noncombative, five-step negotiating style that focuses on interest, develops options, and creates deals that benefit everyone involved.

1-55623-967-X          205 pages

Total Customer Satisfaction
Putting the World's Best Programs to Work
Jacques Horovitz and Michele Jurgens Panak

Excellent customer service is an essential tool for any company competing in today's climate. This book explores the activities of global companies with excellent reputations for customer service. Practical examples and in-depth case studies from the best in business will enable companies to give their customers the best in service quality.

0-7863-0108-2          275 pages

Aftermarketing
How to Keep Customers for Life through Relationship Marketing
Terry G. Vavra

Gives you a clear mandate to help you gain category leadership in the radically changing marketplace of the 90s. Includes ways to identify your customers and build a customer identification file.

1-55623-605-0          292 pages